Terrorism

For my daughter Tamar

Terrorism

A Philosophical Investigation

Igor Primoratz

polity

First published in 2013 by Polity Press

Polity Press
65 Bridge Street
Cambridge CB2 1UR, UK

Polity Press
350 Main Street
Malden, MA 02148, USA

ISBN-13: 978-0-7456-5143-9
ISBN-13: 978-0-7456-5144-6 (pb)

A catalogue record for this book is available from the British Library.

Typeset in 10.5 on 12 pt Plantin
by Servis Filmsetting Ltd, Stockport, Cheshire
Printed and bound in Great Britain by MPG Books Group Limited, Bodmin, Cornwall

The publisher has used its best endeavours to ensure that the URLs for external websites referred to in this book are correct and active at the time of going to press. However, the publisher has no responsibility for the websites and can make no guarantee that a site will remain live or that the content is or will remain appropriate.

Every effort has been made to trace all copyright holders, but if any have been inadvertently overlooked the publisher will be pleased to include any necessary credits in any subsequent reprint or edition.

For further information on Polity, visit our website: www.politybooks.com

Contents

Acknowledgments

My thinking about terrorism and related topics has benefited from responses from audiences at a number of conferences and seminars and from discussion or correspondence with many friends and colleagues, and in particular Andrew Alexandra, C. A. J. (Tony) Coady, Ned Dobos, Nick Fotion, Virginia Held, Georg Meggle, Seumas Miller, Stephen Nathanson, Walter Sinnott-Armstrong, and Rob Sparrow.

I am especially indebted to John Kleinig and Stephen Nathanson, who read the penultimate draft of the book and made numerous queries and suggestions for clarification or revision.

I am also grateful to an anonymous reader for Polity Press for his/her comments on the draft, and to Emma Hutchinson, Sarah Lambert, and Clare Ansell, editors at Polity, for their support throughout the writing and production process.

In writing the book, I have made use of some of my earlier papers on the subject. I thank the publishers of the relevant publications for the permission to do so. The papers I have drawn on are:

"What Is Terrorism?" *Journal of Applied Philosophy* 7 (1990), pp. 129–38. Copyright © 1990 Society for Applied Philosophy. Published by Wiley-Blackwell.

"The Morality of Terrorism," *Journal of Applied Philosophy* 14 (1997), pp. 221–33. Copyright © 1997 Society for Applied Philosophy. Published by Wiley-Blackwell.

"State Terrorism," in Tony Coady and Michael O'Keefe (eds), *Terrorism and Justice: Moral Argument in a Threatened World*, Melbourne: Melbourne University Press, 2002, pp. 31–42. Copyright © 2002 Igor Primoratz.

"Terrorism in the Israeli–Palestinian Conflict: A Case Study in Applied Ethics," *Iyyun: The Jerusalem Philosophical Quarterly* 55 (2006), pp. 27–48. Copyright © 2006 Iyyun: The Jerusalem Philosophical Quarterly. Published by the S. H. Bergman Center for Philosophical Studies, the Hebrew University of Jerusalem.

"Das Bombardement deutscher Städte im Zweiten Weltkrieg: Eine moralische Frage," *Deutsche Zeitschrift für Philosophie* 56 (2008), pp. 585–98. Copyright © 2008 Akademie Verlag GmbH, Berlin.

"Civilian Immunity, Supreme Emergency, and Moral Disaster," *Journal of Ethics* 15 (2011), pp. 371–86. Copyright © 2011 Springer Science+Business Media B.V.

Melbourne, February 2012

Introduction

The Subject

Since the terrorist attacks in New York on September 11, 2001, and those that came in their aftermath in London, Madrid, Bali, and elsewhere, terrorism has been the focus of a worldwide public debate. This debate has involved a wide array of participants, from political scientists and historians to politicians and common citizens. Yet the debate has not been very fruitful: there is little agreement on any of the main questions raised by terrorism, whether conceptual, moral, or political. It has often been plagued by lack of clarity about what its subject is: Who is a terrorist? What is terrorism? It has often been affected, and indeed informed and directed, by all manner of emotions, passions, and interests. It has been plagued by double standards and has often led to talking at cross purposes.

Perhaps this should not be surprising; after all, any debate greatly affected by emotion is liable to get confused and confusing. And terrorism is bound to stir some strong emotions. For, on all plausible accounts, terrorism is a type of violence, and violence is obviously an emotion-laden matter, in particular when directed at life and limb, as most terrorist violence is. Moreover, in an important respect, terrorism is the most frightening type of violence. For, although it is normally on a much smaller scale than the violence of war, unlike war, it is utterly unpredictable and potentially ubiquitous. As a civilian, I may not be under any threat of deadly violence even though my country is at war. But if my country is undergoing a campaign of terrorism, there is not much I can do to make sure that I and those I most care about are not killed or maimed. To be sure, we can avoid going to certain particularly dangerous places, or being out at all at particularly dangerous times. But that will only make for a somewhat better chance of not being hit – it will not provide real and long-term protection.

But the subject of terrorism is not emotion-laden only because terrorism is so frightening. In addition to triggering our apprehension or outright fear for our own life and the lives of family and friends, it often stirs our distinctively moral emotions. Many feel that terrorism is highly morally provocative and repugnant – indeed, a paradigm example of moral atrocity.

Of course, some will find terrorism morally repugnant because they consider all violence repugnant. But if one is not a pacifist, if one allows that violence, including state violence, and including war, too, may be morally justified, one might still draw the line at terrorism. In that case, what would be the crucial consideration concerning terrorism? Just why would one think that recourse to violence in law enforcement or war might be morally right, while terrorism is always morally wrong, and extremely wrong at that?

One possible reason is lack of authority. Terrorists act without any authorization, and indeed in opposition to and in contempt of the authorities. Whereas the violence employed by police officers in law enforcement, or by soldiers in war, is employed on behalf of the state, with its express authorization, terrorists "take the law into their own hands." Their violence is unlawful; indeed, it poses a challenge to the very idea of the rule of law.

Another reason is that terrorists operate in the dark, rather than fighting openly. Unlike soldiers and police officers, they do not identify themselves as such, but rather act as a "secret army." In this way they avoid taking chances of the sort they impose on those they attack.

Yet another way of explaining the deep moral repugnance most of us feel in relation to terrorism is to highlight those on the receiving end of terrorist violence. Unlike soldiers, who fight enemy soldiers, or police officers, who may resort to violent means in apprehending (suspected) criminals, terrorists aim their violence at randomly selected common citizens – that is, people who, by any plausible criterion, neither deserve nor are liable to be killed or maimed.

Each of these explanations can be challenged. The first and the second might be faulted as predicated on the widespread yet questionable assumption that terrorism is by definition employed only by non-state agents. The third might be accepted as relevant to some instances of terrorism, but not to terrorism in general. For, it might be said, some terrorists, just like soldiers (or guerrilla fighters), attack legitimate military targets. Of the three planes that reached their intended targets on September 11, 2001, two crashed into the World Trade Center, where they killed almost three thousand common citizens of the United States and many other countries. But the third crashed into the Pentagon, where it killed 125 people who certainly were not innocent civilians.

What moral considerations are relevant to attempts at a moral assessment of terrorism, then, depends on just what we take "terrorism" to mean. The moral and the conceptual questions are closely related. Before we set out in search of a moral account of terrorism, we need to decide what definition of "terrorism" we will be working with in our search.

Such a definition will need to relate to the actual use of the word "terrorism" in history, in social sciences, and in everyday discourse. In search for a helpful definition we should not be trying to craft one that would cover the entire range of actual use. In such matters, a measure of prescription is quite acceptable, and indeed necessary. But, of course, only a measure: if we wade too far afield, we risk ending up with an elegant definition, but one that leads to a discussion that is no longer of a piece with actual debates about terrorism among historians, political scientists, politicians, and our fellow citizens.

A plausible definition of terrorism – one that is both descriptive and (reasonably) prescriptive – should take us beyond the relativism indicated by the cliché "one person's terrorist is another's freedom fighter." It should also help us display and eliminate double standards that corrupt so much of public debate about terrorism. But the main point of trying for a helpful definition of "terrorism" is that it should provide a proper focus for our investigation of the moral questions posed by terrorism: Just what is morally wrong with it? Is it wrong in some special, distinctive way? Is it always wrong, or can it sometimes be morally justified? If it can, just what would it take to justify it?

This book is a discussion of these two topics – how "terrorism" should be defined and what its moral standing is. These are distinctively philosophical questions about terrorism, which are not discussed – at any rate, not systematically and in detail – in any other discipline. Of course, questions about the causes, main varieties, and various psychological, political, economic, and cultural effects of terrorism are highly important too. But such empirical questions are properly discussed in the social sciences rather than in philosophy. How terrorism has evolved throughout history is also very important.

But that is something best investigated by historians rather than philosophers.

The practical importance and timeliness of the subject of terrorism need no emphasizing. But the subject is also of great theoretical interest, both in itself and in its ramifications. It brings up the vexing issue of the morality of violence in general, and political violence in particular, in an especially dramatic form; for terrorism is, by any standard, a particularly morally and politically provoking type of violence. It poses yet again the problem of collective responsibility, since some terrorists and some apologists of terrorism seek to justify it by portraying its victims as sharing collective responsibility for the oppression, injustice, and misery they allege and want to see eliminated. It also raises, in a particularly sharp way, a fundamental ethical problem: Should most basic moral prohibitions, such as that of killing or maiming innocent people, be adopted as absolute, or do they sometimes give way to other extremely weighty moral considerations?

Plan of the Book

For the most part, the discussion in this book falls into two parts: chapter 1 deals with the question of defining "terrorism," while chapters 3 to 7 discuss the moral questions posed by terrorism. Chapter 2 straddles this division: it spells out the implication of my discussion of the meaning of "terrorism" that states, too, may engage in terrorism, and offers a moral assessment of state terrorism. Chapters 8 and 9 are case studies, showing how the view of the nature and moral status of terrorism offered in the book can be applied in understanding and judging particular campaigns of terrorism. The concluding remarks sum up the main points I seek to make in the book.

In chapter 1, I highlight some confusions and double standards plaguing ordinary use of the term and most everyday moral and political debates and then review some attempts at defining "terrorism" in philosophical literature. These attempts have included both definitions that acknowledge the core meaning of "terrorism" in ordinary use – violence for the purposes of intimidation – and definitions that sever the connection between "terrorism" and violence or between "terrorism" and terror. I go on to present a definition I believe should be particularly helpful in moral discourse about terrorism, focusing on four traits that cause most of us to regard it with great moral repugnance: (i) violence, (ii) innocence of its direct victims, (iii) intimidation, and (iv) coercion. I also look into the ways the question of definition of "terrorism" and that of its moral justification are related.

Government agencies and, more often than not, the media and the general public, too, tend to assume that terrorism is the preserve of non-state agents and find it difficult to discern and acknowledge the terrorist character of certain acts and policies of states. Yet, there is such a thing as state terrorism. In chapter 2 I review the varieties of state involvement with terrorism and argue that, by and large, state terrorism is morally worse than terrorism employed by non-state agencies.

Chapters 3 to 6 address the fundamental ethical question posed by terrorism: Can terrorism ever be morally justified? One might try to justify some acts or campaigns of terrorist violence by arguing that, appearances notwithstanding, its direct victims, common citizens, are not really innocent and therefore should not be deemed morally protected against deadly violence. Rather, they are complicit in the unjust or inhumane practices the terrorist fights against, and accordingly are liable to be attacked with such violence. I discuss some arguments along these lines in chapter 3.

Alternatively, one could concede the innocence of direct victims of terrorism and go on to argue that there are moral considerations weighty enough to override the moral protection against violence enjoined by their innocence. Adherents of consequentialist ethics might argue that, under certain circumstances, the consequences of resorting to terrorism can rationally be expected to be better, or less bad, on balance than the consequences of any other available course of action. In such cases, recourse to terrorism will be morally justified. Consequentialist justifications of terrorism are the subject of chapter 4.

Yet another option is to argue that, although terrorism violates some of the most important rights of its victims and constitutes a grave injustice, there are other, even weightier considerations of rights and justice that tell in its favor. This line of argument is discussed in chapter 5.

In each of these three chapters, I reach the conclusion that the arguments under discussion do not succeed. If so, we do not have a cogent general defense of terrorism. Terrorism is not justified by the involvement of its direct victims in the wrongs the terrorist fights against, or by the balance of its consequences, or, finally, by some considerations of rights and justice. It is morally wrong: not only because, and insofar as, its rationally expected consequences are bad on balance, but rather in itself, because of what it is. Moreover, it is extremely morally wrong. Is terrorism, then, absolutely wrong, whatever the consequences of failing to resort to it? I address this question in chapter 6. While quite a few philosophers endorse absolute moral rejection of terrorism, some argue that it may be justified *in extremis*. A widely discussed version of this position proposes that terrorism may be justified in a "supreme emergency," as the only way of staving off an imminent threat to the survival and freedom of a political community. I argue that this view is vague and overly permissive and go on to present a position that is structurally similar, but much more restrictive, which I term the "moral disaster" view. Terrorism is *almost* absolutely wrong, and may be considered only in the face of a "moral disaster," understood in a special, highly restrictive sense.

In addition to holding that terrorism is absolutely, or at least extremely, morally wrong, many feel that it is wrong in its own distinctive way. However, it is difficult to justify this feeling: to give a reasoned account of the distinctive moral atrociousness of terrorism. In chapter 7 I take a critical look at a string of attempts at providing such an account.

The discussion of the basic conceptual and moral questions raised by terrorism in chapters 1 to 7 is followed by two case studies. In chapter 8 I look into a campaign of state terrorism prosecuted in the course of a conventional war: the terror bombing of German cities in World War II. In chapter 9 I review and assess the role of both insurgent and state terrorism in an ethnic, religious, and political conflict that has been going on for almost a century now and still shows no signs of coming to an end: the conflict between the Zionist movement and the state of Israel, on the one hand, and the Palestinian people, on the other. Each of these cases of the use of terrorism is of considerable interest in its own right; but their discussion also helps test the relevance and cogency of the understanding and ethical evaluation of terrorism advanced in the book.

1

Defining Terrorism

Ordinary Use

What is terrorism? Current ordinary use of the word displays wide variety and considerable confusion; as a result, discussing terrorism and an array of moral, political, and legal questions it raises is difficult and often frustrating. Only two things stand out clearly in most instances of this use: terrorism is, or has to do with, violence and terror, and it is a bad thing, not something to be proud of or to support. Virtually nobody applies the word to their own actions or to the actions of those with whom they have sympathy or whose struggle they support. As the cliché has it, one person's terrorist is another's freedom fighter. This suggests that in discussions of terrorism, as in so much public debate, a double standard is at work: one of the form "us vs. them."

Another type of double standard, less obvious and thus perhaps even more of an obstacle to coming to grips with the notion of terrorism, is the tendency to accuse insurgents who resort to violence of resorting to terrorism, without pausing to take a closer look at the type of violence employed and just who its victims are, coupled with an unwillingness to mention terrorism when talking about violent actions and policies of a state, especially one's own state – even when *what* is done is the same. This indicates a double standard of the form "state vs. non-state agents" – the assumption that, whatever it is, terrorism is by definition something done by insurgents, and never by the state.

Much of this is apparent in the public debate about the use of terrorism in the Israeli–Palestinian conflict, for example. Both Palestinians and Israelis are committing what many among the uninvolved would call terrorism; both sides deny that they are engaging in terrorism; each accuses the other side of doing so; and both attempt to justify the violence they employ, wholly or in part, by the terrorist acts of the other side. Palestinians claim that theirs is a just struggle to put an end to occupation and oppression and to attain self-determination. We are morally and legally entitled to use violence to this end, they say. That is not terrorism, but rather fighting for freedom. Israelis retort that the state of Israel is certainly not engaging in terrorism. It is rather facing a terrorist onslaught, and is merely doing what any state in such circumstances would be morally and legally entitled and indeed obligated to do: it is using its armed forces and security services in defense of the country and the security of its citizens.

Those speaking on behalf of Palestinians are thus assuming that the decisive criterion of terrorism is the ultimate goal of the agent who resorts to violence. If it is a legitimate goal, such as national liberation, that cannot be terrorism. From their point of view, "terrorists fighting for freedom" is a contradiction in terms.

A classic statement of this position is given in Yasir Arafat's speech at the United Nations General Assembly on November 13, 1974:

> Those who call us terrorists . . . seek to hide the terrorism and tyranny of their acts, and our own posture of self-defense. The difference between the revolutionary and the terrorist lies in the reason for which each fights. For whoever stands by a just cause and fights for the freedom and liberation of his land from the invaders, the settlers and the colonialists, cannot possibly be called terrorist; otherwise the American people in their struggle for liberation from the British colonialists would have been terrorists, the European resistance against the Nazis would be terrorism, the struggle of the Asian, African and Latin American peoples would also be terrorism, and many of you who are in this Assembly Hall were considered terrorists. [Ours] is actually a just and proper struggle consecrated by the United Nations Charter and by the Universal Declaration of Human Rights. As to those who fight against the just causes, those who wage war to occupy, colonize and oppress other people – those are the terrorists, those are the people whose actions should be condemned, who should be called war criminals: for the justice of the cause determines the right to struggle. (Arafat 1995, pp. 334–5)

On the other hand, those speaking on behalf of Israel typically assume that it is the identity of the agent that determines whether some act or policy of violence is terrorist or not. This is apparent in the policy of both government spokespersons and the media of portraying as terrorism all violence on the part of Palestinians, whether directed at common Israeli citizens, at holders of high political office, or at members of military and security agencies. If an act or campaign of violence is carried out by insurgents, then it is terrorism; if by the state, then it is either a policing action or warfare. From their point of view, "state terrorism" is a contradiction in terms.

Moreover, this game of denying that one's own side is guilty of terrorism while accusing the other side of resorting to it, in a conflict in which both sides engage in the same type of violent activity, suggests that an additional assumption may be at work. Both sides may well be assuming that, if there is a violent conflict between two parties and one is guilty of terrorism, the other party is thereby absolved of the charge. If *they* are terrorists, *we* cannot be.

Efforts by the United Nations to develop a definition that could be accepted universally and open the way to dealing with terrorism by means of international law seem to have fallen victim, at least so far, to the same sort of relativism and confusion. Trudy Govier describes the impasse these efforts have reached:

> The United Nations has been trying to define terrorism for some thirty years, and has given up in its quest for a definition that everybody can agree upon. A major problem is that Western governments wanted to make sure that state agents could never be considered terrorist, while Islamic countries wanted to make sure that national liberation movements in the Middle East and Kashmir could never be considered terrorist. (Govier 2002, p. 89)

Once they are brought into the open, none of the three assumptions seems plausible. There is no reason whatsoever why two parties to a conflict cannot both be using terrorism, just as two criminals can be at each other's throats, or two states at war can both be waging an unjust war, whether in terms of *jus ad bellum* (justice of going to war) or *jus in bello* (justice in fighting) or both. The bias in favor of the state and against insurgents will not withstand scrutiny either. Although there is much to be said for having a state rather than living in a "state of nature," that is not to say that, in any conflict between a state and an insurgency, we should be on the side of the state. We sometimes find that an insurgency is morally justified and the attempts of the state to put it down are not; this is typically the case in a struggle for national liberation. Even in such a struggle, however, not every means will do, morally speaking. We sometimes have much sympathy with a people fighting to push out the occupying power, but still object if its fighters seek to achieve that by attacking enemy civilians rather than the military.

These remarks suggest that we will be in a better position to understand and therefore also to evaluate terrorism if we discard all three assumptions and try for a definition that does not define terrorism in terms of the agent or the agent's ultimate goal, and which allows for the possibility that victims of terrorism might themselves make use of it in response. Such a definition should focus on just what is done and what the proximate aim of doing it is, and put to one side the identity of the agent and their ultimate and allegedly justifying aim.

Terrorism and Violence

Etymologically, "terrorism" derives from "terror." Originally the word meant a system, or regime, of terror: at first that imposed by the Jacobins, who applied the term to themselves without any negative connotations. Subsequently it came to be applied to any such policy or regime and to express a strongly negative attitude, as it generally does today. Since I am seeking a definition that will cover both a single act and a policy of terrorism, I propose to put aside the notions of "system" and "regime" but preserve the connection with terror. Terrorism is meant to cause terror (extreme fear) and, when successful, does so. But if someone did something with a view to striking terror in the hearts of others with no further aim, just for the fun of it, I think we would not see that as a case of terrorism. Terrorism is intimidation with a purpose: the terror is meant to make others do things they would otherwise not do. Terrorism is coercive intimidation.

This is just the definition offered in one of the early philosophical discussions of the subject, Carl Wellman's paper "On Terrorism Itself": "the use or attempted use of terror as a means of coercion" (Wellman 1979, p. 250). Wellman remarks that violence often enters the picture, as it is one of the most effective ways of causing terror, but hastens to add that "the ethics of terrorism is not a mere footnote to the ethics of violence because violence is not essential to terrorism and, in fact, most acts of terrorism are nonviolent" (ibid., p. 251).

The ethics of terrorism is indeed more than a footnote to the ethics of violence, but not for the reason given by Wellman. Moreover, it seems to me that it does not make much sense to speak of "nonviolent terrorism" (taking this to exclude threats of violence as well). Wellman has three counterexamples, none of which strikes me as convincing. One is a judge who sentences a convicted criminal to death in order to deter potential criminals. I should think that execution is one of the more violent things we can do to a person. Then there is blackmail, in which the prospect of exposure is used as a means of intimidation and coercion. I think we would need to know just how serious the harm caused by the exposure would be in particular cases. If the harm threatened were great, and if we understand acts of violence as acts that characteristically inflict great harm in a striking manner, as Wellman does, then such instances of blackmail might indeed qualify as threats of violence. Finally, Wellman says:

> I must confess that I often engage in nonviolent terrorism myself, for I often threaten to flunk any student who hands in his paper after the due date. Anyone who doubts that my acts are genuine instances of the coercive use of terror is invited to observe the unwillingness of my students to hand in assigned papers on time in the absence of any such threat and the panic in my classroom when I issue my ultimatum. (1979, p. 252)

This seems quite fanciful. But if Wellman's students were indeed as given to panic and terror as he suggests, and if to be failed in his course was indeed such a great and dramatically inflicted harm that their reaction becomes understandable, then his threat was a threat of violence after all. It was not terrorism, though; nor is blackmail, or the meting out of the death penalty to a convicted criminal – but not for the reason adduced by Wellman.

A more radical version of Wellman's position on the definition and moral wrongness of terrorism is offered in Robert E. Goodin's book *What's Wrong with Terrorism?* While Wellman's understanding of terrorism is broad enough to allow for both political and nonpolitical terrorism, Goodin emphasizes its political role. He finds both its "analytic core" and its "core wrong" in the use of terror as a means for achieving a political purpose. Terrorism, he writes, is "fundamentally a political tactic, involving the deliberate frightening of people for political advantage. That is not the worst thing that terrorists commit. But it is the *distinctive* wrong that terrorists commit, making them terrorists and not mere murderers" (Goodin 2006, p. 49). On Wellman's account, one can commit an act of terrorism without using or threatening to use violence and without inflicting any great harm in some nonviolent way, merely by threatening to inflict such harm (see Wellman 1979, pp. 253–4). On Goodin's account, one need not even make a threat of any sort: one acts as a terrorist merely by issuing a warning about the acts of *others* that is meant to intimidate and thereby procure one's own political advantage. Thus Goodin casts his net widely enough to catch both many of those who would be generally perceived as terrorists and a relatively small, yet highly significant group of those who would not be so perceived: those who do not engage in violence of any sort, but do engage in the politics of fear. Accordingly, "*if* (or *insofar as*) Western political leaders are intending to frighten people for their own political advantage, *then* (to *that extent*) they are committing the same core wrong that is distinctively associated with terrorism" (2006, p. 2). When committing this wrong, they stimulate visceral responses instead of rational thinking, and thereby undermine democratic self-government. This is "a capital crime against democratic politics" (ibid., pp. 179–80). Osama Bin Laden is guilty of this crime; apparently, George W. Bush, too, should be charged with it. For, in many of his speeches, he was "clearly himself acting with the intention of instilling fear of terrorism to advance his own political agenda" and, on Goodin's definition, "that would count as an act of terrorism in itself" (ibid., pp. 169–70).

Now it is one thing to argue that deliberate generation of terror (great fear) is *one* defining trait of terrorism, and another to argue that doing so for the sake of coercion (Wellman), or for one's own political advantage (Goodin), *sufficiently* defines terrorism. The latter claims are quite implausible; they confuse terrorism and terrorizing. But, while terrorism is meant to terrorize, not every type of terrorizing with a view to coercion or to gaining political advantage is tantamount to terrorism. The terrorizing must be achieved by violence, whether actual or threatened. From the point of view both of history and of current use, "nonviolent terrorism" looks much too odd, and neither Wellman nor Goodin give us good reason to think of terrorism in a way that allows for it.

Whatever else it is, terrorism is (a type of) violence. But the notion of violence is itself in need of clarification. Just like "terrorism," "violence" has no universally accepted definition and tends to be used in a string of different senses. Just like "terrorism," "violence" is very much a contested concept, and its ordinary use often indicates confusion and displays double standards. This is not the place for an extended, systematic discussion of the subject; for the purposes of this chapter (and the book), some brief remarks must suffice.[1]

One characteristic way of defining violence is in terms of force. Of course, a simple equation of the two will not do: we do not want to say that every use of force is an instance of violence, and therefore also *prima facie* morally wrong. We can act firmly yet gently to restrain someone from doing something desperate, thus using force, but not violence, and doing the right thing under the circumstances rather than something wrong. Therefore we might define violence as "the illegal use of force, or threat of such force, against person or property" (Miller 1984, p. 403). But this implies that, whatever state agents do, as long as they are acting within the bounds of law, they can never be charged with violence – surely an unwelcome implication. A street brawl will count as violence, but a war between two states will not. Replacing "illegal" by "morally illegitimate" does not help. Given the amended definition, a fight between two persons that is clearly violent in the usual sense of "violence" cannot be described as such; we must find out first who is attacking and who is merely defending himself. Only the former is using violence, whereas the latter, while giving as good as he gets, is not. The same goes for war: the side fighting an unjust war is using violence, while the side fighting a just war is not. Both "legalistic" and "legitimist" definitions of violence are overly narrow, run together conceptual and normative considerations, and are bound to generate much too much relativism in discussions of the subject.

There is a different and broader approach to violence – broad enough to include a wide range of oppression and injustice in society. It is argued that these should count as violence because of their consequences. These consequences are not less damaging, and tend to be more pervasive and long term, than the application of brute physical force, which is commonly taken as the paradigm of violence. The fact that they are less dramatic, indeed less palpable, should not make us blind to the fact that they are often as pernicious as violence in the more usual, narrow sense. Thus John Harris argues that, when people are injured or made to suffer, it does not really matter just how that is done; what counts is the result, the injury or suffering caused. He proposes the following definition: "an act of violence occurs when injury or suffering is inflicted upon a person or persons by an agent who knows (or ought reasonably to have known) that his actions would result in the harm in question" (Harris 1980, p. 19). It is not important even whether people are injured by someone's action or as a consequence of failure to act; accordingly, the word "actions" in his definition is to be taken broadly enough to include omissions as well. This helps highlight "the violence of normal times" or "structural violence," the type of violence that is impersonal and psychological, rather than personal and physical, and results largely from people's inaction rather than from their positive actions. In this way, it may be possible to conscript the widely felt repugnance towards, and opposition to, "rape, murder, fire-and-sword"-type violence in the struggle against "structural violence" involved in injustice and oppression. That, indeed, is the main point in adopting a broad conception of violence.

However, it is not clear that much will be achieved along this path. Murder and rape, on the one hand, and injustice and oppression, on the other, are similar in that they are all brought about by human action (or inaction) and that they are all great wrongs; but they are also dissimilar in some important respects. For one thing, there is not only general agreement that murder and rape are wrong, but also a wide consensus on what clear-cut cases of murder or rape are. There is general agreement, too, that injustice and oppression are wrong; but there is very little consensus on what clear-cut cases of injustice or oppression are. Some would go further and say that both "injustice" and "oppression" are *essentially* contested concepts, and that we should not expect ever to reach much consensus on their application (see Gallie 1956). This makes the prospect of any great advance in eliminating or greatly reducing injustice or oppression by this particular method rather dubious. Moreover, we can run together things such as murder and rape, on the one hand, and injustice and oppression, on the other, under a single conceptual and moral heading of "violence" only if we ignore the distinction between acts and omissions. But it is not clear that we should do so. Surely there is a moral difference "between what is done, on the one hand, in stabbing a beggar to death and, on the other hand, in ignoring his plea for assistance" (Coady 2008, p. 31).

Yet another way to understand violence is to focus on the notion of force and qualify it in terms of its direct effects rather than, as in the first approach, in terms of its legality or moral legitimacy. Definitions along these lines reflect common use much better than the previous two approaches, and accordingly are often found in dictionaries. Thus the *Oxford English Dictionary* defines "violence" as "the exercise of physical force so as to inflict injury on or damage to persons or property." This is on the right track, but it raises two queries. Are the words "so as" to be taken in an objective sense, as "apt to," or in a subjective sense, as "meant to"? It seems to me that, if someone were to exercise physical force of the sort likely to cause injury or damage upon someone else, and did so without meaning to do so, that would still count as violence. If the idea of unintended violence makes sense, we should take the words "so as" in the objective sense. The other query is: Must violence always be physical? It would seem not: one can readily think of cases where injury or damage to a person is done by forceful psychological pressure rather than by physical force.

One type of such psychological violence is bullying at school or in the workplace; another is psychological battering that characterizes some intimate relationships. When the *OED* definition is amended to allow for such cases, it reads: "the exercise of physical or psychological force so as to inflict injury on or damage to persons or property."

Unlike definitions produced by the first approach, this one does not preempt discussion of the legality and moral justification of violence. Unlike definitions offered by the second approach, it does not run together injury or damage inflicted by humans on humans with intent, directly, by physical or psychological force, with moral wrongs or states of affairs that fall short of the ideal and are caused unintentionally, indirectly, without the use of force, by omission. I find the definition quite helpful, and will be assuming it throughout the book whenever I refer to violence.

Indiscriminate Violence

It is often said that the most distinctive characteristic of terrorism is that it employs violence indiscriminately. This is certainly not true if construed literally: terrorists do not strike blindly and pointlessly, left and right. They plan their actions carefully, weighing the options and trying for the course of action that will best promote their objective at the lowest cost to themselves. But the claim is true, and of crucial importance, if taken to refer to the terrorists' failure to discriminate between those who are and those who are not innocent and to direct their violence only at the latter while respecting the immunity of the former.

Terrorism has a certain structure. It has two targets: the immediate, direct target, which is of secondary importance, and the indirect target, which is really important. This indirect strategy is a feature of everyday life, and there is nothing wrong with it as such. But when the indirect, but really important, aim is to force someone to do something they would otherwise not do, when that is to be achieved by intimidation, and when intimidation is effected by using violence against innocent people – by killing, maiming, or otherwise severely harming them – or by threatening to do so, then the indirect strategy is that of terrorism. The primary and secondary targets are different persons or groups of people. The person or persons who constitute the primary but indirect target of the terrorist may or may not be innocent themselves; what is essential is that those who are made the terrorists' secondary but direct target are. Thus terrorists may attack a group of civilians with the aim of intimidating the civilian population at large and getting it to leave a certain area. Or they may attack such a group with the purpose of cowing the government into accepting their demands, as is usually the case in airplane hijacking. Those attacked are people who are innocent and who, by virtue of this innocence, enjoy immunity against attack. In war, these are innocent civilians: everyone except members of armed forces and security services, those who supply them with arms and ammunition, and political officials directly involved in the conflict. In political conflict that falls short of war, this class has a similarly wide scope: it includes everyone except certain government officials, police, and members of security services.

What is the sense in which the direct victims of the terrorist are "innocent"? They are not guilty of any action (or omission) the terrorist could plausibly bring up as a justification of what he does to them. There is nothing those victims have *done* (or failed to do) that makes them deserve, or liable, to be killed or maimed. They are not attacking him, so he cannot justify his action as one of self-defense. They are not waging war on him or on those in whose behalf he presumes to act; therefore he cannot say that he, too, is merely fighting a war. They are not responsible, on any credible understanding of responsibility, for the (real or alleged) injustice or suffering that is inflicted on the terrorist or on those whose cause he has adopted, an injustice or suffering so enormous that it could justify a violent response. Or, if they are, he is not in a position to know that. They are, therefore, morally protected from violent attack: as innocent civilians rather than soldiers, if the context is one of war, or as common citizens rather than those devising or implementing policy, if the conflict falls short of war.

Notice that I am not making the sweeping claim that the direct victims of terrorist violence are not responsible in any way and to any degree for the injustice or suffering the terrorist fights against, and that they are accordingly not liable to criticism or other unfavorable response of any sort. I am rather saying that they are not responsible, *on any credible understanding* of responsibility and liability, for the injustice or suffering the terrorist fights against – not responsible at all, or at least not responsible to the degree that makes them liable to be killed or maimed on that account. Moreover, the injustice or suffering at issue need not be *real*; it may be merely *alleged*.

To take up the latter point first, I am not speaking of innocence of injustice or infliction of suffering and the immunity that comes with it from a point of view independent of that of the terrorist. Adopting such an approach would introduce an unacceptable degree of relativity into discussions of terrorism. For example, the killing of Italian politician Aldo Moro by the Red Brigades would be seen as a case of terrorism by most of us. For, whatever we might think of Moro's policies, most of us do not consider them so extremely unjust and morally intolerable as to make him deserve to die on account of them; that is, most of us think of Moro as innocent in the relevant sense and therefore immune against killing. But the Red Brigades would deny that, and claim that what they did was political assassination, not terrorism; for they judged his policies quite differently. In general, if we adopted this approach, whether we thought an act of violence was a case of terrorism or not would depend on whether we thought the actions and policies of its direct victims were causing great injustice or suffering; and that, of course, would normally be open to much disagreement. The bottom line would be that, to paraphrase *the* cliché about terrorism, one person's terrorist would be another's political assassin. In order not to have to grant that, I am saying that being responsible for a merely alleged great injustice or suffering – a great injustice or suffering that is alleged by the terrorist, but not considered as such by others – is enough to lose one's immunity against violence. This is in line with the view adopted in mainstream versions of just war theory and international laws of war that one does not lose one's immunity against acts of war only by fighting in an unjust war, but rather by fighting in any war. Similarly, one does not lose one's immunity against political violence only by holding office in a gravely unjust government or implementing policies of such a government, but by holding office in or implementing policies of any government. As King Umberto I of Italy said after an unsuccessful attempt on his life, this kind of risk is part of the job.

Members of these two classes who fall victim to violence are not considered innocent and morally protected against violence by those attacking them. The latter rather think of their acts as acts of war or political assassination, respectively. I submit that we should grant that. In other words, I submit that the terrorist's victim is innocent *from the terrorist's own point of view* – that is, innocent even if we grant the terrorist her assessment of the policies at issue. Of course, this should not be thought to imply that, if someone holds that a government is being gravely unjust to, or is inflicting intolerable suffering on, its subjects, they have a moral license to kill its officials, but only that, if they do so, that will not be terrorism but, rather, political assassination. We can still condemn their actions as harshly as we feel we should if we reject their judgment of the policies at issue. We can do so even if we accept that judgment, if we believe that they could and should have opposed those policies by nonviolent means. We will not be condemning their actions *qua* terrorism. But to say of an action that it is not terrorism but political assassination is neither to justify nor to excuse it.

This means that, if the terrorist subscribes to some credible understanding of responsibility and liability, she kills or maims people she herself, in her heart, believes to be innocent. By a credible view of these matters I mean a view that, first, grounds a person's *responsibility* for some state of affairs in that person's acts or omissions that are significantly voluntary – that is, informed and free – and have a sufficiently strong connection with that state of affairs. Second, I mean a view that requires an intelligible and morally acceptable proportion between what a person is responsible for and the unfavorable response to which he or she is *liable* on that account.

This fact – that the terrorist kills and maims people she herself thinks innocent – goes a long way in explaining why most of us view terrorism with such repugnance. To be sure, there are terrorists who adhere to crude notions of collective responsibility and liability that take membership in an ethnic or religious group or citizenship of a state as a sufficient ground, or an indication of a sufficient ground, for ascription of such responsibility and liability. For example, the perpetrators of the attacks in New York on September 11, 2001, seem to have held such views. I will discuss several instances of such views in chapter 3. Still other terrorists are amoralists and will not be bothered by questions of responsibility and liability. Terrorists belonging to these two classes do not believe their victims to be innocent. The atrociousness of their type of terrorism must be located elsewhere: in their preposterous views of responsibility and liability and the gory consequences these views have in their practice.

Since terrorism is indiscriminate in the sense specified – since it does not discriminate between the guilty and the innocent – it is also unpredictable. One can never count on keeping clear of the terrorists by not doing the things the terrorists object to: for example, by not joining the army or the police, or by avoiding political office. One can never know whether, at any time and in virtually any place, one will become a target of a terrorist attack.

Walter Laqueur objects to accounts of terrorism as indiscriminate violence:

> Many terrorist groups have been quite indiscriminate in the choice of their victims, for they assume that the slaughter of innocents would sow

panic, give them publicity and help to destabilize the state and society. However, elsewhere terrorist operations have been quite selective. It can hardly be argued that President Sadat, the Pope, Aldo Moro or Indira Gandhi were arbitrary targets. Therefore, the argument that terrorist violence is by its nature random, and that innocence is the quintessential condition for the choice of victims, cannot be accepted as a general proposition; this would imply that there is a conscious selection process on the part of the terrorist, that they give immunity to the "guilty" and choose only the innocents. (Laqueur 1987, pp. 143–4)

Neither of the two objections is convincing. To take the latter first, the way Laqueur presents it contains a contradiction: if it is claimed that terrorist violence is *random*, then it cannot also be claimed that it is directed *solely* against the innocent, while the guilty are given immunity. What *is* claimed is that the defining feature of terrorism, and the reason why many of us find it extremely morally repugnant, is its failure to discriminate between the innocent and the guilty, and its consequent failure to respect the immunity of the former and to attack only the latter. Terrorists do not take on the army or the police, nor do they attempt to kill a political official, but choose, say, to plant a bomb in a city bus, either because that is so much easier or, perhaps, because that will better serve their cause. They know that their victims are innocent civilians, but that is no good reason for them not to do it. If a couple of soldiers get on the bus along with the civilians and get killed as well, they will not see that as a fly in the ointment, but will either consider it irrelevant or welcome it as an unexpected bonus. As for Laqueur's first objection, it is predicated either on a definition of terrorism that includes political assassination, and is thus question-begging, or on the assumption that every act of a terrorist is a terrorist act, which is absurd. The Red Brigades, for instance, were a terrorist organization, for they committed many terrorist acts; but when they abducted and killed Aldo Moro, that was political assassination, not terrorism.

This targeting of the innocent is the essential trait of terrorism, both conceptually and morally. The distinction between guilt and innocence is one of the basic distinctions in the moral experience of most of us. Most of us require that the infliction of serious harm on someone be justified in terms of some free, deliberate action, or culpable inaction, on their part. If this cannot be done, people are innocent in the relevant sense, and thus immune against the infliction of such harm. A discussion of the way terrorism should be defined is not the right context for establishing this claim. But I would not be greatly tempted to try to prove it in any context. The belief that innocence implies a far-reaching (though perhaps not absolute) immunity against the infliction of severe harm is a brute fact of the moral experience of most of us. For those who find it compelling, it is as simple and compelling as anything, and more so than anything that might be brought up as a supporting argument. Accordingly, as Michael Walzer puts it, "the theoretical problem is not to describe how immunity is gained, but how it is lost. We are all immune to start with; our right not to be attacked is a feature of normal human relationships" (Walzer 2000, p. 145 n.). One may lose this immunity by attacking someone else, or by enlisting in the army in time of war, or by joining security services, or by holding office in a regime or an organization that is resisted by violence because of its unjust, or allegedly unjust, policies. But one who has done none of the above is innocent of anything that might plausibly be brought up as a justification for a violent attack on her, or a threat of such an attack, and is thus immune against it. When she is attacked nevertheless, with the aim of intimidating someone else and making them do something they otherwise would not do, that is terrorism. Terrorism is different, both conceptually and morally, from violence employed in self-defense, from war in general and guerrilla war in particular, and from political assassination.

My account of terrorism is motivated by the need to overcome relativism that infests most debates about the subject and makes them barren. I have argued that, in order to arrive at an understanding of terrorism that is not plagued by relativism, we must put aside both the identities of those employing terrorism *and* their ultimate aims and the related issue of the moral standing of the policies and practices they oppose. We must focus instead on *what is done* and what is the *proximate aim* of doing it. The conceptually and morally salient trait of terrorism is that it is violence against the innocent: against those who, on any credible understanding of responsibility and liability, are not responsible, or not responsible enough, for the real or alleged injustice or suffering the terrorist fights against. Since not only real, but also merely alleged, injustice or suffering should count in determining the innocence of the direct victims and deciding who is a terrorist, my account does not make this decision hostage to endless debates about the moral standing of contested policies and practices. My conception of terrorism and its application does not presuppose any particular type of agent, any particular ultimate aim, any particular moral and political views. It presents terrorism as a way of acting that could be adopted by different agents and could serve various ultimate objectives (most but perhaps not all of them political). It can be employed by states or by non-state agents and may promote national liberation or oppression, revolutionary or conservative causes (and may possibly pursue some nonpolitical aims as well). One can be a terrorist *and* a freedom fighter; terrorism is not the monopoly of enemies of freedom. One can hold high government or military office *and* design or implement a terrorist campaign; terrorism is not the preserve of insurgents. In this way much of the relativism concerning who is and who is not a terrorist that has plagued contemporary public debate can be overcome.

However, there is a residuum of relativity: my account does presuppose a certain understanding of responsibility and liability, whereby a person is *responsible* for a state of affairs only by virtue of that person's voluntary – that is, informed and free – act or omission that has a sufficiently strong connection to that state of affairs, and thereby becomes *liable* to some proportionately unfavorable response. Given this understanding of responsibility and liability, the victims of terrorist violence will be found innocent from the terrorist's own point of view. Yet when an individual or group resorts to violence which we perceive as terrorist, but rejects the label by deploying a view of responsibility and liability based on some extremely far-fetched connection between states of affairs and human choices and actions, and argues that entire social classes or nations are responsible for certain policies and practices and liable to be attacked by deadly violence, I can only discount such arguments as preposterous. I will then insist on describing and judging their actions as terrorist, although they reject this label. I do not see how this last remnant of relativity can be eliminated; we may have to live with it.

Further Issues

The next three points are suggested by C. A. J. Coady's definition of a terrorist act as "a political act, ordinarily committed by an organized group, which involves the intentional killing or other severe harming of noncombatants or the threat of the same or intentional severe damage to the property of noncombatants or the threat of the same" (Coady 2008, p. 159).

While Wellman and Goodin want to preserve the connection between terrorism and terror, but to disconnect terrorism from violence, Coady's definition suggests the opposite: terrorism is a type of violence which, indeed, often causes terror, but this is "an important insight into the sociology of terrorism" and should not be included in the definition. The connection is merely contingent (2008, p. 162). Moreover, do not all uses of political violence effect some degree of fear?

That is true, but there is an important difference between the sort of violence most of us would want to call terrorist and other kinds of violence, where the fear caused is either a less important objective or not an objective at all, but merely a welcome byproduct. In terrorism proper, the causing of fear and coercion through fear is *the* objective. Even if in certain contexts coercion through fear may not seem important enough to single out this particular type of violence, things look different from a moral point of view. Most of us feel that terrorism is so very wrong primarily, but not solely, because it is violence inflicted on the innocent; intimidation and coercion through intimidation are *additional* grounds for moral condemnation, an insult added to injury.

This should not be taken to suggest a simplistic, overly rationalistic picture of terrorism: a picture of the terrorist making a clearly specified threat to his primary target, who then rationally considers the matter and comes to the conclusion that it pays to comply. This picture may fit some cases of terrorism – for instance, airplane hijacking – but it certainly does not fit others. For terrorism often aims at generating long and complex social processes, involving much irrational behavior, that are meant to disorient the public and destabilize various social arrangements and institutions, if not social life in general. However, intimidation plays a central role in such cases as well, while the ultimate aim of the terrorists is, again, to make those who constitute their primary target do things they otherwise would not do. Therefore such cases do not call for a revision of the definition of terrorism as a type of coercion through intimidation.

The violence perpetrated by terrorists is typically killing, maiming, or otherwise severely harming their victims. Must terrorist violence be directed against persons? According to Coady's definition, it need not be. Suppose a terrorist organization decided to stop killing and maiming people and took to destroying valuable works of art instead. Or suppose it started destroying the crops that are the only source of livelihood of a village. Would that mean giving up terrorism for a non-terrorist struggle, or would it rather be substituting one terrorist method for another? In the latter case, I think, we would still speak of terrorism – because the destruction of property would threaten people's lives. In the former case, however, the word "terrorism" might no longer seem clearly appropriate. As Jenny Teichman puts it, "it may indeed be grossly unfair and unjust to destroy the property of non-combatants, but unless that property is needed for life itself it isn't terroristic. For one thing it is not likely to produce terror – only fury" (Teichman 1986, p. 92).

Terrorism is often defined in various overly restrictive ways. The identification of terrorism with political terrorism, as in the definition offered by Coady, is quite typical. Yet the method of coercive intimidation by infliction of violence on innocent persons has often been used in nonpolitical contexts: one can speak of religious terrorism (e.g. that of the Hizballah) and criminal terrorism (e.g. that of the Mafia). Much of the former type of terrorism can perhaps be subsumed under political violence, if "political" is understood broadly enough; but the latter cannot. Philosophical discussion of terrorism, in particular, should allow for its nonpolitical varieties. Such discussion aims at determining the moral status of terrorism, and that need not depend on whether it is employed for political or nonpolitical purposes. It might be said that, other things being equal, the use of violence is morally worse if its aim is self-interested, as in criminal activities, than if it is other-regarding, as it is in politics. On the other hand, some political views and practices are so morally repugnant that violence used in implementing them may be morally worse rather than better on that account.

Even more restrictive are definitions couched in terms of *who* uses terrorism. Terrorism is often presented as a method employed solely by rebels and revolutionaries, and state terrorism is thus defined out of existence. This may be good propaganda, but it is poor analysis. As I remarked at the outset, the word "terrorism" was used originally to refer to the reign of terror set up by the Jacobins – that is, to a case of *state* terrorism. And liberal and democratic states too have engaged in terrorism: witness the bombing of Hamburg and Dresden, Hiroshima and Nagasaki. In all these cases the targets were neither military nor industrial, but rather major centers of civilian population of enemy countries. The objective was to destroy the morale and break the will of the population and in that way either secure capitulation of the enemy (Germany) or shorten the war (against Japan). This kind of bombing has come to be known as "terror bombing." Furthermore, there is a type of state – the totalitarian state – whose most fundamental principle is permanent, institutionalized terrorism. For nothing less than such terrorism, exercised by the omnipotent state and, in particular, its secret police, would do as a means of an attempt at total domination of society. (I will have to say more on state terrorism in the next chapter.)

The preceding discussion results in the following definition of terrorism: the deliberate use of violence, or threat of its use, against innocent people, with the aim of intimidating some other people into a course of action they otherwise would not take.

Let me summarize the most important points about this definition.

- Terrorism has a certain structure. It has two targets, the primary and secondary. The latter target is directly hit, but the objective is to get at the former, to intimidate the person or persons who are the primary target into doing things they otherwise would not do.
- The secondary target, which is hit directly, consists of innocent people. Thus acts of terrorism are distinguished from acts of war proper – whether conventional, civil, or guerrilla war – in which innocent civilians are not deliberately attacked. They are also distinguished from acts of political assassination, whose victims – political officials and police officers – are responsible for certain policies and their enforcement. This, of course, does not mean that an army cannot engage in terrorism; many guerrilla and even conventional armies have done so. Nor does it mean that political assassination does not often intimidate the government or the public, or is not often meant to do so.
- The definition preserves the connection of "terrorism" with "terror" and "terrorizing," which has a long history and is well entrenched in current ordinary use.
- The definition covers both political and nonpolitical (e.g. religious or criminal) terrorism.
- With regard to political terrorism, it makes it possible to speak both of state and non-state terrorism, of revolutionary and counter-revolutionary terrorism, of terrorism of the left and of the right. The definition is politically neutral.
- The definition is both narrower in some respects and wider in others than ordinary use might warrant. Attacks of insurgents on holders of high political office, soldiers, or police officers, which the authorities and the media portray, and the public perceives, as terrorist, would *not* count as such, but rather as political assassination or guerrilla warfare. The bombing of German and Japanese cities in World War II, or numerous Israeli army attacks on Lebanon, on the other hand, are commonly presented as acts of war, but *would* count as terrorism on my definition. That, I submit, is just as it should be. A helpful definition of "terrorism" should not depart from ordinary use drastically and for no good reason. At the same

time, if we hope for more discerning and critical moral understanding of terrorism, we cannot be unduly bound by such use. What
matters here is that, in attacks of the former type, the targets are
holders of high political office, soldiers, or police officers, and not
innocent people. In attacks of the latter type, innocent people are
deliberately targeted with the aim of intimidation and coercion. On
the other hand, whether the bomb is planted by hand or dropped
from an aircraft or who does or does not wear a uniform can hardly
be decisive, morally speaking.

- By highlighting the innocence of direct victims of terrorism, the
definition helps relate the debate about the morality of terrorism to
the traditional discussion of the morality of war, and in particular
connects it with just war theory. The main provision of that theory
under the heading of *jus in bello*, the morality of ways and means
of fighting in war, is the principle of discrimination, enjoining bel-
ligerents to discriminate between military and civilian targets and
to refrain from intentionally harming innocent civilians.

Definitions and Justifications

Can terrorism be morally justified? There is no single answer to this
question, since there is no single understanding of what terrorism is.
The focus of any attempt at answering it will be determined by the
conception, or definition, of terrorism that is adopted at the outset.

Philosophical literature on terrorism offers a wide variety of definitions of the term, as almost every philosopher starts with at least a
brief discussion of the question of definition and proffers his or her
own answer to it. The definitions on offer – those I have and those
I have not discussed – differ in various respects and can be classi-
fied in more than one way. But the most important difference is
between definitions that might be termed, respectively, narrow and
wide: those, such as my own, C. A. J. Coady's, and many others,
that restrict terrorism to violent attacks on innocent people (civilians,
noncombatants, common citizens) and those that do not. There are
many examples of the latter, too. Thus Georg Meggle defines acts of
terrorism as "acts that (attempt to) achieve aims by means of terror
induced by violence" (Meggle 2011, p. 133). Another good example
is the definition proposed by J. Angelo Corlett:

> Terrorism is the attempt to achieve (or prevent) political, social, eco-
> nomic, or religious change by the actual or threatened use of violence

against other persons or other persons' property; the violence (or threat thereof) . . . is aimed partly at destabilizing (or maintaining) an existing political or social order, but mainly at publicizing the goals or causes espoused by the agents or those on whose behalf the agents act; often, though not always, terrorism is aimed at provoking extreme counter-measures which will win public support for the terrorists and their goals or causes. (Corlett 2003, pp. 119–20; emphasis deleted)

Both Meggle and Corlett bring up reasons for rejecting narrow definitions and adopting a wide one instead. Meggle does not want to be prevented from following traditional use of the term and apply-ing it to such activities as assassination of holders of high political office, which was the preferred type of political violence on the part of some nineteenth-century Russian revolutionary organizations (Meggle 2011, p. 138 n. 13). Corlett insists that we keep the question of the nature of terrorism and that of its moral justification separate. In order to do so, we must have a morally neutral definition of ter-rorism, and that means a wide one. Narrow definitions "unwarrant-edly sneak into the construal of terrorism" a feature that is obviously morally unjustified. This makes terrorism morally wrong by defini-tion and preempts all discussion of its moral standing (Corlett 2003, pp. 114–21, 135).

Let me address Corlett's objection first. In one sense, he is right: one might be tempted to move from an understanding of terrorism as violence against the innocent to the moral conclusion that terror-ism is obviously and always wrong. Thus Rüdiger Bittner starts an essay written for a collection on the ethics of terrorism by claiming that there is no such ethics. "There is nothing worth asking here. It is wrong, and obviously wrong . . . to kill innocent people, for political aims without political authority. [. . .] Terrorism . . . is a matter as clear as can be. [. . .] The ethics of terrorism is a subject as interesting as the ethics of murder" (Bittner 2005, p. 207). However, this move is invalid: it is predicated on the confusion of "intrinsically wrong" and "absolutely wrong." If a way of acting is absolutely wrong then it must be wrong in itself; bad consequences can make a way of acting only conditionally wrong – wrong on condition that they indeed follow (or are rationally expected to follow). But the converse does not hold: a way of acting may be wrong in itself, yet not wrong abso-lutely, always, in any actual or possible circumstances. It may be wrong as long as there are no other moral considerations that tell in its favor and are weighty enough to override its intrinsic wrongness. That is, a way of acting may be wrong *prima facie*, some or most of the time, even almost all the time, rather than wrong all things considered and always.

Now violence against the innocent is wrong in itself, and obviously so, if anything is. If that is what terrorism is, then it is indeed obviously wrong intrinsically, because of what it is. But to say this amounts to saying that it is *prima facie* wrong – to stating a general presumption against terrorism, not its sweeping moral condemnation in each and every actual or possible instance, whatever the circumstances and whatever the consequences of desisting from it. A narrow definition, then, does not rule out that in certain circumstances terrorism might not be wrong, all things considered. It does not preempt ethical investigation of the subject: particular acts and campaigns of terrorism still have to be judged on their merits. Many, perhaps most, will turn out to be wrong both *prima facie* and all things considered. But we do not know that this will always be the case: that we will never come across an act or campaign of terrorism that is wrong *prima facie*, but is not wrong all things considered.

Meggle, too, has a point: a wide definition has the advantage of being faithful to ordinary use, both historical and current, whereas a narrow one has a more restricted application. Large-scale terrorism in the sense captured by a narrow definition is very much a phenomenon of the twentieth and twenty-first centuries. To be sure, the targeting of the innocent as a means of coercive intimidation was occasionally advocated and practised in the nineteenth century as well: advocated, for instance, by the radical democrat Karl Heinzen (see Heinzen 1978) and practised in particular in the last decades of that century by some Irish nationalists and some of the anarchists who believed in "propaganda by deed." But most of those who were called, and often called themselves, terrorists throughout the nineteenth century – most anarchists, various revolutionary groups in Russia – did not practise terrorism in this sense, but rather engaged in political assassination. Russian revolutionaries in particular were given to constant probing of the moral questions raised by their struggle. They accepted the use of violence only unwillingly and generally insisted that it be employed sparingly; in the words of Peter Lavrov, "not one drop of unnecessary blood shall be spilled" (quoted in Ivianski 1989, p. 232). They considered assassination of some of the most prominent officials of the oppressive regime as a grave sin that must be committed, but must also be expiated by dying on the gallows. They would never contemplate deliberate killing and maiming of the innocent. If a planned assassination turned out to involve deaths of innocent people as an inevitable side effect, they called off the action, even if that meant taking an extreme risk to themselves (see Ivianski 1989). The moral distance between them and present-day terrorists is immense. This may not be decisive for those engaged in historical or social science research of terrorism; they may well prefer a definition that applies to the entire range of practices termed "terrorist" throughout history. Philosophers, however, are interested above all in ethical assessment of terrorism, and therefore are better off adopting a narrow definition and focusing on contemporary terrorism and its morally salient traits. That is best done by restricting the term "terrorism" to the latter, rather than applying it to both types of violence and then distinguishing between them in some such terms as "direct" and "indirect" or "individual" and "mass" terrorism.

I need not go into the causes of the shift from assassination of chiefs of state and other high political officials to indiscriminate attacks on the innocent which took place at the beginning of the twentieth century. At the practical level, the explanation may well be that "mass" terrorism promises to be much more effective than the "individual" variety. As Edward Hyams has written, "chiefs of state are more carefully guarded than they used to be, and revolutionaries have learnt that the elimination of individual leaders is apt to resemble driving out Satan with Beelzebub" (Hyams 1974, p. 166). At a more general level, one might cite Walter Laqueur, who points out that, "in the twentieth century, human life became cheaper; the belief gained ground that the end justified all means, and that humanity was a bourgeois prejudice" (Laqueur 1987, p. 84).

In this connection, it is telling that, more often than not, philosophers who adopt a wide definition normally do not mean to deny or belittle the difference between violence against the innocent and violence against those who cannot claim innocence of the wrongs at issue. This difference is fully acknowledged in Meggle's account of terrorism: it is the basis of his distinction between "terrorism in the strong sense," which deliberately, recklessly, or negligently harms innocent people, and "terrorism in the weak sense," which does not (Meggle 2002). Corlett distinguishes between terrorism that is selective – that is, directed "only against those clearly guilty of committing acts of significant injustice" (Corlett 2003, p. 127) – and terrorism that is not selective in this way. Moreover, both philosophers see great *moral* difference between the two types of what they call "terrorism." Meggle submits that terrorism that targets, or otherwise culpably harms, innocent persons – that is, terrorism in the strong sense – is morally prohibited without any exception. On the other hand, terrorism that does not culpably cause harm to the innocent – that is, terrorism in the weak sense (which does not count as "terrorism" on a narrow definition of the term) – may live up to the requirements of the ethics of violence and war and thus be morally justified (Meggle 2002, pp. 155–7). Corlett presents a list of conditions on which terrorism might be morally justified; the condition to the point here is that it be "as conscientiously selective as possible." That means that only "selective" terrorism (which, again, does not qualify for "terrorism" on a narrow definition of the word) can be morally justified, whereas terrorism that is not selective cannot (Corlett 2003, pp. 126–7). In a similar vein, Robert Young rejects wide definitions of terrorism as "moralized" and question-begging, and adopts a narrow characterization. He then submits that "it is a general truth that the more indiscriminate the terrorist action the harder it will be to give a moral defense of it" (Young 2004, pp. 56–7). He goes on to argue that, on certain conditions, terrorism of the discriminating kind – that is, directed at those who cannot claim innocence of the wrongs at issue (which does not count as terrorism on a narrow definition) – may be morally justified.

This, too, is a possible way of approaching the problem of moral assessment of violence in general and terrorism in particular, for it does not deny or obfuscate, but rather takes into account, the crucial moral difference between killing or seriously injuring those deeply involved with a government, war, or policy considered to be gravely unjust and killing or seriously injuring innocent civilians or common citizens. But I find this approach unnecessarily roundabout. It seems more helpful to highlight the immense moral difference between the two types of violence by reserving the term "terrorism" for the latter and describing the former as political assassination – that is, to opt for a narrow definition of terrorism such as the one I have proposed here. Accordingly, my discussion throughout the book will focus on terrorism in the narrow sense of violence against innocent civilians or common citizens, intended to intimidate and coerce.

2
State Terrorism and Counterterrorism

Varieties of State Involvement with Terrorism

The upshot of the preceding chapter was that, for the purposes of philosophical discussion, terrorism is best defined as the deliberate use of violence, or threat of its use, against innocent people, with the aim of intimidating some other people into a course of action they otherwise would not take. The definition says nothing about the identity of terrorists: they can be rebels or revolutionaries, or criminals, but they can also be soldiers of a state at war or members of a state security organization. Indeed, when it first appeared in political discourse, the word "terrorism" was used to describe a case of state terrorism – the "Reign of Terror" imposed by the Jacobin regime. Historians of the French Revolution have analyzed and discussed that case in great detail. There are also historical studies of some other instances of state terrorism, most notably of the period of "the Great Terror" in the Soviet Union.

Closer to home, however, state terrorism is apparently much more difficult to discern. Discussions of terrorism in social sciences and (to a lesser degree) in philosophy tend to focus on insurgent terrorism. In common parlance and in the media, terrorism is as a rule assumed to be an activity of non-state agents in virtue of the very meaning of the word. If one suggests that the army or security services are doing the same things that, when done by insurgents, are invariably described and condemned as terrorist, the usual reply is: "But these are actions done on behalf of the state, in pursuit of legitimate state aims: the army, waging war, or the security services, fending off threats to our security." As British poet Roger Woddis put it in "Ethics for Everyman" (quoted in Coady 2008, p. 154),

Throwing a bomb is bad,
Dropping a bomb is good;
Terror, no need to add,
Depends on who's wearing the hood.

As far as everyday discourse and the media are concerned, this can perhaps be explained by two related tendencies. One is the widely shared assumption that, at least normally, what the state does has a certain kind of legitimacy, while those challenging it tend to be perceived as forces of disorder and destruction, engaged in clearly unjustifiable pursuits. The other is the double standard of the form "Us vs. Them." In states facing insurgency, more often than not, the general public and the media take the side of the state. This tends to affect the usage. An offshoot of this tendency is that, when insurgents abroad are sponsored by our state, we do not call them terrorists but, rather, guerrillas or freedom fighters.

The focusing on non-state terrorism in social sciences is given a different explanation: that whatever the similarities between state and non-state terrorism, the dissimilarities are more prominent and instructive. Walter Laqueur, a leading authority on the history and sociology of terrorism, tells us that the two "fulfil different functions and manifest themselves in different ways" and that "nothing is gained by ignoring the specifics of violence" (Laqueur 1987, p. 146). I am not convinced that this approach is to be preferred in social sciences.[2] But, be that as it may, this certainly will not do in philosophy. If some acts of state agents are basically similar to and exhibit the same morally relevant traits as acts of non-state agencies commonly termed terrorist, that will clearly determine our moral judgment of both. Accordingly, philosophers have been less reluctant than sociologists and political scientists to recognize and discuss state terrorism (see Glover 1991; Ryan 1991; Gilbert 1994; Ashmore 1997; Lackey 2004).

But the philosophical work on the subject done so far leaves room, and indeed suggests the need, for a typology of state involvement in terrorism. There is also a need for a fuller statement of the argument for a claim philosophers sometimes make in passing: that state terrorism is worse, morally speaking, than terrorism by non-state agents. In this chapter, I discuss these two topics. I also briefly consider some issues raised by counterterrorism.

Philosophers are given to introducing all manner of distinctions where none were acknowledged before. With respect to state terrorism, this has been the case to a lesser degree than on most other issues. Thus Alan Ryan discusses the claim that "a terrorist state" is logically impossible by virtue of the definition of "state," and brings up Stalin's Soviet Union and Nazi Germany as obvious counterexamples. Further on he writes: "If Syria paid for, protected, equipped, and assisted hijackers and would-be bombers of El Al aircraft, that makes the Syrian regime a terrorist regime" (Ryan 1991, p. 249). For the purpose of moral assessment, this is clearly much too rough. However repugnant Syria's sponsorship of Palestinian terrorism may have been, it is certainly not in the same moral league as the regimes of Stalin and Hitler. Surely we ought to differentiate more carefully.

With regard to state involvement in terrorism, there are distinctions to be made both in terms of degree of such involvement and with regard to its victims.

Concerning the degree of state involvement in terrorism, we should resist the temptation to classify every state that has made use of terrorism, either directly or by proxy, as a terrorist state. I suggest that we reserve this label for states that do not resort to terrorism merely on certain occasions and for certain purposes, but employ it in a lasting and systematic way, and indeed are defined, in part, by the sustained use of terrorism against their own population. These are totalitarian states, such as Nazi Germany or the Soviet Union in Stalin's time.

The "Reign of Terror" the Jacobins imposed in France from the fall of 1793 to the summer of 1794 was a precursor of full-fledged totalitarian terrorism employed by those states. The ultimate aim of the Jacobins was the reshaping of both society and human nature. That was to be achieved by destroying the old regime, suppressing all enemies of the revolution, and inculcating and enforcing civic virtue. These tasks were to be carried out by a revolutionary government, which is by its very nature transitory, and whose radical methods would be inappropriate, indeed intolerable, in normal times, but are indispensable in revolutionary situations. French citizens were considered to fall into one of two groups: "good citizens" or "patriots" – that is, active supporters of the revolutionary regime – and "enemies of the people." The latter group was taken to consist not only of active opponents of the revolution, but of all those who were not seen to be "good citizens." This left no room for neutrality or an apolitical stance. As E. V. Walter explains, the revolutionary regime

was concerned not only with active hostility against the state but also with various kinds of passivity and noncooperation, which were also interpreted as resistance. The well-known Law of Suspects . . . marked

as subject to arrest not only émigrés and unreconstructed persons associated with the nobility but also anyone who by conduct, connections,
remarks, or writing showed himself a partisan of tyranny, federalism,
and the enemies of liberty, as well as anyone who could not demonstrate . . . active patriotism, and a positive contribution to the revolution. (Walter 1967, pp. 139–40)

Whereas the Law of Suspects determined who could be interned,
the next major step in revolutionary legislation, the Law of 22
Prairial, provided for setting up revolutionary tribunals. These tribunals had wide authority, were constrained by very few rules of
procedure, and saw their task as implementing revolutionary policy
rather than meting out legal justice of the more conventional sort.
They went after "enemies of the people" actual or potential, proven
or suspected. The law on the basis of which they were operating
"enumerated just who the enemies of the people might be in terms so
ambiguous as to exclude no one" and "to include whosoever might
need to be so identified" (Carter 1989, p. 142). The standard punishment was death; as Robespierre said, "to good citizens the revolutionary government owes the nation's every safeguard; to enemies of
the people it owes only death" (quoted ibid., p. 140).

Trials and executions were meant to eliminate all "enemies of the
people." If that were all, the "Reign of Terror" would not qualify
as terrorism on my definition; it would rather constitute large-scale
political murder pure and simple. But that was not all; the trials and
executions were also meant to strike terror in the hearts of all those
in the public at large who lacked civic virtue, and in that way coerce
compliance with, and indeed active support of, revolutionary laws
and policies. Michael Phillip Carter is right to point out that the direct
victims of the Terror, who were sent to the guillotine, were not *mere*
scapegoats (1989, p. 146). But the vast majority *were* innocent in the
sense assumed in the definition of terrorism I work with: nothing they
had done or had failed to do could, on any credible understanding of
responsibility and liability, make them deserve, or become liable, to
die on the guillotine. That is what makes the "Reign of Terror" a case
of state terrorism. Jacobins believed such terrorism was a necessary
means of consolidating the new regime. As Robespierre put it, terror
was but "an emanation of virtue"; without it, virtue remained impotent. Therefore the Jacobins applied the term to their own actions
and policies quite unabashedly, without any negative connotations.

The terrorism employed by the Bolsheviks during the Russian
Revolution and Civil War was in important respects a throwback to

that of the Jacobins. The government they set up in Russia was totalitarian. So was the Nazi regime in Germany. Both sought to attain total political control of society and to impose total political unanimity on its members. Such a radical aim could only be pursued by a similarly radical method: terrorism inflicted by an extremely powerful political police on an atomized and utterly defenseless population. Its efficiency is due, for the most part, to its arbitrary character: to the unpredictability of its choice of victims. In both countries, the regime first brutally suppressed all opposition; when there was no longer any opposition to speak of, political police took to persecuting "potential" and "objective" enemies. Those were not persons who had engaged in opposition activity, voiced opposition views, or even entertained such views. They were rather persons who, for objective reasons such as race (in Nazi Germany) or social background (in the Soviet Union), *might* hold opposition views and eventually act on them – persons seen as "carriers of undesirable tendencies," rather like carriers of a disease – and in any case would not really fit in the projected national community or communist society, respectively. In the Soviet Union, terrorism was eventually unleashed on masses of victims chosen at random (see e.g. Weissberg 1952, chapters I and X). Its direct victims were subjected to investigations that more often than not involved extreme pressure or outright torture; they were tried, convicted, and sentenced for imaginary crimes in procedures that fell short of the requirements of basic legality and finally punished – or, more accurately, "punished" – by death or by years of forced labor in camps.

In the words of Carl J. Friedrich and Zbigniew K. Brzezinski, totalitarian terrorism

aims to fill everyone with fear and vents in full its passion for unanimity. Terror then embraces the entire society . . . Indeed, to many it seems as if they are hunted, even though the secret police may not touch them for years, if at all. Total fear reigns. [. . .] The total scope and the pervasive and sustained character of totalitarian terror are operationally important. By operating with the latest technological devices, by allowing no refuge from its reach, and by penetrating even the innermost sanctums of the regime . . . it achieves a scope unprecedented in history. The atmosphere of fear it creates easily exaggerates the strength of the regime and helps it achieve and maintain its façade of unanimity. Scattered opponents of the regime, if still undetected, become isolated and feel themselves cast out of society. This sense of loneliness, which is the fate of all but more especially of an opponent of the totalitarian regime, tends to paralyze resistance . . . It generates the universal longing to "escape" into the anonymity of the collective whole. (Friedrich and Brzezinski 1965, pp. 169–70)

Totalitarian terrorism is the most extreme and sustained type of state terrorism. In Hannah Arendt's words, "terror is the essence of totalitarian domination," and concentration and extermination camps are "the true central institution of totalitarian organizational power" (Arendt 1958, pp. 464, 438). While students of totalitarianism talked of terrorism as its method of rule, representatives of totalitarian regimes, sensitive to the pejorative connotation of the word, portrayed the practice as defense of the state from internal enemies.

Only totalitarian states use terrorism in this way and with such an aim. But many states that clearly are not totalitarian, including democratic and liberal states, have used terrorism on a much more limited scale and for more specific purposes. They have done so directly or by sponsoring non-state organizations whose *modus operandi* is, or includes, terrorism. But, as their resort to terrorism is occasional rather than sustained, let alone essential, they should not be termed terrorist states. When they are, an important moral, political, and legal divide is blurred.

Another distinction is that between the use of terrorism by a state against its own citizens and the use of terrorism beyond its borders, as a means of foreign policy, war, or occupation. Other things being equal, state terrorism of the former type seems worse, morally speaking, than that of the latter type. For in the former case the state is attacking the very population for which it should be providing order, security, and justice.

Quite a few non-totalitarian states have made use of terrorism against their own population. Some have done so directly, by having state agencies such as the armed forces or security services employ terrorism. Many military dictatorships in South America and elsewhere are examples of this; the most extreme cases are Chile under Pinochet and Argentina under the generals. Other states have done the same indirectly, by sponsoring death squads and the like.

Many states, both totalitarian and non-totalitarian, have used terrorism abroad as a means of achieving foreign policy objectives, in the course of waging war, or as a method of maintaining their occupation of another people's land.

These types of state involvement in terrorism are not mutually exclusive; actually, they are often complementary. A terrorist state will see no moral reason for hesitating to make use of terrorism beyond its borders too, whether in the course of waging war or in peacetime, as a means of pursuing foreign policy objectives. Both Nazi Germany and the Soviet Union provide examples of that. The same is true of states that do not qualify as terrorist, but do resort to terrorism against their own population on certain occasions and for some specific purposes. Such states, too, are not likely to be prevented by moral scruples from using terrorism abroad as well, whether directly or by proxy, when that is found expedient.

On the other hand, the fact that a state has resorted to terrorism in the international arena need not make it more prone to do the same at home, as there is a fairly clear line between the two. But it might. Since its establishment, Israel has often made use of terrorism in its conflict with the Palestinians and the neighboring Arab states. The suppression of the second Palestinian uprising (*intifada*) was carried out, in part, by state terrorism. (Israel's neighbors, on their part, have supported Palestinian terrorism against Israel.) The way Israeli police put down the demonstrations of Palestinians living in Israel proper, as its citizens, in October 2000 – by shooting at them with rubber-coated and live ammunition and killing thirteen – may well qualify as state terrorism. If it does, that shows how the willingness to resort to terrorism abroad can eventually encourage its use at home.

To be sure, in practice the dichotomy of state and non-state terrorism does not always readily apply. Attempts at drawing hard and fast lines cannot succeed because of the widespread phenomenon of terrorist organizations receiving various types and degrees of support from states. Since in such cases a simple division of terrorism into state and non-state is no longer feasible, the moral assessment too becomes much more complex.

State Terrorism Is Morally Worse than Non-State Terrorism

All terrorism is *prima facie* extremely morally wrong. But not everything that is extremely morally wrong is wrong in the same degree. State terrorism can be said to be morally worse, by and large, than terrorism by non-state agents. There are several reasons for this claim.

One is sheer scale of killing and destruction. Although unwilling to extend the scope of his discussion of terrorism to include state terrorism, Walter Laqueur remarks that "acts of terror carried out by police states and tyrannical governments, in general, have been responsible for a thousand times more victims and more misery than all actions of individual terrorism taken together" (Laqueur 1987, p. 146).

He could also have mentioned terrorism employed by democracies (mostly in wartime), although that would not have affected the striking asymmetry very much. Now this asymmetry is not just another statistical fact; it follows from the amount and variety of resources that even a small state normally has at its disposal. No matter how much some non-state terrorist groups have managed to enrich their equipment and improve their organization, planning, and methods of action, none has ever come close to changing the score. No insurgent, no matter how well funded, organized, determined, and experienced in the methods of terrorism, has ever come close to the killing, maiming, and overall destruction on the scale the Royal Air Force and United States Army Air Force visited on German and Japanese cities in World War II, or to the psychological devastation and physical liquidation of millions in Nazi and Soviet camps.

The terrorist attacks in the United States carried out on September 11, 2001, were in some respects rather unlike what we had come to expect from non-state terrorism. The number of victims, in particular, was unprecedented. Mostly because of that, I suspect, the media have highlighted these attacks as "the worst case of terrorism ever." So have quite a few public intellectuals. Thus Salman Rushdie, in his monthly column in the Melbourne daily *The Age* (October 4, 2001, p. 15), wrote of "the most devastating terrorist attack in history." The number of people killed, believed to be approaching seven thousand at the time, was indeed staggering. Yet "the worst case of terrorism ever" mantra is but another instance of the tendency of the media to equate terrorism with non-state terrorism. When we discard the assumption that it is only insurgents who engage in terrorism, as I submit we should, the overall picture changes significantly. Let me give just one, admittedly extreme, example from the Allies' terror bombing campaign against Germany. In the night of July 27–8, 1943, the RAF carried out the second of its four raids on Hamburg, known as the "Firestorm Raid." In the morning, when both the attack itself and the gigantic firestorm it had created were over, some forty thousand civilians were dead.[3]

But it is not only its scale that makes state terrorism morally worse than terrorism employed by non-state agents. In one way or another, state terrorism is bound to be compounded by secrecy, deception, and hypocrisy. When involved in terrorism, whether perpetrated by its own agencies or by proxy, a state will be acting clandestinely, disclaiming any involvement and declaring its adherence to values and principles belied by its actions. Or, if it is impractical and perhaps even counterproductive to deny involvement, it will do its best to present its actions to at least some audiences in a different light: as legitimate acts of war or acts done in defense of state security. It will normally be able to do that without much difficulty, given the tendencies of common use I mentioned at the beginning of this chapter.

Those engaging in non-state terrorism, on the other hand, need not be secretive, need not deceive the public about their involvement in terrorism (except, of course, at the operational level), and need not hypocritically proclaim their allegiance to moral principles violated by their actions. Some of them are amoralists. Others exhibit what Aurel Kolnai termed "overlain conscience" – conscience completely subjected to a non-moral absolute (the leader, the party, the nation), which will permit and indeed enjoin all manner of actions incompatible with mainstream moral views, including terrorism (see Kolnai 1977, pp. 14–22). Still others adhere to some version of consequentialist moral theory, which will readily justify terrorism under appropriate circumstances. In none of these cases will there be a need for deception and hypocrisy concerning the performance of specific terrorist acts or the adoption of policies of terrorism.

A further argument for the claim that state terrorism is worse, morally speaking, than terrorism employed by non-state agents has to do with certain international commitments by which contemporary states are bound. Virtually all actions that constitute terrorism are prohibited by one or another of the various international human rights declarations or conventions and agreements that make up the laws and customs of war. The latter provide for immunity of civilians in armed conflict and thus prohibit terrorism by belligerent parties. Most, if not all, remaining types of terrorism – terrorism in wartime perpetrated by groups not recognized as belligerent parties, and terrorism in time of peace perpetrated by anyone at all – are covered by declarations of human rights. Now those engaging in non-state terrorism are not signatories to these declarations and conventions, while virtually all states today are signatories to most if not all of them. Therefore, when a state is involved in terrorism, it acts in breach of its own solemn international commitments. This particular charge cannot be brought against non-state agents resorting to terrorism.

Finally, non-state terrorism is often said to be justified, or at least that its wrongness is mitigated, by the argument of no alternative. In a case where, for instance, a people is subjected to foreign rule with the usual attendant evils of oppression, humiliation, and exploitation, when that rule is utterly unyielding, and when it deploys overwhelming power, a liberation movement may claim that the only effective method of struggle at its disposal is terrorism. To refrain from using terrorism in such circumstances would be tantamount to giving up the hope of liberation altogether.

This argument is exposed to two objections. Since terrorism is extremely morally wrong, the evils of foreign rule, grave as they may be, may not be enough to justify, or even mitigate, resort to it. After all, its victims would by definition be innocent people rather than those responsible for such evils. Moreover, one can hardly ever be confident that terrorism will indeed achieve the aims adduced as its justification or mitigation. What people has ever succeeded in liberating itself by terrorism?

This brings up the question as to whether terrorism – that is, deliberate killing and maiming of innocent persons for the sake of intimidation and coercion of others – can ever be morally justified and, if so, just what would it take to justify it. This question is the subject of the next four chapters of this book, and there is no point in anticipating the outcome of that discussion. At this stage, let me just say, provisionally, that the two objections to the argument of "no alternative" are weighty and may well be enough to dispose of most attempts at justifying particular cases and policies of terrorism; but they do not show that the argument will *never* apply. Perhaps persecution and oppression of an ethnic, racial, or religious group can reach such an extreme point that even a resort to terrorism in response may properly be considered. And the question of its efficiency, being an empirical one, cannot be settled once and for all. So it is possible that a national liberation movement should be facing such circumstances where resort to terrorism is indeed the only feasible alternative to the continuation of persecution and oppression so extreme as to amount to an intolerable moral disaster. In such a situation, the "no alternative" argument might provide moral justification for terrorism or, at least, might mitigate somewhat our moral condemnation of its use. On the other hand, it seems extremely unlikely that a state should find itself in such circumstances where it has no alternative to the use of terrorism.

One counterexample to this claim that is sometimes cited is the terror bombing campaign of the Allies against German cities in World War II. The campaign, a clear case of state terrorism, is sometimes said to have been morally justified as the only possible way of preventing victory of Nazi Germany, which would have ushered in a period of Nazi rule in most of Europe – surely a prospect that had to be prevented at any cost. The Allies had no alternative. I will discuss this campaign in some detail in chapter 8 and will try to show that none of the attempts at its defense can withstand critical scrutiny.

If so, it does not provide a counterexample to my argument that, in contrast to an insurgent movement, it is extremely unlikely that a state could morally justify or mitigate its resort to terrorism by the argument of no alternative.

Another way of challenging my argument might be to point out that what I have called terrorist regimes can maintain themselves only by employing sustained, large-scale terrorism against their own population. Furthermore, a state that would not qualify as terrorist in this sense may be waging a war whose aims can be achieved only by means of terrorism. The successive Serbian onslaughts on Croatia, Bosnia-Herzegovina, and Kosovo in the 1990s present a clear example. Their aim was conquest, "ethnic cleansing," and annexation of territories whose inhabitants included a non-Serb majority or large minority. Under the circumstances, and given the constraints of time, the "cleansing" had to be accomplished by large-scale terrorism. The Serbs had no alternative (see e.g. Danner 2009).

All this is true, but not to the point. In such cases terrorism is indeed the only efficient option and, if the aim is to be achieved, there is no alternative to its use. But in such cases, unlike at least some conceivable cases of non-state terrorism justified or mitigated by the "no alternative" argument, the aim itself – the continuation of a Nazi or Stalinist regime or the setting up of a greatly expanded *and* "ethnically homogeneous" Serbia – can justify or mitigate nothing. Its achievement, rather than failure to achieve it, would amount to an intolerable moral disaster.

Yet another objection would refer to the "balance of terror" produced by the mutual threat of nuclear attack that marked the Cold War period. The type of such threat relevant here was the threat of attacking the other side's civilian population centers. (In Cold War jargon, this was known as "countervalue deterrence.") If that threat was morally justified, it was a case of state terrorism justified by the "no alternative" argument.

I am not convinced that it was justified. Clearly, carrying out the threat and actually destroying major population centers of the enemy and killing hundreds of thousands, if not millions, of enemy civilians could never be morally justified. But does that mean that a threat to do so – made with the aim of preventing the chain of events that would make such destruction a serious option – is also morally impermissible? A positive reply to this question assumes that, if it is wrong to do X, it is also wrong to intend to do X, and therefore also to threaten to do X. This assumption has been questioned (see e.g. Kavka 1978). I have not made up my mind on this matter. Perhaps the problem can be circumvented by arguing that the threat need not involve the intention of ever carrying it out; a bluff will do. Yet one might well wonder if a threat of this sort can be both credible and a bluff. Of course, if the threat is not credible, it will not be morally justified either.

But this is too large a subject to go into here. Therefore I will only say, in conclusion, that, even if the "balance of terror" generated by the threat of use of nuclear weapons against civilian targets turned out to be a convincing counterexample to my fourth argument for the claim that state terrorism is, by and large, morally worse than terrorism employed by non-state agents, the first three arguments would still stand and, I trust, suffice.

Counterterrorism

This discussion of state terrorism has some fairly straightforward implications with regard to moral assessment of and constraints on counterterrorist measures in general and the "war against terrorism" the United States and its allies have waged since the fall of 2001 in particular.

One concerns the moral high ground the state usually claims in the face of insurgent terrorism. What is at issue is a certain policy contested by the insurgents or a certain political setup the state wants to maintain and the insurgents want to do away with. But at the same time the conflict is seen as much more basic: since the insurgents have resorted to terrorism, the conflict is also about the very fundamentals of the political and social order, and indeed about certain moral values and principles, which terrorists are challenging and the state is defending.

Now it is true that terrorism challenges some of our fundamental moral beliefs and rides roughshod over some highly important moral distinctions. Therefore opposition to terrorism can and should be motivated, above all, by moral concern. But that is not the only condition for claiming the moral high ground in the face of terrorism. The other, equally necessary condition is that of moral standing. A thief does not have the moral standing required for condemning theft and preaching about the paramount importance of property. A murderer does not have the moral standing necessary for condemning murder and pontificating about the sanctity of life. By the same token, a state which has made use of terrorism, or sponsored it, or condoned it, or supported governments that have done any of the above – in a word, a state which has itself been involved in or with terrorism to any significant degree – lacks the moral standing required for *bona fide* moral criticism of terrorism. Those speaking on behalf of such a state would do better to leave such criticism to others, whose record with regard to terrorism is different.

This simple point bears emphasizing. More often than not, it is completely ignored. As a result, we are treated, time and time again, to moral condemnations of terrorism by representatives of states that have much to answer for on the same count. Much of the quaint moralistic rhetoric that accompanies the "war against terrorism" currently waged by the United States and its allies is as good an example as any.

Another point has to do with the nature of counterterrorism. Insurgency that makes use of terrorism poses a difficult challenge to the state. Not only does it contest the state's monopoly of violence – any violent opposition activity does that – but it also demonstrates that the state is no longer capable of performing efficiently enough its most important task, that of providing basic security to its citizens. For the indiscriminate nature of terrorism poses a threat of deadly violence to virtually everyone; there is next to nothing a citizen can do to ensure his or her lasting physical security.

Faced with such a challenge to its very *raison d'être* and the difficulties of fighting terrorism while remaining within the bounds of morality and the law, the state may well be tempted to resort to terrorism itself, as Israel has done in response to Palestinian terrorism. Since the 1950s, a central part of Israel's response to terrorism has consisted of reprisals in which civilian targets in the neighboring countries were attacked in order to force their governments to restrain Palestinian terrorists operating from their soil. Israel occasionally acknowledged the terrorist nature of its strategy, most memorably when its prime minister (and defense minister) Yitzhak Rabin explained that the aim of shelling and bombing south Lebanon was "to make it uninhabitable" and thereby force the Beirut government to suppress the activities of the Palestinian liberation movement on its territory. Israel has also made extensive use of state terrorism in its rule over the Palestinian territories occupied in 1967 and its fight against Palestinian resistance terrorism. But the temptation to fight terrorism with terrorism ought to be resisted. This type of counterterrorism may well prove a failure in political terms, as it has done in the Israeli case. More to the point, it is utterly indefensible in moral terms. Israel has certainly had other options, and so does virtually every state. (I will have more to say on this in chapter 9.)

What of the current "war against terrorism" prosecuted by the United States and its allies? It raises an array of moral, political, and legal concerns about citizens' rights at home and the treatment of enemies taken prisoner. At a more basic level, it raises questions about the nature and point of the whole enterprise.

Very soon after the attacks on September 11, 2001, a number of states passed laws and introduced policies considerably expanding the authority of state agencies with regard to surveillance, coercive interrogation, and detention. The rationale for these measures was simple: the dangers posed by global terrorism that was at work in those and subsequent attacks were unprecedented and required a new balance to be struck between liberty and privacy, on the one hand, and security, on the other. Yet critics have questioned both the claim about radical novelty of the "new terrorism" (see e.g. Coady 2006) and the "new balance" that was being struck in response (see e.g. Dworkin 2006, chapter 2).

Beyond these specific concerns to do with the right response, there are questions about the character of the response and the constraints to be placed on it. How should the "war on terrorism" be understood: as a kind – possibly, a new kind – of war, as the term suggests, or as law enforcement? From an early stage there has been lack of clarity on this point. In his first response to the attacks on September 11, President Bush announced: "The search is underway for those who are behind these evil acts. I've directed the full resources of our intelligence and law enforcement communities to find those responsible and to bring them to justice. We will make no distinction between the terrorists who committed these acts and those who harbor them" (quoted in Lackey 2006, p. 77). At that point, the terrorists were seen as criminals, and the announced response was to be that of criminal justice. But in the president's subsequent speeches and the policy statements of his administration, the focus shifted from the terrorists themselves to the states that were sheltering them and the threats those states posed to the rest of the world: that of developing and then using weapons of mass destruction, or supplying their terrorist proxies with such weapons and unleashing them on other countries. Accordingly, the understanding of the required response changed too; it was no longer, straightforwardly, law enforcement but also war or, more specifically, preventive war – first on Afghanistan, and then on Iraq (see ibid., pp. 77–81).

Yet the two activities differ in important respects, and so do the rules those engaged in them are supposed to follow. In war, there is a presumption that soldiers will be using lethal force – that is what makes them soldiers. To be sure, this presumption will be rebutted in certain circumstances. There is no such presumption in police work. On the contrary, the norm is that the use of such force should be avoided if at all possible, and resort to it can be justified only on certain strictly specified conditions. Both main approaches in the ethics of war, consequentialism and just war theory, as well as the laws of war, allow for a certain degree of "collateral damage" – that is, of killing or injuring civilians that is not intended, but is a foreseen or foreseeable side effect of attacks on legitimate military targets. Rules regulating police work do not permit incidental killing or injuring of bystanders in the course of pursuing (suspected) criminals. Both consequentialist ethics of war and the mainstream version of just war theory, as well as the laws of war, accord certain minimum legitimacy to soldiers fighting on both sides in a war, whereas criminals compound their crimes when they resist police officers who are trying to apprehend them. The liabilities and rights of those at whom these two activities are directed are different too. Enemy soldiers are liable to be killed or wounded at any time, except when they are *hors de combat*, no longer able to fight, whether because wounded or because they have surrendered. When *hors de combat*, they have certain rights: they may not be tried and punished merely for having fought in the war, treated harshly or threatened with harsh treatment, or held prisoner after the war has ended. Suspected criminals, on the other hand, are liable to be apprehended, tried, and punished. But they are not liable to be targeted with deadly violence, except in certain tightly specified circumstances in which the use of potentially deadly force is considered both necessary and reasonable. And they have rights to be presumed innocent until proven guilty in a fair trial and, if convicted, not to be subjected to "cruel and unusual" punishments.

In the current "war on terrorism," the United States government has run together the two practices, waging war and enforcing criminal law. It has introduced the notion of "unlawful combatants" – those who are neither enemy combatants in the sense the term has in the ethics and laws of war nor criminal suspects pure and simple – and applied it to the enemy it is fighting in this war. In an essay titled "The War on Terrorism and the End of Human Rights," David Luban summarizes the consequences of this approach:

> By selectively combining elements of the war model and elements of the law model, Washington is able to maximize its own ability to mobilize lethal force against terrorists while eliminating most traditional rights of a military adversary, as well as the rights of innocent bystanders caught

in the crossfire. [. . .] The legal status of al Qaeda suspects imprisoned at the Guantanamo Bay Naval Base in Cuba is emblematic of this hybrid war-law approach to the threat of terrorism. In line with the war model, they lack the usual rights of criminal suspects – the presumption of innocence, the right to a hearing to determine guilt, the opportunity to prove that the authorities have grabbed the wrong man. But, in line with the law model, they are considered *unlawful* combatants. Because they are not uniformed forces, they lack the rights of prisoners of war and are liable to criminal punishment. [. . .] Neither criminal suspects nor POWs, neither fish nor fowl, they inhabit a limbo of rightlessness. (Luban 2003, p. 53)

But whatever its flaws from a moral and legal point of view, it will be said that at least the "war on terrorism" is not an instance of state terrorism. There have been civilian casualties in the course of attacks on the Taliban and Al-Qaeda targets in Afghanistan. But the innocent have not been attacked intentionally; civilian casualties have been foreseen, or foreseeable, but not intended side effects of attacks on legitimate military targets. Such "collateral damage" is widely considered inevitable in modern war. Actions that bring it about do not qualify as terrorism, on my own or any other definition of "terrorism" I find helpful.

It is true that the United States and its allies are not guilty of state terrorism, since terrorism is by definition *intentional* attack on the innocent. But that is not the end of the matter. Concerns about the scale of "collateral damage" the "war on terrorism" has been inflicting surfaced early on, as the war was initially conducted exclusively from the air, and from very high altitudes at that. By January 2002, it was clear that these concerns were based on good grounds. Under the heading "News of Afghan Dead Is Buried," Gay Alcorn, the United States correspondent of *The Age*, reported (January 12, 2002, p. 17):

University of New Hampshire economics professor Marc Herold was so disturbed by the lack of coverage of civilian deaths in the war in Afghanistan that he began keeping a tally. [. . .] Professor Herold says, on average, 62 Afghan civilians have died each day since bombing began. The total was now close to 5000, far more than the 3000 killed in the terrorist attacks in America on September 11. [. . .] According to Professor Herold, America's strategy of using air strikes to support local ground forces is designed to minimize American casualties. Only one American soldier has died from enemy fire.

News of innocent civilians being killed or maimed as "collateral damage," often out of any proportion to the military advantage to be achieved by the actions that caused it, have been coming from Afghanistan ever since. They have been coming from Iraq too. And they are still coming at the time of writing.

Now just war theory does not prohibit harming the innocent *simpliciter*, but rather harming them deliberately, with intent. With regard to harming civilians incidentally, without intent, mainstream just war theory applies the doctrine of double effect. According to this doctrine, causing harm to civilians incidentally, as a side effect – that is, an unintended but foreseen consequence of an act of war directed at a legitimate military target – may be permitted if that harm is proportionate to the importance and urgency of the military objective sought. It will not do, say, to shell a village in order to take out a handful of enemy soldiers who have taken up position there if that also involves the unintended but foreseen killing of scores of innocent villagers.

This much is clear in any mainstream version of just war theory. The version advanced by Michael Walzer adds an important qualification. When carrying out an act of war that will also have the unintended but foreseen consequence of harming the innocent, we must seek to reduce that harm to a minimum, and must accept risk to life and limb of our own soldiers in order to do so. The right of the innocent not to be harmed is the centerpiece of the *jus in bello* part of just war theory. It is the soldiers who put the civilians' life and limb in danger; therefore they should accept some risk in order to minimize that danger (Walzer 2000, pp. 155–6).

Now our repugnance of terrorism is motivated, primarily, by the value we place on human life and physical security, and in particular by our commitment to the right of the innocent not to be killed or maimed. This right is violated when the terrorist intentionally kills or maims them in order to achieve his or her aims. But it is also violated when their death or grave physical injury is not brought about as a means, but as a foreseen (or foreseeable) side effect. That violation is compounded when those who do the killing and maiming refuse to take any chance of being harmed themselves in the process. That is not terrorism, but it is not much less repellent, morally speaking, than terrorism proper.[4]

If this is granted, it means that terrorism may not be fought by terrorism. Nor may it be fought by means of a strategy that does not amount to terrorism, but must be condemned on the ground of the same moral values and principles that provide the strongest reasons for our rejection of terrorism. In this respect, so far the record of the "war on terrorism" has been very poor indeed.[5]

3

Complicity of the Victims

Some Crude Versions of the Complicity Argument

How might one try to justify some act or campaign of terrorism? The task could be approached in two ways. One could argue that the direct victims may be civilians or common citizens but are *not* innocent of the wrongs the terrorists are fighting against. Alternatively, one could concede the innocence of the victims and argue that attacks on them are nevertheless justified, either by their good consequences on balance or by some other considerations. In this chapter, I look into the first line of argument.

An obvious objection to any argument of complicity of direct victims of terrorism is that, if the argument is successful, it proves too much. For it proves that the victims are not really innocent. If so, violence directed at them is not terrorism; for terrorism is, by definition, violence against the innocent. But this may not be a major problem. We may want to put it to one side as merely a matter of semantics; surely it cannot be the end of the matter. Even if the use of violence against civilians, or common citizens, with a view to intimidating and coercing some other persons or groups, is not, strictly speaking, terrorism, we still want to know whether or not such violence is morally justified.

There is a more damaging objection. A terrorist act is characteristically the killing or injuring of a random collection of people who happen to be in a certain place at a certain time. An argument to the effect that those people are not innocent of the wrongs the terrorists fight against will have to have a *very* wide reach. Therefore it will have to be based on some highly problematic conception of collective responsibility. Alternatively, the argument will operate with a conception of collective responsibility that is quite plausible, but cannot properly be applied to the issue of the morality of terrorism.

To be sure, many reject the very idea of collective responsibility. They see it as a throwback to pre-modern times, when children were made to pay, often dearly, for the misdeeds of their parents. Writing in the immediate aftermath of World War II, when many were eager to pronounce the entire German people responsible for the crimes committed by the Nazis and their henchmen, H. D. Lewis said: "If I were asked to put forward an ethical principle which I considered to be especially certain, it would be that no one can be responsible, in the properly ethical sense, for the conduct of another. [. . .] . . . The belief in 'individual,' as against any form of 'collective' responsibility is quite fundamental to our ordinary ethical attitudes." He went on to argue that, in the unlikely event that the issues posed by our usual, individualistic understanding of moral responsibility could not be resolved, "then the proper procedure [should] be, not to revert to the barbarous notion of collective or group responsibility, but to give up altogether the view that we are accountable in any distinctively moral sense" (Lewis 1948, p. 3).

It is difficult to take issue with Lewis's claim that moral responsibility essentially belongs to the individual. However, in rejecting *any* form of collective responsibility, he was overstating his case. For some forms of collective responsibility are not incompatible with the view that responsibility is essentially individual.[6] The range of notions of collective responsibility is wide and varied, and its varieties can be distinguished along different dimensions. The distinction to the point here is one between collective responsibility that is completely independent of the choices and actions of individuals and collective responsibility that is grounded in such choices and actions. The former, which might be termed strong, is based on certain assumptions about the distinctive nature of human groups and their agency which cannot be reduced to that of individuals comprising them. It is said to accrue to individual members of certain groups even though they may have done nothing to come to share it, and even though their membership in these groups is not a matter of choice. The latter, which might be termed weak, presupposes no metaphysical claims about irreducibility of groups to the individuals comprising them and the relations between those individuals. It is basically a type of individual responsibility – it is generated by the individual's own choices and actions – which is also collective in that it is mediated by the individual's membership in a group.

Now collective responsibility in the strong sense may seem a good basis for a moral justification of terrorism insofar as it provides a sufficiently wide reach of such justification. If, for example, all Israelis are indeed collectively responsible for the wrongs the state of Israel has been committing against Palestinians – the wrongs which constitute a just cause for their armed struggle against Israel – then Palestinian militants can legitimately direct deadly violence at any random collection of Israeli civilians. Killing and maiming them will not be killing and maiming innocent people. Yet one hardly ever comes across attempts at justifying Palestinian terrorism in these terms; apparently, neither terrorists themselves nor their apologists find this line of argument promising.

In his discussion of terrorism and collective responsibility, Seumas Miller first looks into this particular conception of such responsibility. He terms it "the morality of collective identity," and writes:

> According to the morality of collective identity, the members of some oppressor or enemy group are guilty purely by virtue of membership of that national, racial, ethnic or religious group. So a white South African who opposed apartheid was, nevertheless, guilty in the eyes of extremist anti-apartheid groups simply by virtue of being white. All Americans are guilty of oppressing Muslims simply by virtue of being American citizens, according to some extremist Al-Qaeda pronouncements. [. . .]
> . . . A person is a wrongdoer – and thus liable to lethal attack by way of response – not by virtue of what he or she as an individual has deliberately done, but rather by virtue of (more or less) unchosen aspects of his or her collective identity . . . This collective identity approach to collective moral responsibility is inconsistent with the notions of moral responsibility (individual or collective) that underpin both common morality and criminal justice systems, whether they be contemporary, historical, western or Islamic. (Miller 2009, p. 61)

Not much needs to be said about this view. It says that one can be *guilty* of a policy one has neither devised, nor implemented, nor supported, but rather *opposed*, and that one can be a wrong*doer* without deliberately *doing* (or *omitting to do*) anything. That is, it cannot be stated without incongruity or outright contradiction; therefore, to state it is to refute it. As Paul Gilbert remarks, "such a view can arise only on the wilder shores of identity politics" (Gilbert 2003, p. 95).

However, a justification of terrorism in terms of complicity of its direct victims can also be based on a weak version of the idea of collective responsibility. Let me look into four simple instances of such an argument. They are spread over three centuries and include both insurgent and state terrorism.

In the last decades of the nineteenth century, some anarchist groups became disillusioned with conventional methods of political struggle and took to political violence. They had come to the conclusion that words were not enough and that what was called for were deeds: extreme, dramatic deeds that would strike at the heart of the unjust, oppressive social and political order, generate fear and despair among its supporters, demonstrate its vulnerability to the oppressed, and ultimately force political and social change. This was "propaganda by deed," and the deed was for the most part assassination of royalty or high-ranking government officials. However, in some instances bombs were planted in places where they would kill or maim random collections of common citizens. These included two bombs planted by French anarchist Emile Henry. One was placed at the office of a mining company; had it exploded there, it would have killed or injured a number of people who did not work for the company but lived in the same building. The other was planted in a café and did go off, injuring twenty people, one of whom later died of his injuries. At the trial, when queried about his choice of victims, Henry replied: "What about the innocent victims? . . . The building where the Carmeaux Company had its offices was inhabited only by the bourgeois; hence there would be no innocent victims. The whole of the bourgeoisie lives by the exploitation of the unfortunate, and should expiate its crimes together" (Henry 1977, p. 193). When commenting on the second attack, he said: "Those good bourgeois who hold no office but who reap their dividends and live idly on the profits of the workers' toil, they also must take their share in the reprisals. And not only they, but all those who are satisfied with the existing order, who applaud the acts of the government and so become its accomplices . . . in other words, the daily clientele of Terminus and other great cafés!" (ibid., p. 195). What Henry is saying, then, is that all members of a social class – men and women, young and old, adults and children – are liable to be killed or maimed: some for operating the system of exploitation, others for supporting it, and still others for benefiting from it.

Another, recent example is provided by Osama Bin Laden, the mastermind of the September 11, 2001, attacks. In an interview he gave on November 12, 2001, he said:

The American people should remember that they pay taxes to their government and that they voted for their president. Their government makes weapons and provides them to Israel, which they use to kill Palestinian Muslims. Given that the American Congress is a committee that represents the people, the fact that it agrees with the actions of the American government proves that America in its entirety is responsible for the atrocities that it is committing against Muslims. (Bin Laden 2005, pp. 140–1)

The claim is that all Americans ("America in its entirety") are eligible to be killed or maimed: some for devising and implementing America's policies, others for voting in elections that decide who will be devising those policies, and still others for paying taxes that make the implementation of those policies possible.[7]

In World War II, the Allies bombed German cities, attempting to break the morale of the civilian population and force the government to halt the war. (I will discuss the bombing campaign in some detail in chapter 8.) Hans Magnus Enzensberger, who was to become a prominent writer after the war, was in his early teens at the time. He spent many nights in a cellar, hoping to survive a terror bombing raid on his city. Yet he did not share the general indignation at the deliberate and systematic violation of civilian immunity on the part of the RAF and USAAF. He tells us why:

> I well remember the . . . terrors of the air-raids. And the grown-ups who cowered on the benches in the cellar, at whom these "terror raids" were aimed; they were the "innocent civilians." . . . But it wasn't always like this. A strange transformation had occurred in the "innocent civilians" who sat in the cellars while all around them phosphor bombs turned the city into a sea of fire. I remember how their eyes lit up every time the Führer spoke and let them know what he had in mind: "a titanic and unprecedented struggle," a fight to the bitter end. . . . Without their enthusiastic support the Nazis could have never come to power. (Enzensberger 1994, p. 50)

Enzensberger goes on to say that wars always start with jubilant masses applauding the warmongers who lead them. These leaders are often elected; sometimes their position is confirmed in subsequent elections. They, and the soldiers they send off to war, act as envoys of their society "who feed on its rage, its cruelty, its lust for revenge" (ibid., p. 51). If so, civilians cannot in good faith protest their innocence of the war and claim immunity against being exposed to the killing and destruction. They are not innocent, but rather responsible for what their military do to the other side. Accordingly, when attacked by the other side, they are merely facing the fatal repercussions of their own actions and omissions. That, Enzensberger submits, applied to the entire civilian population of Germany during the war years (with the possible exception of minors).

My final example of this type of argument relates, like Enzensberger, to a (projected) campaign of state terrorism; but that campaign was to be a core component of the "war on terrorism" triggered by the attacks on September 11, 2001. It is an argument presented by Barry Buzan, an international relations expert, in an essay titled "Who May We Bomb?" Buzan starts by deploring the notion that, in war, a distinction should be made between a people and its government, and that they ought to be accorded different treatment, which he sees as "something of a Western fetish" (Buzan 2002, p. 85). He submits that a people can "deserve its government." When it does, it need not be treated differently from its government. If that government is the enemy, then the civilian population it governs is the enemy too and may legitimately be bombed. Wars are conducted "not just between groups of fighters, but between groups of fighters and their networks of support" (ibid., p. 86). Indeed, the civilian population should be bombed. For,

> if people really do deserve their government, and yet only the govern-ment is targeted, the country as a whole remains politically unrecon-structed and thus a continuing danger to itself and to the international community. [. . .] To delink people from their governments, when they are in fact closely linked, is to undermine the political point of resort-ing to war in the first place. In the end, war is about changing people's minds about what sort of government they want. (Ibid., pp. 90–1)

How does a civilian population come to deserve its government? The simplest way to do so is by voting for it. To be sure, not everyone takes part in voting, but having the option of voting, even if no use is made of it, is enough to become deserving of whatever the outcome of the voting turns out to be. Therefore civilians in a democracy are legitimate targets. So are civilians under an authoritarian regime where the regime has wide support or acquiescence (passive accept-ance). To be sure, acquiescence can be coerced, but "such coercion is usually visible, allowing distinctions to be drawn between passive acceptance and terrorized obedience" (Buzan 2002, p. 88). Only civilians living under "blatant tyrannies" such as Uganda under Idi Amin or Burma under the generals are clearly off the hook. In general, "the question whether people get the government they deserve can often be answered quite simply on the basis of day-to-day observa-tions about the relationship between the demos and the government" (ibid., p. 90). In Buzan's view, then, whenever civilians participate in the political process by voting, or have the option of doing so even though they do not make use of it, or when they support the government or merely acquiesce in its policies, they all become legitimate targets of deadly violence, just like their leaders and armed forces. Since that violence will be deployed with a view to making people change their minds about the kind of government they want to have, it will qualify as terrorism. Buzan does not call it that, but what his argument seeks to justify is state terrorism as part and parcel of the "war on terrorism."

These four arguments are meant to show that civilians, or common citizens, are complicit in wrongs that constitute a just cause for resort to violence, and therefore are not protected against violence; and they deploy the idea of collective responsibility. However, they do not employ the preposterous notion of collective responsibility in the strong sense I mentioned earlier. Common citizens are not said to be complicit in the wrongs at issue simply because of who they are – because of an ascribed rather than chosen identity, defined by membership in a certain social, political, cultural, or racial group. It is rather collective responsibility in a weak sense: a type of responsibility that is essentially individual in that it is generated by some action or omission of the individual, but also collective, in that the individual can act as she does only in virtue of her membership in the group, and that this membership is an indication that she is guilty of such action or omission.

Considerations deployed in these arguments for the claim that the direct victims of terrorism, whether insurgent or state, are not really innocent, although they are but common citizens, include the following:

- common citizens perform organizing, overseeing, or servicing roles in the unjust social and economic system
- in some general, unanalyzed sense they "support" their government and its unjust policies
- . . . or at least acquiesce in those policies
- they have installed their government in power by voting, or could have voted even if they did not
- they pay taxes which the government spends on devising and implementing unjust policies
- they benefit from their government's unjust policies or their society's unjust practices
- their government, armed forces, and security services are their "envoys," acting on their behalf.

Now, such actions and omissions may well be the ground for moral condemnation, perhaps harsh moral condemnation, of those found guilty of them. Of course, such condemnation will presuppose harsh moral condemnation of practices or policies involved. In line with what I said in chapter 1 on how terrorism should be defined, I will grant, for the sake of argument, that the practices and policies at issue are indeed gravely unjust – unjust to a degree that can justify resort to violence when that is the only way of putting an end to them. The questions to ask are two. First, are all those on the receiving end of terrorist violence guilty of such acts or omissions? Is their group membership a reliable indication that they are? Second, with regard to those who are guilty of those acts or omissions, is that enough to justify targeting them with such violence?

With regard to most of the acts and omissions listed above, group membership is an unreliable indicator. Being a citizen of a polity may, but need not, involve voting for its government, supporting it in any way, including by paying taxes, or even acquiescing in its policies. A citizen may be completely apolitical. Or she may oppose the government or the policy at issue and work for a change of policy or even a change of government. Her income may be below the taxation threshold. By the same token, being a citizen of a polity may, but need not, indicate that what the government of that polity, its military, and its security agencies are doing represents one's views, wishes, or interests – that it is done on one's behalf. It may, but need not, indicate that one reaps benefits from the government's unjust policies. Those policies may benefit only a small part of the population. Even if they benefit most of the population, a citizen may belong to a disadvantaged minority. Or she may not be culpable for benefiting from them, because she cannot really avoid doing so. Finally, more often than not, a random collection of common citizens is likely to include minors; and minors, for obvious reasons, cannot be charged with, or at any rate cannot be held to account for, acts or omissions that are at issue here. This means that, in almost every terrorist attack, some of the direct victims may satisfy the terrorists' criteria of complicity with the wrongs they fight against, and some may not. A bomb planted in a coffee shop or on a city bus, or dropped from a plane on a city, has no way of killing or maiming only those common citizens who are complicit in the iniquities of their government while staying clear of those who are not.

Even if we suppose, counterfactually, that lethal violence can be employed in a way that harms only those common citizens who do vote for the government, or who support it and its unjust policies in some way, or acquiesce in those policies, or pay taxes which the government uses for devising and implementing those policies, or culpably benefit from them, is that enough as a moral justification of the violence? Those citizens are not innocent in the strongest sense of the word, in which only small children and a few saintly adults may be innocent – they are not completely free of any wrongdoing. They are not innocent in the more down-to-earth sense of having nothing to do with the policies the terrorist seeks to abolish. On the contrary, they are implicated in them in certain ways. That may well call for moral criticism, and perhaps some further unfavorable response. But surely they are innocent in the sense relevant to the issue under discussion: surely there is nothing they have done, or omitted doing, that makes them deserve, or liable, to be killed or maimed. If, at this point, the terrorist were to point out that A voted in the last elections, B was paying taxes, C was expressing support for the contested policies while D was acquiescing in them, and E was benefiting from those policies, and go on to say that that made the lot of them a legitimate target of deadly violence, that, it seems to me, would be a very ineffective rebuttal. For it would ignore, instead of addressing, the drastic disproportion between their offense and his response to it.

On the other hand, membership of a social class does indicate certain things. If one is a member of the bourgeoisie in a capitalist society and if one works, it is highly likely that one will be organizing, overseeing, or servicing the functioning of the system rather than performing simple wage labor. Moreover, whether one works or not, one is almost certain to benefit from the existing social and economic arrangements. While minors cannot be held responsible for benefiting from them and some adults may be benefiting inculpably, many, if not most, adults will have no excuse for doing so. If the capitalist social and economic system is indeed deeply oppressive, exploitative, and unjust, as many of its anarchist (and other) critics have argued, then a person's role in operating it and her benefiting from it will expose her to moral criticism, and perhaps some further unfavorable response. But surely she is innocent in the sense relevant to the issue under discussion: surely there is nothing she has done, or omitted doing, that makes her deserve, or liable, to be killed or maimed. If, at this point, the terrorist were to point out that A was the owner of a company that employed, and exploited, many workers, while B, C, D, and E were his dependants who benefited from the unjust social and economic arrangements, and go on to say that that made the lot of them a legitimate target of deadly violence, that, it seems to me, would be a very weak rebuttal. Again, it would ignore, instead of addressing, the drastic disproportion between their offense and his response to it.

With regard to each of seven types of complicity listed above, we would need to consider just how causally significant it is for the injustice at issue, and just how voluntary it is. Having established that, we would need to ask whether the nature and degree of wrongdoing and culpability that come to the fore are enough for the persons concerned to deserve, or become liable, to be targeted by the kind of violence terrorists employ – that is, to be killed or maimed. To fail to examine every type of complicity in its own right and to continue instead to take any of them as indication enough of non-innocence and ground enough for liability to be killed or maimed would indicate a superficial and implausible, indeed preposterous, view of responsibility and liability. As I pointed out in chapter 1, a credible view of these matters is one that grounds a person's responsibility for some wrongdoing in that person's acts or omissions that are significantly voluntary – that is, informed and free – and have a sufficiently strong connection with that wrongdoing. Further, it provides for a certain morally acceptable proportion between what a person is responsible for and the unfavorable response to which he or she is liable on that account.

Of course, a terrorist may also adopt a very different view of responsibility and liability: one which does make a person liable to be blown to pieces if, for instance, that person voted in the last elections (even if her vote was for the opposition), or if she has been paying taxes (even if there is no way of avoiding paying them), or if she has benefited from the contested policies (even if she is a minor, or for some other reason has no way of avoiding benefiting from them). If the terrorist cannot be persuaded to revise his view of responsibility and liability – say, by considering whether he would like to see that view applied to his family and friends by some militants with an agenda he does not share – then there is not much room for further discussion. The terrorist will insist that his direct victims are not innocent of, but rather complicit in, the policies he fights against, and that therefore what he does when killing and maiming them is not terrorism, but rather morally justified armed struggle. I will point out the problematic, indirect, fractional contribution of his victims' acts and omissions to the policies he fights against and the insufficiently voluntary character of such acts and omissions, as well as the drastic disproportion between those acts and omissions and the violence he inflicts on them; reject his views of responsibility and liability as preposterous; and portray and condemn what he does as terrorism.

Collective Political Responsibility

The four instances of the argument from complicity reviewed so far operate with much too superficial a notion of collective responsibility. However, a defense of terrorism in terms of collective responsibility of its direct victims can operate with an understanding of collective responsibility that is neither superficial nor implausible.

In *Terrorism and Collective Responsibility*, Burleigh Taylor Wilkins argues that "any adequate answer to the question when, if ever, terrorism is justified must take into account the problem of collective guilt, which . . . has been entirely neglected by those who have written on terrorism" (Wilkins 1992, p. 19). Wilkins adopts a wide definition of terrorism and presents it in two versions, a shorter and a more detailed one. The shorter version, which will do for present purposes, reads: "terrorism is the attempt to achieve political, social, economic, or religious change by the actual or threatened use of violence against persons or property" (ibid., p. 2). But his justification of terrorism is also expressly applied to terrorism in the narrow sense of violence against common citizens, who are usually considered innocent.

If terrorism is to be justified, Wilkins argues, it must be undertaken in collective self-defense. It must also be selective, in two senses. First, it must be directed against members of the community which is "collectively guilty" of the aggression or injustice at issue. Second, at least initially, it must be directed against the perpetrators of the aggression or injustice. If that is of no avail, then the scope of the group targeted may be gradually expanded until it encompasses the entire civilian population of the aggressor polity.

When can a group be collectively guilty? In this regard, Wilkins says, "solidarity in the sense of a shared or common interest is our best guide" (1992, p.19). This rules out humanity as a whole, since the interests an individual has in common with it are much too restricted or tenuous. Smaller groups, such as family, neighborhood, business organization, cultural institution, and perhaps an entire social class, can have significant shared interests and exhibit solidarity based on those interests. So can a polity. A good indication of this solidarity and shared interests that generate it are pride and shame one can feel on account of actions done by members of such a group, or by the group as a whole, or on its behalf.

If a group does exhibit solidarity and common interests, if it is indeed collectively guilty of some injustice grave enough to justify a violent response, and if nonviolent means have been tried and failed, or there is an emergency that rules out trying other means, then, Wilkins argues, terrorism directed at members of the group may be justified. But it must be used in a judicious, gradual way.

- At first, as far as possible, it should be directed against the perpetrators of the injustice at issue – the decision-makers and those who are implementing the decisions taken. Wilkins terms these the "primary targets" of terrorism.
- Where that is not feasible, the terrorists may attack a "secondary target": those who are "as guilty or nearly as guilty, in the sense of being responsible for initiating or participating in the violence" the terrorists respond to. Wilkins calls such persons "criminal accomplices" of the initiators and perpetrators.
- If that, too, does not work, the terrorists may attack the "moral accomplices" of the initiators and perpetrators of the injustice they have set out to fight: those who know of the injustice at issue, but choose to look the other way and are rewarded for their silence and acquiescence. Wilkins's examples are editors, bankers, university professors, and film-makers.
- Should that, too, prove ineffective, the terrorists may turn against "the silent majority" – that is, against common citizens. At that stage, "some judicious, highly selective terrorism aimed at members of the 'silent majority' might become morally appropriate and tactically necessary, as a reminder that no one is safe until the injustice is ended" (Wilkins 1992, pp. 29–31).

Some of this is not very clear. The difference between those constituting the "primary target" and those comprising the "secondary target" is unclear. We are not told just why those Wilkins calls "moral accomplices" of the initiators and perpetrators of the injustice at issue should be more liable than common citizens generally. Is it because they are particularly well placed to identify, condemn, and oppose the injustice being perpetrated in their name by their government, or for some other reason? Then again, once all members of the "silent majority" are liable to be attacked, just how can attacks on them be "highly selective"? In one place in the final pages of the book, Wilkins seems to be suggesting that terrorist attacks on common citizens might be restricted to their property (1992, pp. 143–4). However, what he says about the fourth and final stage of escalation of violence against an obtuse and unyielding polity – namely, that at that stage the message of terrorist violence must be that "no one is safe" – rather suggests attacks on life and limb.

These details can be put to one side. The main question is: How can attacking common citizens – destroying their property, but also killing and maiming them – be morally justified? If it can, will that amount to justifying violence against innocent people? Here, Wilkins writes,

> the answer is a yes and a no. Yes, it may involve inflicting violence upon those who in their individual capacity may have done or intended no harm to the would-be terrorists or to the community or group to which they belong; but no, the individuals in question by virtue of their membership in the community or group which has done or threatened to do violence to the would-be terrorists or the community or group to which they belong are collectively guilty of the violence in question. (1992, p. 31)

Theirs is "political responsibility," which should be understood by analogy with corporate responsibility. The latter, under certain circumstances, involves vicarious and strict liability – that is, liability for somebody else's action, which is imposed on a person without any fault on her part. An employer may be personally completely innocent of a certain wrongdoing committed by an employee, and yet be held strictly liable for the wrongdoing. Now states, Wilkins argues, are in some relevant respects similar to corporations. By the same token, common citizens can be held liable for the acts and policies of their government although they had no part in framing or implementing them (see ibid., pp. 129–35). That is so

> because members of a group typically stand to benefit from belonging to it: it is in their interest to belong, or else they would not, though, of course, this assumes that membership is voluntary. In cases where membership is not voluntary . . . the picture changes significantly, but the burden of proof . . . falls upon the member to show that his membership was not voluntary. Since few if any of our choices are fully voluntary, what usually has to be shown is that there was some coercive element which excuses membership and which, if sufficiently strong, may negative membership altogether. But the coercion . . . has to be a deliberate and intentional act by some would-be coercer; 'natural necessity' or 'economic necessity' would not by themselves suffice. (Ibid., pp. 138–9)

This argument is flawed in several respects. First, like other proponents of the argument from complicity, Wilkins forgets that, more often than not, an indiscriminate attack on "the silent majority" of common citizens is likely to kill or maim minors – that is, those to whom his notion of "collective political responsibility" cannot be applied.

Second, the crucial claim that common citizens typically benefit from membership of their polity, do so voluntarily, and therefore may be made to pay a price for that is simply not true. The restriction Wilkins imposes on the type of consideration establishing that a person has not freely chosen the country he lives in seems arbitrary. Why should only pressures exerted on an individual by intentional human action count? If a person prevented by law from emigrating is not to be held to share in the "political responsibility" for the country's policies, why should another person, who is not prevented from leaving the country by its laws, but by the simple fact that he could never make a living outside it, be thought to bear a share of such responsibility? Here Hume's classic objection to social contract theory of political obligation is to the point:

> Can we seriously say, that a poor peasant or artisan has a free choice to leave his country, when he knows no foreign language or manners, and lives, from day to day, by the small wages which he acquires? We may as well assert that a man, by remaining in a vessel, freely consents to the dominion of the master; though he was carried on board while asleep, and must leap into the ocean and perish, the moment he leaves her. (Hume 1963, p. 462)

However, once we admit that all coercion counts, whatever its source, it becomes clear that much too often – perhaps even more often than not – membership of a polity is *not* a matter of voluntary choice.

Finally, as Seumas Miller points out (Miller 2009, p. 63), there are important differences between strict liability of corporations and "political responsibility" of common citizens. Employers and employees cooperate within a highly structured, legally regulated organization. In accordance with the relevant regulations, employers undertake vicarious and strict liability with regard to a specified range of their employees' actions and omissions. Membership of a political community is not regulated in a similar way, and common citizens undertake no such liability for acts and policies of their government. The actions and omissions of employees for which an employer undertakes to be vicariously and strictly liable are work-related offenses, rather than unjust or inhumane policies that might provoke violent resistance. An employer would not be required to undertake to be liable for such policies, and would have no good reason to do so if required. Finally, strict liability normally exposes employers to fines; it could never extend to being killed or maimed.

Therefore Wilkins's attempt at moral justification of terrorism in terms of collective responsibility of its direct victims for the wrongs terrorists fight against does not succeed.

Responsible Bystanders

A different justification of terrorism in terms of complicity of its direct victims is suggested in Kai Draper's paper "Self-Defense, Collective Obligation, and Noncombatant Liability." Draper discusses the problem as one of the ethics of conventional war and speaks of soldiers and enemy civilians, but his discussion also applies, *mutatis mutandis*, to conflict that falls short of (conventional) war and involves insurgent terrorists and common citizens.

Draper takes as his point of departure the claim made by a senior United States Air Force officer at a briefing during the First Gulf War that Iraqi civilians were not entirely innocent and therefore were not entirely immune against lethal violence either, since "ultimately the people have some control over what goes on in their country" (Draper 1998, p. 57). Admittedly, Iraqi civilians took no part either in the decision-making process that led to Iraq's aggression on Kuwait or in the military aggression itself. As far as the actual aggression was concerned, they were bystanders: persons present at, but not involved in, the aggression. But they had some control over their government and military with regard to the aggression. They failed to prevent it, and thereby lost their immunity against deadly violence. When harming them serves a military purpose, they may legitimately be harmed.

It might be objected that, as long as one does not authorize a morally wrong action or policy, takes no part in it, or contributes to it, one remains a bystander. One's failure to prevent the action or policy does not undermine one's bystander status and the immunity that comes with it. But a closer look into the connection between being a bystander and having immunity from deadly violence shows that things are not quite as simple as the objection assumes.

Consider the following scenario. A is about to kill B, with no moral justification for doing so. C is a bystander who could, at no great cost to himself, prevent A from killing B. But C fails to do so, without having a justification or excuse for that. B cannot save her life by killing A, but can do that by killing C. C's death will affect A in such a way that he will no longer want or be able to kill B.

In such a case, it seems to me, C is indeed a bystander. But he is not a *mere* bystander; he, too, is responsible for B's death, if B is killed. This responsibility is not quite the same as that of A but is nevertheless extremely serious. If, on the other hand, B saves her life by killing C, she will not have violated C's immunity against deadly violence. C could and should have acted to prevent A from attacking B, and had lost this immunity by failing to do so. *Responsible* bystanders, unlike mere bystanders, have no such immunity.

If so, the question to ask about Iraqi civilians during the First Gulf War, and more generally about civilians in war and common citizens in violent conflicts that fall short of war, is this: Can they, or some of them, be seen as C in the above scenario? For them to lose the immunity they have as civilians or common citizens, it would have to be true that

- they could prevent the aggression
- they could do so at no great cost to themselves
- they have a moral duty to do so
- they have no moral justification or excuse for not doing so.

These conditions are interrelated. "Ought" implies "can": if I cannot do something, I cannot have a duty to do it. Then again, when the price bound up with doing one's duty goes beyond a certain threshold, the duty no longer binds (putting aside duties that bind absolutely, if any). Finally, the first two conditions are jointly sufficient for generating the third condition. Draper cannot make up his mind on this. But it seems to me that, at least with regard to very serious harms, when one is facing the prospect of such harm being unjustifiably inflicted on another human being and is able to prevent that at no great cost to oneself, one has a moral duty to act; no previous undertaking to do so should be required.

Of course, no common citizen of Iraq could have prevented the country's aggression against Kuwait on his or her own. But it might be maintained that Iraqi civilians *collectively* should have acted to prevent it. If it is true that they could have prevented their country's aggression had they acted collectively to that purpose, that they would not have had to pay too high a price for so acting, that accordingly they as a group had a duty to do so, and that they had no justification or excuse for not doing so, then they are collectively at fault for failing to prevent the aggression. They make up a group of responsible bystanders. Moreover, their collective responsibility is distributive. It can be assigned to individual Iraqi civilians by means of some such principle as the one advanced by Draper: "The failure of a group to act as it should can be blamed on all those members who, without exculpating [reason], were unwilling to take part in the group acting as it should" (1998, p. 73). Accordingly, when military exigency requires it, they may legitimately be attacked.

However, the circumstances of Iraqi civilians at the time of the First Gulf War were not at all like that. Spontaneous individual action held no hope of preventing the aggression on Kuwait. Even if a large number of individuals had chosen to act without coordinating their action with that of others, they would not have achieved this end. In order to stand a chance of preventing their country's aggression, Iraqi civilians would have had to act in a concerted, organized way to that purpose. Given the nature of the regime, that was clearly not feasible. Thus the first condition for considering them responsible bystanders does not hold. The second condition does not hold either, and for the same reason. Given the nature of the regime, any vigorous public opposition to the attack on Kuwait, whether individual or collective, would have been bound up with a prohibitive price. Consequently, the third condition was not satisfied: Iraqi civilians did not have a moral duty to prevent the aggression on Kuwait. They cannot be considered responsible bystanders and were not fair game for the Allied military.

Is that but an instance of the circumstances that tend to prevail in countries at war or in the grip of internal violent conflict? It seems so, at least as long as we are dealing with countries with authoritarian regimes. Draper does not embark on a separate discussion of the issue as it arises in a democratic polity. But surely the circumstances are different in a democracy. When a democracy wages an unjust war, its citizens need not lack opportunities of coordinating and organizing their anti-war activities and need not fear drastic response from the government to their actions. However, in such a case the prospect of success will be relevant and indeed decisive. When their country is at war, whether just or unjust, people tend to rally around the flag and to give strong, indeed uncritical support to the government and the military. Such support becomes the touchstone of patriotism; anything less tends to be perceived, and criticized, as unpatriotic (see e.g. Somerville 1981). This is true of a democracy, just as of a country ruled by unrepresentative, undemocratic government, although, of course, citizens of a democracy should know better. And when a war, whether just or unjust, enjoys strong support of the vast majority of the population, attempts of a small, marginalized, disliked and suspected bunch of dissenters to prevent or stop it will be bound to fail. That will be reason enough, both in prudence and in morality, not to make such attempts.[8]

To be sure, circumstances may be different: the support for the war may not be so widespread and strong that dissent stands no chance of preventing the government from starting an unjust war, or stopping the war if it is already under way. In such a case, those who are in a position to undertake concerted action to that purpose do have a duty to do so, and can properly be considered responsible bystanders if they fail to discharge it. If so, may the military of the unjustly attacked country attack them too, if they hold that doing so would contribute significantly to defeating the aggression? A powerful practical consideration suggests that the answer is no. Enemy civilians who could be considered eligible for attack on the basis of the responsible bystander argument will virtually always live thoroughly intermingled with other enemy civilians who are not eligible: those who mistakenly but excusably believe their country's cause to be just; those who know that the cause is not just, while mistakenly but excusably believing that there is no chance of affecting the events for the better; those who are not in a position to contribute anything to the opposition to the war, such as the sick and the very infirm; and, last but not least, minors. There is no way of making sure that, in an attack on a civilian target, only the former are hit while the latter emerge unscathed.

Thus I concur with Draper that, as far as civilians in war are concerned, the responsible bystander line of argument will have very little purchase on reality (1998, p. 78). It will virtually never apply in the type of case Draper considers: in countries similar in the relevant respects to Iraq at the time of the First Gulf War. For somewhat different reasons, it will virtually never provide moral justification for targeting civilians or common citizens in the type of case Draper does not consider: in countries dissimilar in the relevant respects to Iraq at the time.[9]

Therefore attempts at moral justification of terrorism in terms of complicity of its direct victims in the wrongs terrorists fight against do not succeed. If terrorism is to be morally justified, the justification will have to concede innocence of its direct victims and provide some moral considerations showing that they may nevertheless be killed or maimed. Such justifications will be examined in the next three chapters.

4

The Consequences of Terrorism

Consequentialism and the Morality of Terrorism

Consequentialist ethics judges human action solely by its rationally expected consequences. When they are good (on balance), an act is right; when they are bad (on balance), it is wrong. Rules of action, policies, practices, institutions – everything that can be understood in terms of human actions – are judged in the same way, in terms of their rationally expected consequences. Nothing is right or wrong, obligatory or prohibited, in itself, but only in light of its consequences. The goodness or badness of consequences is understood as the way in which they affect those they affect. Different versions of consequentialism interpret this in different ways: in terms of causing happiness or suffering, or satisfying or frustrating preferences, or promoting or setting back interests. But they are all at one concerning the view that only consequences matter.

Terrorism, too, is judged solely in terms of its consequences. That means that it, too, is not considered wrong in itself, but only if its rationally expected consequences (on balance) are bad. The innocence of its victims does not change this. One of the standard objections to consequentialism has been that it allows, and indeed enjoins, punishment of the innocent, when its consequences are rationally expected to be good (on balance). This objection can get off the ground only because consequentialism denies that in such matters a person's innocence is morally important in itself.

Those who judge terrorism from a consequentialist point of view differ in their judgment of its morality. Their judgment depends on two things: on their view of the good to be promoted by terrorism and on their assessment of the usefulness of terrorism as a means of promoting it.

Terrorism: "Red" and "White"

A classic example of a defense of terrorism from a consequential-ist point of view is found in the writings of Leon Trotsky: *Terrorism and Communism*, published in 1920 as a reply to a book with the same title published by Karl Kautsky in 1919, and the essays "Their Morals and Ours" and "The Moralists and Sycophants against Marxism," written in the late 1930s in a debate with some disil-lusioned Marxists. Trotsky was one of the leaders of the Bolsheviks throughout the Russian Revolution and the Civil War that followed it. He had played a crucial role in the planning and implementa-tion of the "Red Terror," and Kautsky's condemnation of the "Red Terror" was also a condemnation of Trotsky's views and actions. In their debate, neither Kautsky nor Trotsky felt the need to define "ter-rorism." What they had to say was meant to bear on terrorism in the wide sense of violence aiming at intimidation and coercion, but what matters here is how their arguments apply to terrorism in the narrow sense of such violence directed against the innocent.

Both Kautsky and Trotsky were Marxists, committed to the same view of the human good: the untrammeled flourishing of human nature, which is essentially social and therefore possible only in a "truly human society" – society no longer plagued by class division and conflict. But they differed on the necessity of large-scale violence, and in particular of terrorism, as a means of dismantling the existing capitalist society and replacing it with a socialist political and eco-nomic system. Kautsky acknowledged the violent nature of previous revolutions, but argued that in the twentieth century a revolutionary transformation of society could be accomplished without imposing party dictatorship and a reign of terror. Yet the Bolsheviks set up a dictatorship, with revolutionary tribunals and extraordinary com-missions that deliberated in secret and had extremely wide, indeed arbitrary powers. They suppressed all dissent by a system of large-scale executions and took hostages. The means the Bolsheviks were using in order to achieve their aims were in fact compromising those aims, and the "Red Terror" was altogether a moral fiasco: "They could discover nothing, these Marxists, these bold revolutionaries and innovators, except the miserable expedient with which the old society endeavours to absolve itself from the results of its own sins, namely, the *tribunal, prison and execution*, in other words, Terrorism. [. . .] Shooting – that is the Alpha and Omega of Communist government wisdom" (Kautsky 1973, pp. 181, 211).

Trotsky rejects Kautsky's optimism concerning the possibility of avoiding violence and terrorism. The liberation of humanity is possible only through revolution; therefore the revolutionary cause is the supreme moral law. In pursuit of the cause, all means are right, if they are efficient. Although aiming to take us beyond class society, revolution is still a product of that society and exhibits its traits and limitations. Therefore it cannot dispense with violence. The type and degree of violence is a question not of principle, but of expediency. To Kautsky's charge that, by resorting to terrorism, the Bolsheviks were employing the same methods as the forces of the old order and therefore were no better, Trotsky's reply is that of an unflinching consequentialist and a revolutionary. The end justifies the means; the same means can be right or wrong, depending on the end they serve. "Red Terror" is right, "White Terror" is wrong (Trotsky 1961, p. 59).

Against this background, Trotsky advances two specific arguments in defense of the "Red Terror." The first seeks to show continuity between war, revolution, and terrorism. Revolution is a type of war; accordingly, what is permissible in war will also be permissible in revolution. Now war is waged with the aim of breaking the enemy's will to resist, and that is done by violence. The more strongly the enemy resists, the harsher and more massive the violence employed against him must get. At a certain point in the conflict, it will include terrorism:

> *Intimidation* is a powerful weapon of policy, both internationally and internally. War, like revolution, is founded upon intimidation. A victorious war, generally speaking, destroys only an insignificant part of the conquered army, intimidating the remainder and breaking their will. The revolution works in the same way: it kills individuals, and intimidates thousands. In this sense, the Red Terror is not distinguishable from the armed insurrection, the direct continuation of which it represents. (Trotsky 1961, p. 58)

In view of this continuity, Trotsky argues, one must either accept terrorism as a legitimate method of struggle in certain circumstances or reject as morally impermissible all war, all revolution, indeed every type of violence.

This argument is not sound. Where Trotsky sees only continuity, one can see both continuity and discontinuity. It is true that, in war in general and in revolutionary war too, one uses intimidation and coercion through intimidation: one kills and wounds a certain number of enemies, and thereby intimidates and subjugates all or most of the others. In this respect, terrorism can be considered similar to war and revolution. But there is also an important, indeed morally decisive, difference between war and revolution, on the one hand, and terrorism, on the other. In war and revolution this intimidation is (or can and ought to be) effected by attacks on *legitimate* targets: on members of the enemy's armed forces and security services, other military targets (e.g. arms factories), and political leadership. Terrorism, on the other hand, is always an attack on *illegitimate* targets, on innocent people, with the aim of intimidation and coercion. Terrorism is therefore morally impermissible even when employed by a side that otherwise wages a war, or a revolution, which is morally justified in terms of its character and goals.

Trotsky's second argument in defense of terrorism seeks to undermine this distinction between legitimate and illegitimate targets in war and revolution – the distinction between civilians and soldiers, or those who are and those who are not innocent in the relevant sense. He claims that this distinction is irrelevant, if not in general, then at least with regard to contemporary wars. For one thing, many soldiers of a modern army have been drafted against their will. Moreover, "modern warfare, with its long-range artillery, aviation, poison gasses . . . with its train of devastation, famine, fires, and epidemics, inevitably involves the loss of hundreds of thousands and millions, the aged and the children included, who do not participate directly in the struggle" (Trotsky, Dewey, and Novack 1973, p. 57).

Now Trotsky is right to point out that the distinction between legitimate and illegitimate targets, which should make possible a moral demarcation between war and revolution, on the one hand, and terrorism, on the other, is not as clear-cut as one might wish, at least on the face of it, and that there will be difficulties and borderline cases in its application. Nevertheless, these difficulties are not such that we should give up the distinction. If we were to do that, we would have to get used to the idea that there is no moral difference between deliberately killing or wounding soldiers on the battlefield and deliberately killing or wounding civilians, including children and the aged, in the rear. Just war theory does provide a criterion for distinguishing between legitimate and illegitimate targets of armed attacks in war: who is, and who is not, "currently engaged in the business of war" (Walzer 2000, p. 43). Soldiers and those who supply them *qua* soldiers, as well as those who make decisions concerning

the war and oversee its course, are so engaged, and therefore constitute legitimate targets. Others – even if they are in some way related
to, or involved in, the war effort – are not *engaged* in war in the way
soldiers and those supplying or overseeing them as soldiers are. They
are innocent civilians in the pertinent sense, and accordingly are
morally protected from such attacks.

The fact that many modern armies include those who have been
drafted against their will and participate in war only unwillingly
does not bring the whole distinction into question. If a soldier is not
responsible for the fact that he has been drafted, he is responsible for
remaining in uniform, armed, on his post. There is always the possibility of throwing away the rifle, taking off the uniform, leaving the
post, either openly, by refusing to obey the commands, or secretly,
by deserting. To be sure, such a choice always has a price. But even
when the price is the highest possible, namely summary execution
by a firing squad, it does not mean that the choice is not available,
and that those who do not make it are absolved from responsibility
for taking part in war. The fact that A was threatening to kill B if B
refused to kill C is neither a justification nor an excuse for B's killing
C – neither in morality nor in law.

As for the suffering of civilians, it has been part and parcel of
warfare throughout history. Over the last hundred years or so, in
particular, it has been constantly on the rise. Still, we need not accept
Trotsky's way of dealing with it as if it were all of a piece, independently of the way it is brought about. Nor do we need to accept the
stark choice he seeks to foist on us: either embrace a version of pacifism that rejects all war and revolution, or permit and justify any type
and amount of harm inflicted on civilians, when its consequences are
expected to be good on balance. For there is considerable middle
ground between these two extremes.

One possible position within that middle ground is that taken by
mainstream just war theory, which adopts the doctrine of double
effect as the best way of dealing with the problem of harm to civilians. The doctrine is based on the distinction between harm inflicted
with intent and that caused without intent but with foresight; its
central claim is that there is a considerable moral difference between
the two. Acknowledging this difference makes it possible to uphold
an absolute prohibition of deliberate attacks on civilians and, at the
same time, allow for a degree of incidental – that is, unintended but
foreseen – harm to civilians as a side effect of legitimate acts of war.

The doctrine lays down the following conditions that an act that
has both a good and a bad effect must satisfy:

- the act is not wrong in itself
- its direct and intended effect – that is, the effect for the sake of which the act is performed – is good
- its other effect, which is bad, is not intended, whether in itself or as a means, but only foreseen – that is, it is a side effect of the act
- the intended good effect is sufficiently valuable to compensate for the unintended but foreseen bad effect.

Applied to the ethics of war, the doctrine says that employing lethal violence in war, which is not wrong in itself (otherwise no war could ever be legitimately waged), may be morally acceptable even if it also harms civilians, provided that the harm to civilians is incidental – that is, not intended but only foreseen – and that it is proportionate to the importance of the military objective sought. For instance, it may be morally justified to bomb an enemy position with intent to kill the soldiers manning it even though the bombing will also kill some civilians who happen to be nearby, if killing the civilians is incidental to, and proportionate to the importance of, killing the soldiers.

This might be thought a rebuttal of Trotsky's argument that, morally speaking, terrorism is of a piece with war and revolution, since they all involve the killing of civilians. They do, but in war or revolution civilians can be harmed legitimately – namely, in accord with the doctrine of double effect – whereas terrorism cannot live up to the requirements of the doctrine and therefore cannot harm civilians legitimately. For, in terrorism, the killing and maiming of civilians is by definition intended (as the means to the objective sought) rather than merely foreseen.

But this view might be considered too permissive. It requires of soldiers not to intend the killing of civilians, and to make sure that their incidental killing is not disproportionate to the importance and urgency of the military objective they seek. It says nothing about the chances the soldiers should take in the course of their action. Michael Walzer argues that this is not enough, and proposes an amendment of the doctrine as it applies to the problem of harming civilians in war. It is not enough *not to intend to harm* civilians; soldiers must *intend not to harm* them, or at least to reduce the unavoidable harm to them to a minimum. Moreover, soldiers must give expression to the latter intention by themselves accepting risk to life and limb:

> Simply not to intend the death of civilians is too easy . . . What we look for in such cases is some sign of a positive commitment to save civilian lives. Not merely to apply the proportionality rule and kill no

more civilians than is militarily necessary – that rule applies to soldiers as well; no one may be killed for trivial purposes. Civilians have a right to something more. And if saving civilian lives means risking soldiers' lives, the risk must be accepted. (Walzer 2000, pp. 155–6)

It is important to mark the words "right" and "must": taking risks to ensure that harm to the innocent is reduced to a minimum is not a matter of supererogation, but rather a *duty* of soldiers and a correlative *right* of civilians. The right of the innocent not to be killed or maimed is the point of departure of just war theory and, indeed, of any plausible ethics of war. Since it is the soldiers who put the life and limb of civilians in danger, it is only fair that they, too, should have to take some risk to life and limb in order to reduce that danger to a minimum.

That risk is not unlimited: "These are, after all, unintended deaths and legitimate military operations, and the absolute rule against attacking civilians does not apply. War necessarily places civilians in danger . . . We can only ask soldiers to minimize the dangers they impose." Just what degree of risk is required cannot be determined in a general way; it will depend on such things as the nature of the military target, the urgency of attacking it, the technology to be used in the attack, etc. The only guidance of a general nature Walzer feels he can offer is "to say simply that civilians have a right that 'due care' be taken" (2000, p. 156).

Walzer's amended version of the doctrine of double effect, just as the traditional version, makes it possible to contrast terrorists and soldiers of a conventional or revolutionary army: whereas terrorists intend to harm civilians, soldiers must not intend to harm them and, moreover, must seek to reduce the unavoidable harm to civilians to a minimum and, if need be, take risks to their own life and limb in the process. Thus this version, too, provides a rebuttal of Trotsky's argument about the continuity of terrorism with war and revolution.

By amending the traditional version of the doctrine of double effect, Walzer makes his position significantly more restrictive. For it says that, "even if the target is very important, and the number of innocent people threatened relatively small, they must risk soldiers before they kill civilians" (2000, p. 157). The traditional doctrine does not require that. This makes the amended version of the doctrine more plausible. But both versions are still at one on the central point: the moral asymmetry of harm caused with intent and harm caused without intent but with foresight. It is this asymmetry that makes it possible to justify a degree of unintended harm to civilians.

Now the distinction between what we intend (what we set as our end and choose as the means for achieving it) and what we only foresee is conceptually sound; however, its moral significance can be questioned. Some critics feel it has no moral significance whatever. Other critics ask: Even if the distinction has *some* such significance, can that be *decisive* for discriminating between morally permissible and morally impermissible killing? A civilian killed as a side effect of an attack on a military target is just as dead as a civilian killed with intent in a terror bombing raid. The right to life of the former has been violated just as the right to life of the latter has. Nor is it clear that the attitudes evinced in the two types of killing are very different. Adherents of the doctrine of double effect point out that a soldier who kills civilians incidentally, without intent, does so with regret and would much rather achieve his objective without harming the civilians if that were possible. But a soldier who kills civilians deliberately, as a means to achieving his objective, can also regret the necessity of doing so, and may well prefer achieving his objective by some other means if that were possible. Why, then, should we think that killing civilians with intent is always wrong but that killing them without intent, but with foresight, in the course of pursuing a sufficiently important military objective, is permissible?[10]

If one finds the intention/foresight distinction a conceptual distinction without a (significant) moral difference, one might put it aside and deal with the problem of incidental harm to civilians in war by taking a cue from Walzer's remark, quoted above, that civilians have a *right* that soldiers should take "due care" not to harm them, or to reduce the harm they inflict on them to a minimum. If civilians have this right, then soldiers have the corresponding duty: the duty to take precautions against inflicting harm on civilians as a side effect of attacks on military targets. This much might be thought to be implied by the very notion of civilian immunity. This is how international law of armed conflict regulates this matter. Article 57 of the First Protocol Additional to the Geneva Conventions (1977) decrees that, "in the conduct of military operations, constant care shall be taken to spare the civilian population, civilians and civilian objects." It goes on to specify that military commanders must do "everything feasible" to verify that the objects of attack are not civilians or civilian objects, and must "take all feasible precautions in the choice of means and methods of attack with a view to avoiding, and in any event to minimizing, incidental loss of civilian life, injury to civilians and damage to civilian objects." This is also the approach adopted by Stephen Nathanson, who terms it the precautionary principle: "While actions that cause civilian deaths are morally wrong if they result from insufficient precautions to spare civilians from harm, actions that cause civilian deaths are permissible if precautionary measures have been taken to avoid or minimize civilian harm" (Nathanson 2010, p. 261).

This position, too, undermines Trotsky's claim that terrorism is of a piece with war and revolution because all three involve the killing of civilians. They do, but, whereas a soldier or a revolutionary can, and should, take precautions to avoid or at least minimize harm to civilians, a terrorist *qua* terrorist seeks to inflict it.

Now this position does not seem to differ significantly from Walzer's amended version of the doctrine of double effect with regard to practical guidance offered; the difference is rather one of rationale. Both Walzer and Nathanson allow for causing a degree of unintended but foreseen harm to civilians. If that, too, is found too permissive, there is yet another possible view to consider: one that prohibits all incidental harm to civilians. This view looks at the way killing is regulated in criminal law. Many legal systems distinguish five types of killing:

- intentionally
- knowingly
- recklessly
- negligently
- accidentally.

One kills intentionally when one sets the death of another as one's aim or chooses it as a means to achieving one's aim. One kills knowingly when one does not intend to kill but foresees that one's action will bring about another's death as a side effect. One kills recklessly when one is aware that one's action is likely to kill and goes ahead nevertheless, disregarding the risk. One kills negligently when one brings about another's death while being unaware that one's action was likely to do so, although one could and should have been aware of the risk. Finally, one kills accidentally when one causes another's death without intent or foresight and, through no fault of one's own, is unaware of the risk involved in one's action.

The psychology of each of these five types of killing is different. But, as far as the law is concerned, the main line of demarcation is that between the first four types, on the one hand, and the fifth, on the other. Notwithstanding all the differences between the first four types with regard to intention, foresight, or awareness of the risk involved, they are all considered criminal homicide and severely punished. The precise legal qualification may differ (first vs. second degree murder, murder vs. manslaughter), and the attendant punishments may differ too. But because all four types of killing – killing intentionally, knowingly, recklessly, and negligently – exhibit significant degrees of voluntariness, choice, and control on the part of the agent, they also involve responsibility and invite punishment. The fifth, accidental type of killing is not voluntary, does not indicate the agent's choice, and remains beyond his or her control; therefore the agent is not held responsible and is not punished for it.

It can be argued that the law of homicide reflects an important moral distinction. If the principle of civilian immunity is to provide robust protection against lethal violence to those who have done nothing to deserve, or become liable, to such violence, it must be taken to prohibit all acts that are morally equivalent to criminal homicide – that is, all non-accidental killing. This is the conclusion reached by Colm McKeogh in what is still the sole book-length philosophical study of civilian immunity in English:

> We are responsible not only for that which we directly intend; we are culpable also for our negligence and for the foreseeable avoidable consequences of our acts. To be excusable, the deaths of civilians in war must be accidental. The deaths must be, not only unintended but also unforeseen and reasonably unforeseeable ... [. . .] For an attack on a military objective to be just, there must be, not only an intention but also a likelihood of no civilian deaths occurring as a result. (McKeogh 2002, pp. 169–70)

Obviously, this position makes for a sharp contrast between soldiers and revolutionaries, who can and ought to attack only legitimate targets and refrain from harming civilians in any way – whether intentionally, knowingly, recklessly, or negligently – and terrorists, who deliberately kill and otherwise harm innocent civilians.

I will not go into this issue any further and try to decide which of these four positions on incidental harm to civilians is most convincing. For present purposes, it should suffice to have shown that we are not facing the choice Trotsky's defense of terrorism seeks to impose: that of either adopting (a certain kind of) pacifism and refusing to take up arms, no matter what aggression or oppression we may be facing, or allowing for any kind and degree of harm to innocent civilians necessary for the achievement of an important objective in armed struggle. We can also adopt one of the views that constitute the middle ground between these extremes. There is some continuity between war, revolution, and terrorism, but there is also an important, indeed morally decisive discontinuity between war and revolu-tion, on the one hand, and terrorism, on the other, concerning harm to innocent civilians. Trotsky was right to point out the continuity but wrong to ignore the discontinuity; as a result, his argument does not succeed.

Beyond Trotsky's two specific arguments, there are problems with his defense of the "Red Terror" at the fundamental level. Most of them plague any consequentialist account of terrorism, and I will bring them up shortly. But there is one problem that is distinctive of the particular type of consequentialism exemplified by Trotsky's posi-tion. In order to agree with Trotsky's defense of the "Red Terror," one would have to accept both his judgment about the value, and necessity, of terrorism as a means of bringing about "a truly human society" as portrayed by Marxists and the claim about the paramount value of that society. But, of course, one may well resist the latter claim. Indeed, historically, this claim has been widely rejected, not only by those who stand to lose in such a society, but also by those who are supposed to be its primary beneficiaries – by members of the working class. In other words, the paramount end which is said to justify the killing and maiming of innocent people as a means to it is defined in ideological terms by terrorists themselves, rather than grounded in settled preferences, interests, or values of actual people. (This has been a problem facing a wide range of terrorist organiza-tions promoting both right-wing and left-wing political agendas.) Accordingly, for those who do not embrace the vision of the just, or good, or "truly human society" which terrorists seek to realize, justifications of terrorism such as Trotsky's never get off the ground.

Terrorism and the Principle of Humanity

While radical groups that resort to terrorism, whether on the left or on the right, typically define the social and political change they seek to bring about in ideological terms, the aim to be promoted by ter-rorism can also be understood in non-ideological terms – in terms of what actual people would prefer, consider to be in their overall, long-term interest, or acknowledge as basic and universal values. This is the approach of Ted Honderich in a string of writings on political violence and terrorism, including the books *After the Terror* (2002) and *Humanity, Terrorism, Terrorist War* (2006).

Honderich's statement of consequentialism starts with a list of what anyone would recognize as "great human goods": a decent length of life, quality of life, freedom and power, relationships with individuals and belonging to groups, respect and self-respect, the goods of culture. Human lives are good when humans' desires for these goods are satisfied and bad when they are deprived of, or insufficiently provided with, these goods. Now the lives of millions of human beings are bad: much too short, of poor quality, lacking freedom and power, bereft of respect and self-respect, and so on. This, Honderich argues, is a fact of central moral importance, and the basic principle of ethics, which he terms "the principle of humanity," reflects that: "we must actually take rational steps to the end of getting and keeping people out of bad lives" (Honderich 2006, p. 60). An act is right when it can be rationally expected to serve this end better than, or at least as well as, any other act possible in the circumstances and wrong when it cannot. Only rationally expected consequences count; distinctions such as that between act and omission, or between intention and foresight, have no moral significance. The intrinsic nature of acts, too, has no such significance. Deontological ethics, which insists that some acts are right or wrong in themselves, independently of their consequences, in Honderich's view amounts to "an abandoning of humanity" (ibid., p. 78).

Terrorism, and political violence in general, should be assessed in the same way. Since both affect human lives for the worse much of the time, both are wrong much of the time. However, neither can be rejected completely. When either harms some people but helps more people out of bad lives, it will be morally justified. Honderich operates with a wide definition of terrorism, which includes lethal violence against soldiers and highly placed government officials *and* against common citizens (2006, p. 88). But his discussion of the attacks on September 11, 2001, and of the use of terrorism in the Israeli–Palestinian conflict clearly shows that this consequentialist justification is meant for terrorism in the narrow sense too. In his discussion of the latter topic, Honderich offers two historical examples of a morally justified campaign of terrorism. In his judgment, the use of terrorism by the Zionist movement in the course of setting up the state of Israel was morally justified. So was its use by the Palestinian Liberation Organization and other Palestinian resistance groups in the following decades and to this day (ibid., pp. 94–118). (I will take a closer look at Honderich's stand on these instances of terrorism in chapter 9.)

The distinctive character of and the basic flaw in this approach to the morality of terrorism are displayed in Honderich's final conclusion about the morality of the attacks in New York on September 11,

2001. Most of us would say that September 11 was as clear a case of morally unjustified, indefensible, atrocious mass killing as we are ever likely to see. Honderich, too, holds that the attacks were morally unjustified. Most of us would say that on the basis of what these attacks involved: the killing of up to three thousand common citizens of the United States and a number of other countries as they were going about their daily business. Many, perhaps most of them, died in some extremely frightening and painful way. And virtually all of them, as far as one can tell, were innocent in the sense in which I am using the word in this book: the sense of not having done, or having failed to do, anything that could be plausibly adduced as making them deserve, or become liable, to be blown to pieces, asphyxiated, or burnt to death. For Honderich, however, a mere description of what happened, what was done, is not enough to ground the moral judgment. The attacks were wrong for a different reason – a reason to do with the future, rather than the past and present:

> What was done was wrong because there could be no certainty or significant probability . . . that it would work to secure a justifying end, but only a certainty that it would destroy lives. [. . .] The killers and those behind them . . . could not know that the killing of several thousand people would in due course serve the end of the principle of humanity, saving people from bad lives. They could have no such rational confidence. (Honderich 2002, pp. 118–19)

Unlike the case of terrorism driven by some ideology, the problem here is not the nature of the end, but rather the view that the end justifies the means, and that a sufficiently good end can justify virtually any means, however atrocious, including terrorism. The view that we may always snuff out or wreck the lives of some innocent people, when that is the only way to help more people out of bad lives, will be thought by many to be much too permissive. For it offends against certain fundamental moral beliefs many of us hold:

- the separateness of persons
- respect for persons
- the distinction between guilt and innocence
- moral dialog
- moral equality.

The first, most fundamental of those beliefs comes under different descriptions but is perhaps best termed "the separateness of persons" (see Rawls 1971, pp. 22–7). A terrorist who justifies his actions in consequentialist terms has one paramount goal: to bring about the state of affairs to which he accords the highest value. That can be the good, just, truly free and human society, or the liberation of the homeland and setting up an independent state, or the victory of the one true faith, or, as in Honderich's philosophy, the getting and keeping people out of bad lives – lives bereft of, or insufficiently provided with, the basic human goods. Since this commitment is to the highest value, that value overrides all other values that might conflict with it, all considerations that might stand in the way of its realization. He may also have certain beliefs about society according to which the way to bring about the desired state of affairs is, or includes, terrorism. It is often said that terrorism is indiscriminate violence, but that is not true if taken in the most obvious sense. The terrorist does not strike mindlessly, but rather carefully plans his actions, considering the situation and the resources at his disposal and choosing the course of action likely to be most effective under the circumstances. In his calculations he takes into account, on the debit side, his victims: the men, women, and children he is going to kill, maim, or otherwise seriously harm. They are part of the price that has to be paid on the way to the ultimate goal; he will have no great difficulty proving this by his calculations. It is precisely these calculations, in which human beings figure as units to be added and subtracted, that many find morally inappropriate and indeed offensive. Many will endorse the claim of Nikolai Rubashov, the hero of *Darkness at Noon*, Arthur Koestler's philosophical novel about the "Great Terror," that "twice two are not four when the mathematical units are human beings" (Koestler 1968, p. 125). For every human being is an individual, a person separate from other persons, with a unique, irreproducible thread of life and a value that is not commensurable with anything else. The terrorist will find this preposterous: arithmetic, he will say, applies to human beings just as it does to everything else.

Since the terrorist does not take seriously the separateness of persons, she is not in a position to show respect for persons. The principle of respect for persons can be construed in more than one way (see Atwell 1982); but the terrorist is bound to offend against it on any plausible construal. On one interpretation, the principle enjoins respect for the core of individuality of each and every person, a concern for seeing things from the point of view of the other person, in terms of his or her character or "ground project." As Melvin Rader put it, "there is always something about me that is never common to you and me. Respect for a person includes respect for this core of individuality. It means appreciation of the real man of flesh and blood – the individual and human *me* – not just a grammatical abstraction" (quoted in Atwell 1982, p. 22). This deeply personal way of relating to another person is the direct opposite of the impersonal, objective, calculating way in which the terrorist relates to her victims.

According to another interpretation, the principle demands that we recognize and respect certain basic human rights of every human being, which safeguard an area of personal freedom; persons are to be respected as holders and claimers of rights:

> Having rights enables us to "stand up like men," to look others in the eye, and to feel in some fundamental way the equal to anyone. To think of oneself as the holder of rights is not to be unduly but properly proud, to have that minimal self-respect that is necessary to be worthy of the love and esteem of others. Indeed, respect for persons . . . may simply be respect for their rights, so that there cannot be one without the other; and what is called "human dignity" may simply be the recognizable capacity to assert claims. To respect a person then, or to think of him as possessed of human dignity, simply *is* to think of him as a potential maker of claims. (Feinberg 1980, p. 151)

There is no way the terrorist can show this kind of respect to her victims; for, if they have any basic rights at all, surely the right not to be killed or maimed in order that the terrorist's cause be promoted is one of them.

On still another interpretation, the principle prohibits using the other person as a mere means. This is Kant's principle of humanity as end in itself, one of the formulations of the supreme law of morality. Kant distinguishes between things, which can have only relative value and are there to be used as means, and persons, whose value is absolute, and who therefore must not be used as mere means. Humans are rational beings and therefore persons. Accordingly, the principle reads: "Act in such a way that you always treat humanity, whether in your own person or in the person of any other, never simply as a means, but always at the same time as an end" (Kant 2005, pp. 106–7; emphasis deleted). Kant's account of the exact meaning and practical implications of this principle is not as clear as could be desired, and has generated debates about the best interpretation and correct application. But, at a minimum, the principle requires that the other be able to "share in the end" of one's action – that is, to consent to it (ibid., pp. 107–8). This is just what the terrorist's victim is normally not in a position to do. Indeed, terrorism is often brought up as a paradigmatic example of reducing other people to mere means – of treating human beings as things rather than persons.

The distinction between guilt and innocence is generally considered one of the most fundamental moral distinctions. It lies at the basis of the entire realm of what Peter Strawson terms "participant reactive attitudes" – that is, "essentially natural human reactions to the good or ill will or indifference of others towards us, as displayed in their attitudes and actions" (Strawson 1982, p. 67; emphasis deleted). We tend to accord this distinction central significance in a range of contexts, from personal relationships, to moral judgment, to the practice of criminal courts. It also has pride of place when war and other types of violence are to be judged and circumscribed from the moral and legal point of view. Terrorists deliberately and systematically attack, kill, and otherwise severely harm innocent people; this, and the intimidation and coercion they seek to effect by doing this, is what makes them terrorists. To be sure, some terrorists and apologists of terrorism argue that the direct victims of terrorist violence are collectively guilty; I reviewed some characteristic examples of this line of argument in chapter 3. Some such arguments are based on an extension of the notion of guilt so extreme that the whole distinction between guilt and innocence no longer makes much sense, at least in the context of moral appraisal of things terrorists do to their victims. Others operate with an understanding of collective guilt that is plausible but does not apply to the issue at hand. Many terrorists do not even bother to pay lip service to the distinction.

We often hope for moral dialog with those whose moral views differ from our own. In particular, we feel a need for such a dialog with those who propose to do to us something we find extremely objectionable. We want to hear how they can justify their actions *to us*. In general, it seems that, other things being equal, a theory of punishment that goes some way in convincing the person punished that the punishment is justified is better than a theory that does not try to address him in particular. A moral justification of progressive taxation that appeals to the rich is better than one that remains on the most abstract level, and does nothing in particular to convince those who are to pay the highest price when it is put into effect. The terrorist does not try to justify her actions *to* her victims in a free and equal dialog with them, and is not in a position to do so.

We hope for moral dialog with others because we believe in basic moral equality of humans. We believe that every mature and sane human being, *qua* human being, is qualified to exercise moral judgment and to reason with us on an equal footing. We accept that there are experts on certain factual questions relevant to moral issues; but we acknowledge no *moral* experts. We admire certain individuals as morally saintly or heroic; but we do not believe in moral elites. Terrorists who justify their actions in consequentialist terms see themselves as members of such an elite and relegate us to the status of lesser beings, to whom they need not, and indeed cannot, try to explain and justify their actions. They feel themselves called and authorized to perform what Herbert Marcuse calls "historical calculus," with its "inhuman quantifying character" (Marcuse 1968, p. 140), which decides who will live and who will die. We have no say in it, although it is our lives that are at stake.

These objections to terrorism, I believe, show that it is a type of action incompatible with some of the most basic moral beliefs many of us hold. Those who hold these beliefs will find its consequentialist justifications quite unconvincing. Indeed, such justifications will be seen not as showing that terrorism is morally permissible under certain circumstances, but rather as telling against the ethical theory which implies that terrorism is justified whenever such circumstances obtain.

Terrorism and Rule-Consequentialism

At this point, it might be objected that there are different versions of consequentialism, and that it is only one version that allows for resort to terrorism whenever that is the option with the best rationally expected consequences. But there is also a version of this approach that does not.

The basic principle of consequentialist ethics enjoins us to judge human action solely by its rationally expected consequences. Now "human action" can be taken to refer either to particular acts or to classes of acts. If our moral judgment is to focus on particular acts, then our ethical theory is act-consequentialism. It tells us to consider the balance of good and bad consequences that each option in a particular case can be rationally expected to have and to choose the option with the best balance. Act-consequentialism applies the basic principle of consequentialism directly to particular acts; the anticipated good and bad consequences to which the principle refers are the consequences of particular acts. But "human action" can be understood as referring to classes of acts; in that case, our theory is rule-consequentialism. According to this theory, the basic principle of consequentialism normally does not enter the picture when we judge particular acts. Such acts are judged by being subsumed under moral rules, which determine certain classes of acts as right or wrong. The rules are selected and justified from a consequentialist point of view: adopting them can be rationally expected to have better consequences than adopting some alternative rules or having no rules at all. The expected good and bad consequences to which the consequentialist principle refers are the consequences not of particular acts, but of classes of acts. The principle itself is a second-order rule; it is normally applied to moral rules as rules of the first order and only indirectly, through those rules, to particular acts.

Recasting consequentialism in this way has two advantages. First, rule-consequentialism acknowledges the role of moral rules in our actual moral deliberation and action. Normally, when considering what we ought to do in a particular situation, we do not look into and compare the good and bad consequences of every single option. We rather bring the relevant moral rule to bear on the situation at hand and decide that the right thing to do is what the rule requires. Second, this version of consequentialism does not tell us that we may lie, break our promise, cheat, or resort to violence whenever that can be rationally expected to have somewhat better consequences on balance than not doing so. Rather, it enjoins adherence to moral rules that prohibit such actions, which almost all of us have adopted as the basics of morality. For it is adoption of those rules, rather than some alternative rules or no rules at all, that can be rationally expected to have the best consequences on balance. Accordingly, while act-consequentialism will be rejected by most people as leading to strongly counter-intuitive conclusions with regard to lying, promise-keeping, and so on, and generally being much too permissive with regard to moral rules, rule-consequentialism is not exposed to these objections. It comports with moral rules, and indeed provides their justification.[11]

Act-consequentialist accounts of the morality of terrorism such as Honderich's will be rejected by those who understand the basics of morality in terms of separateness of persons, respect for persons, the distinction between innocence and guilt, and so on. But a rule-consequentialist account of terrorism is a different matter. Such an account will not advise that we assess the consequences of each and every act or campaign of terrorism on its merits, and resort to terrorism whenever doing so can rationally be expected to have better consequences on balance than refraining from it. It will rather tell us to go by the relevant moral rule. And the moral rule concerning terrorism will, of course, prohibit its use; for both history and contemporary experience show that, in the vast majority of cases, the balance of consequences of terrorism has been very bad indeed.

However, critics of rule-consequentialism have argued that it is not a great improvement upon act-consequentialism, since it does not succeed in ruling out those numerous departures from basic moral rules that compromise the latter. A moral rule – say, that we must not resort to terrorism – is selected because it is rationally expected that its adoption will be for the best. The adoption of this rule is justified by this expectation. We then keep to this rule until we face a situation where we rationally expect that, atypically, we will achieve better consequences on balance if we depart from the rule and engage in terrorism than if we stick to the rule and desist from it. Our assessment takes into account not only direct and short-term consequences of resorting to terrorism but also various indirect and long-term consequences of doing so, including the ways in which that will affect the general acceptance of the rule. Now there are various nonconsequentialist reasons for keeping to the rule that forbids terrorism in such a situation: the separateness of persons, respect for persons, innocence of the direct victims of terrorism and their immunity against deadly violence this innocence entails, and so on. But what *consequentialist* reason for sticking to the rule could there be? How can a rule-*consequentialist* argue for upholding the rule prohibiting terrorism that has been selected and justified because of its good consequences in a situation where such consequences will not transpire, and so the justification of the rule no longer applies? But if she cannot, then rule-consequentialism allows for as many departures from this and other basic moral rules as does the old, "act" variety of the theory.[12]

If we cannot accept the act-consequentialist account of the morality of terrorism because we find it much too permissive, then we must reject the rule-consequentialist account as well, for the same reason. There is more to the morality of terrorism than its various good and (mostly) bad, direct and indirect, short-term and long-term consequences.

5

Terrorism, Rights, and Justice

Nonconsequentialist Ethics and the Morality of Terrorism

Within a nonconsequentialist approach to morality, terrorism is not considered wrong only because (and insofar as) its rationally expected consequences are bad on balance. It is rather held to be wrong in itself, because of what it is. Yet it would be a mistake to think that nonconsequentialist ethics rules out all discussion about the morality of terrorism. This is an elementary mistake, but is nevertheless made occasionally, even by philosophers; I cited an instance in chapter 1. It consists in moving from "the morality of terrorism is not a matter of its consequences; rather, terrorism is wrong in itself" to "therefore, as far as terrorism is concerned, there is no moral question to ask, no moral discussion to have." The move is based on the mistaken assumption that, if something is wrong intrinsically, then, by the same token, it is also wrong absolutely – that is, always, in any circumstances. For something can be wrong intrinsically, for being what it is, but only *prima facie* – that is, as long as there are no further moral considerations which allow, or even require, that it be done, and which are so weighty that they override its intrinsic wrongness. In fact, most – some would say all – types of action that are intrinsically wrong are wrong in this sense. Lying is an obvious example. Many would say that lying is not wrong only when (and insofar as) it has bad consequences on balance but, first of all, in itself. But very few (Kant is a notorious exception) would want to claim that lying is wrong absolutely, always, whatever the circumstances. Sometimes there are moral considerations in favor of lying; and sometimes such considerations are weighty enough to override the intrinsic wrongness of lying (and whatever bad consequences it might have), so that lying is not wrong all things considered. Of course, terrorism is an incomparably more serious matter than lying. Still, it is worth inquiring whether terrorism, too, may be both *prima facie* morally wrong and in certain cases, at the same time, morally justified all things considered.

A nonconsequentialist might try to justify an act or campaign of terrorism in one of two ways. One is to invoke some deontological considerations, such as justice or rights, in favor of resorting to terrorism under certain circumstances. Alternatively, it might be argued that the obvious, and obviously very weighty, considerations of rights (of the victims of terrorism) and justice (which demands respect for those rights) that tell against terrorism may sometimes be overridden by extremely weighty considerations of consequences – an extremely high price that would be paid for *not* resorting to terrorism. For the rejection of consequentialism is of course not tantamount to denying that consequences of our actions, policies, and practices matter in their moral assessment; what is denied is the consequentialists' claim that *only* consequences matter.

I will discuss the first line of nonconsequentialist argument in this chapter and the second line of argument in chapter 6.

Terrorism, Human Rights, and Distributive Justice

The most interesting attempt at moral justification of terrorism from a nonconsequentialist point of view is Virginia Held's paper "Terrorism, Rights, and Political Goals" (originally published in 1991). Hers is a broad definition of terrorism (Held 2008, p. 76), but her discussion explicitly refers to terrorism in the narrow sense of violence against the innocent. The main thesis of the paper is that, under certain circumstances, terrorism can be morally justified in terms of basic human rights. This may be found surprising; for one might think that, if we take human right seriously, terrorism – that is, the killing and maiming of innocent people – must stand unequivocally and unconditionally condemned.

Held begins by emphasizing that social action in general cannot be properly judged solely in the light of its consequences; we must also apply the concepts of rights and duties. When dealing with terrorism, we must focus on the fact that terrorists violate rights and ask whether such violations can be morally justified.

What may we do in order to secure respect for rights? May we, in order to ensure that the rights of one person or group are respected, violate the rights of another person or group? This is a difficult question: "If we say that no violations of rights are justified even in this case, this can become a disguised recipe for maintaining the status quo. If we permit violations, we risk undermining the moral worth of the very rights for which we are making efforts to achieve respect" (Held 2008, p. 82).

In a society in which rights are not respected, we will have to make comparative judgments about rights and their holders. Granting the necessity of such judgments does not amount to accepting consequentialism of rights – the view of rights as (part of) the state of affairs which we ought to bring about and safeguard. On that view, we ought to seek to minimize violations of rights, so that, for example, we may violate a certain right of A, if by doing so we ensure the same right of B and C. For Held, rights are not properly a subject of calculations and trade-offs, with a view to maximizing their respect, or minimizing their violations, in society as a whole. But sometimes rights come into conflict; when they do, we must try to order them according to their importance. Where rights are not respected, we must be able to make comparative judgments about their violations.

According to Held, the question of the moral justification of terrorism is a particular case of the general question whether we may violate certain rights in order to ensure the respect of other rights. Terrorism violates basic human rights of its direct victims. But what if a limited use of terrorism is the only way of securing effective respect of basic human rights of all in a society?

In Held's view, in such circumstances resort to terrorism would still not be justified. But it would become justified if an additional condition were met: that of distributive justice. If, in a society, (a) basic human rights of one part of the population are effectively respected while basic human rights of another part of the population are violated; (b) if the only way of overcoming this state of affairs and ensuring the effective respect of basic human rights of all is a limited use of terrorism – that is, the violation of basic human rights of those who end up as its direct victims; finally, (c) if terrorism is directed against members of the first group, that terrorism will be morally justified. For it will be enjoined by distributive justice, applied to the problem of violations of basic human rights. From the point of view of justice, it is better to equalize violations of rights in a stage of transition to a situation in which the rights of all will be effectively respected than to allow that the group which has already suffered far-reaching violations of rights be exposed to further such violations – of course, assuming that in both cases we have violations of the same, or equally important, basic human rights. "If we must have violations," Held says, "a more equitable distribution of such violations is better than a less equitable one" (2008, p. 88).

The justification of terrorism offered by Held is original and interesting. It is quite different from the usual consequentialist arguments that refer to the good consequences of resorting to terrorism: to the fact that its use in certain circumstances promotes political and social change, serves to bring about a truly human society, or helps get people out of bad lives – arguments of the sort I examined in chapter 4. For this is a justification in terms of rights. It is also different from a justification in terms of consequentialism of rights. Consequentialism of rights will allow recourse to terrorism when that is the only way of maximizing the respect for rights or minimizing their violations. Held does not refer simply to rights and the aim of minimizing their violations, but to a just distribution of violations of rights. A crucial part of her justification of terrorism is the argument of distributive justice.

Is Held's justification of terrorism convincing? Before considering objections to it, I need to attend to a question of interpretation. Rekha Nath has argued that Held's justification of terrorism can be interpreted in two different ways. On the "responsibility-sensitive" interpretation, members of the group whose basic human rights are effectively respected, while the same rights of another group are not, are seen as responsible for this unjust state of affairs, and this responsibility plays a significant, albeit not highlighted, role in the justification of terrorism that targets them. On the other, "responsibility-insensitive" interpretation, members of the former group are not responsible for the unjust asymmetry of respect for basic human rights in their society. They are innocent, and the justification of terrorism directed at them is in no way based on their own actions or omissions (Nath 2011).

I do not find Nath's interpretation plausible, for two reasons. The textual support for construing the argument as "responsibility-sensitive" is extremely thin: a single remark of Held's that, "while some persons' most basic rights are denied respect, it seems worse to continue these violations than to permit some comparable violations of the rights of those who are *participating in this denial*" (Held 2008, p. 83; emphasis added). More importantly, this interpretation greatly detracts from the interest of Held's justification of terrorism. Instead of seeing it as a straightforward attempt at justifying the killing and maiming of innocent people – a drastic violation of their basic human rights and a great injustice by any account – in terms of the same considerations of rights and justice, Nath construes it, in part, as but another version of the kind of argument I discussed in chapter 3: yet another somewhat simplistic attempt to justify the killing and maiming of people who may not be completely innocent, but are surely not guilty enough to deserve such extreme punishment. Therefore I prefer to read Held's argument as unequivocally "responsibility-insensitive."

Objections

Uwe Steinhoff has two objections to Held's account of morally justified terrorism. He points out that using terrorism as a way of securing a more equitable distribution of basic human rights violations would not simply bring about a different distribution of a given number of such violations, but would rather mean adding new violations to those that would occur anyway.

> There is no determined quantity of such violations such that in order to distribute them we only have to select the victims who will receive them. [. . .] . . . The "distribution" of rights violations is not a zero-sum game. This means that if the blacks [in apartheid-time South Africa] march off to kill some whites, they do not thereby redistribute "pre-existing" acts of violence, but . . . produce new ones. While it may be just to distribute a fixed suffering or total rights violations burden equally on all shoulders, it is rather unjust to equalize the suffering of one innocent by making the other innocents suffer, too. "If one group is having a bad time, the others shall also have a bad time" – this does not appear to be a particularly commendable principle of justice. (Steinhoff 2007, pp. 128–9)

This objection is based on a misunderstanding of Held's argument that reduces it to one of its two components. Held does not propose to justify terrorism solely as a way of securing a measure of distributive justice in a very imperfect society. Her argument is not exclusively deontological. Rather, hers is a complex, two-part, deontological *and* consequentialist justification. On her account, terrorism directed at members of a group whose basic human rights have been effectively respected will be morally justified for *two* reasons: because it will bring about (a) a more equitable distribution of violations of those rights in the process of transition to (b) a better society in which basic human rights of all will be effectively respected. Neither of these two reasons – that of distributive justice and that of consequentialism of rights – is sufficient. Each is necessary, and the two are jointly sufficient to justify terrorism in the assumed circumstances.

Another problem Steinhoff brings up is that of identifying the group to be targeted by terrorism:

> Let us assume that Joe, Jim and Jill (group 1) as well as Frank, Fred and Fran (group 2) live in the poor neighbourhood, while Bob, Bill and Berta (group 3) live in the rich one. Let us further assume that the members of group 1 have already been robbed and bear a high risk of being robbed again, while this is not true for the members of groups 2 and 3. (Frank and Fred are monks, Fran is a nun, and this is respected by the criminals in the neighbourhood as sufficient reason not to assault them, apart from the fact that they do not have any valuables anyway.) Why, now, should the redistribution of rights violations or of risks of becoming a victim of violence proceed from group 1 to group 3 – which is probably what Held has in mind – instead of proceeding from group 1 to group 2? (2007, pp. 129–30)

This is not really a problem. The remark about members of group 2 having no valuables spoils the example somewhat. If those monks and nuns take their vows of poverty so seriously that they really have nothing valuable, then the kind of violence at issue, namely assault and robbery, cannot be targeted at them, so they need not be considered. Perhaps we should rather disregard Steinhoff's parenthetical remark and keep group 2 in the picture. What Held should have in mind for such a setup is not for members of group 1 to resort to terrorism and direct it at members of group 3 only, as Steinhoff surmises. The source of the problem which terrorism is to address is that basic human rights of some members of that society are effectively respected, while basic human rights of other members are often violated. This divides the society into two fairly clearly demarcated groups; subdivisions within these groups are not to the point.

Whereas Steinhoff's critique of Held's position targets its deontological requirement, Andrew Alexandra focuses on its consequentialist part – on the requirement that terrorism should be the way, and the only way, of moving from a society in which the basic human rights of some of its members are effectively respected to one in which those rights of all of its members are. Whether this is true will be an empirical question, to be answered in each particular case. Held's defense of terrorism will apply to those cases where the question is answered with a "yes" and will not apply to cases where the answer is "no." Alexandra submits that, in the world we live in, the answer will never be "yes," and that therefore Held's defense of terrorism has no application in it.

We have to imagine that members of (oppressed) group B, whose rights are violated so egregiously by members of group A that they become prepared to kill and maim innocent members of that group, to see them as mere means to their end, will be able to welcome their erstwhile oppressors and victims as their moral equals and partners once they have terrorised them into submission, and similarly that members of (formerly dominant) group A, who saw members of the group B as less than their moral equals *before* members of that group started to kill and maim innocent members of group A, will be willing and able to do so after they have been coerced into letting go of their dominance. That anything like this could happen seems to me to be a philosopher's fantasy, the falsity of which has been repeatedly demonstrated in the melancholy history of inter-ethnic conflicts over the past century. (Alexandra 2006, p. 114)

In the world we live in, acts and, in particular, campaigns of terrorism tend to have very different consequences: "almost invariably concerted terrorism produces in the terrorised group a persisting sense of moral resentment against those in whose name the terrorism is being perpetrated, provokes reciprocal outrages, cements the internal solidarity of the antagonistic groups, and makes co-existence more and more difficult" (ibid.).

The empirical issue is very difficult, if not impossible, to decide, at least in the present context. Any attempt at coming to a better understanding of the middle- to long-term consequences of terrorism would have to involve a close look into a number of violent conflicts generated by racial, ethnic, or religious divisions. Some conflicts, such as that between Israel and the Palestinians, seem to support Alexandra's gloomy picture; others, such as that in Northern Ireland, seem to suggest a very different conclusion; still others, such as that in South Africa during the apartheid years, may be open to different assessments. But let me assume, for the sake of argument, that Alexandra is right about the consequences the use of terrorism in racial, ethnic, or religious conflicts normally has, and that there is not a single historical example of a campaign of terrorism that can be justified in terms of Held's account of the morality of terrorism. Is Alexandra right to conclude that, "even if we accept that Held has given us an argument that supports the conclusion that terrorism *could* be justified, the possible world in which it *is* justified is so remote from ours, that consideration of it can play no part in the kind of judgements we must make about terrorism in this world" (2006, p. 114)? I think not; for we should not start the discussion of the morality of terrorism by assuming that there must be some actual cases of the use of terrorism that are morally justified, and that we need to find out just *what* their justification is. The initial question should rather be: *Is* terrorism ever morally justified? When put this way, the question does not rule out the possibility that no terrorism whatsoever, or no terrorism employed in the world in which we live so far, or which is likely to be employed in it, is morally justified. And, should that be the conclusion we reach, it would be a conclusion of some importance. It would certainly be a conclusion that plays a part – indeed, an important part – in "the kind of judgements we must make about terrorism in this world." If the objection is that Held sets the moral standard for morally justified terrorism much too high and that, as a result, terrorism turns out to be virtually never justified in the world we live in, my reply is that, in view of what terrorism is – the deliberate killing and maiming of innocent people with a view to intimidating and coercing some other people – perhaps that is as it should be.

So far I have reviewed and sought to rebut objections to Held's account of the morality of terrorism I find unconvincing. But I believe that there is another criticism to be made of her account, which does succeed in undermining it. It is best presented by approaching the issue from the perspective of a potential direct victim of terrorism.

If I were a candidate for a victim of a terrorist attack and were offered the usual consequentialist justification of terrorism, I would most likely say that I find it unacceptable to be killed or maimed for the sake of promoting the general interest, satisfying everyone's preferences, or keeping people out of bad lives. I have a *right* to life and bodily integrity, and this right may not be violated in order to promote the general interest, to satisfy preferences all round, or to keep other people out of bad lives. Considerations of rights have in principle greater weight than those of consequences. When offered a justification of the impending attack couched in terms of consequentialism of rights, I would say that I find that justification unacceptable as well. For that justification, too, does not take seriously the separateness of persons, and sacrifices *my* basic human rights for the sake of the greatest possible degree of respect for such rights of a certain *group* of people.

When faced with the justification of terrorism offered by Held – the justification that invokes basic human rights *and* applies distributive justice to violations of such rights – I would make a similar retort. I would say that I find the justification unconvincing and unacceptable; for it too does not take seriously the separateness of persons, but rather sacrifices *my* basic human rights for the sake of a more just distribution of violations of such rights within a *group* of people in the course of transition to a stage where these rights will be generally respected.

Is this retort convincing? The answer to this question will depend on the view of rights one espouses. If one views rights as almost absolute side constraints on our pursuit of individual and collective goals, the way Robert Nozick does (Nozick 1974, pp. 28–33), one is likely to find this retort quite appropriate and to reject the justification of terrorism advanced by Held. But this view of rights has been criticized as much too radical and as one that prevents us from making certain obviously relevant moral distinctions. In Nozick's theory, says H. L. A. Hart, "the basic rights which fill the moral landscape and express the inviolability of persons are few in number but are all equally stringent" (Hart 1979, p. 81). As a result, the theory has unacceptable implications:

> How can it be right to lump together, and ban as equally illegitimate, things so different in their impact on individual life as taking some of a man's income to save others from some great suffering and killing him or taking one of his vital organs for the same purpose? [. . .] Can one man's great gain or relief from great suffering not outweigh a small loss of income imposed on another to provide it? (Ibid., p. 84)

On the other hand, if, in order to avoid these implications of Nozick's radical account, one opts for a more moderate view of rights, Held's argument may appear quite attractive.

However, although Nozick's view of rights is indeed much too radical if one applies it across the board – that is, to property rights, as to the rights to life and bodily integrity, the way Nozick does – this view no longer looks quite as exaggerated if we recall *just what rights* the terrorist typically violates. Are an individual's rights not to be killed or maimed (except in self-defense, defense of others, or as deserved punishment) almost absolute, or are they rights that may be sacrificed for the sake of a more just distribution of violations of the same rights within a group in a transition to a stage where they will be generally respected?

Faced with the prospect of being killed or maimed on the ground of this last justification, I would draw on Nozick's view of rights, and say that I am a person in my own right, that my life is the only life I have and all I have, and that nobody may take it away, or ruin it by making me a cripple, for the sake of a more just distribution of, and subsequently more general respect for, the rights to life and bodily security within a group of people. My life and my basic human rights, or at least some of them, amount to more than mere membership in a group of holders of rights. The meaning and value of my life is not derived from my membership in a group. Nobody may sacrifice it for reasons to do with the group.

If so, Held's attempt to justify terrorism from a nonconsequentialist point of view does not succeed. Nozick's radical view of rights as almost absolute side constraints on our pursuit of individual and collective goals is not too radical when the rights at stake are the rights the terrorist typically violates: the rights of the individual not to be killed or maimed (except in self-defense, defense of others, or as deserved punishment). If it is not, if these rights are indeed almost absolute, then the considerations of rights and distributive justice to which Held appeals cannot override them after all.

The criticism, then, is that Held submerges the individual in the group of rights holders rather than recognizing her as an individual in her own right, one whose rights are not based on her belonging to the group and may not be sacrificed for the sake of a more just distribution of rights violations within the group. In response, Held makes two points. She notes that the criticism is not made from the point of view of extreme pacifism, which claims that the right to life is absolute and accordingly prohibits the killing of human beings in any circumstances whatsoever. It rather allows for killing humans in cases of self-defense, defense of others, and capital punishment. But, if the right to life is not absolute, we still face the questions of *when* one's right to life may be violated, whose rights count, and count for more.

Held goes on to argue that hers is not a collectivist position. "To fail to achieve a more just distribution of violations of rights (through the use of terrorism if that is the only means available) is to fail to recognize that those whose rights are already not fairly respected are individuals in their own right, not merely members of a group . . . whose rights can be ignored" (Held 2008, pp. 89–90). An argument for achieving a just distribution of rights violations need not be collectivistic; it can be an argument about the rights of individuals to basic fairness.

Yet the criticism that Held subordinates the individual holder of rights to the group of rights holders does not presuppose the view of the right to life as absolute. An individual can forfeit this right, and that is precisely what makes it possible to justify killing in self-defense or defense of others, and perhaps capital punishment as well. What the objection to Held's account points out is that an individual belonging to the group whose basic human rights are effectively respected has not done anything, or failed to do anything, that could be construed as forfeiture of his right to life. If he is then killed by a terrorist seeking to make the distribution of right to life violations in the entire population more just, that individual's right to life is violated for reasons to do with the *group*, namely for the sake of more justice within the group. This reason has nothing to do with the *individual's* acts or omissions, and in this sense what we have here is a collectivistic argument.

I still find Held's response unconvincing. She claims that, if we fail to resort to terrorism in the circumstances described in her argument, we thereby fail to recognize that individuals belonging to the disadvantaged section of the population "are individuals in their own right," rather than merely members of a group whose human rights can be ignored. This argument is predicated on a sweeping moral equivalence of acts and omissions and a strong version of negative responsibility: moral responsibility for *everything* we could, but do not, help prevent (see Williams 1973, pp. 93–6). This, too, I find problematic. We do not fail to respect the right to life of disadvantaged individuals when we fail to kill or maim other individuals, personally innocent of the plight of the former. The disadvantaged individuals do not have a right that we should engage in terrorism in their behalf, and we do not have a duty to do that. Indeed, I believe we have a duty *not* to do that.

6

Terrorism, Supreme Emergency, and Moral Disaster

Terrorism and Supreme Emergency

In Virginia Held's justification of terrorism, discussed in the preceding chapter, it is justice that requires that violations of human rights be more evenly distributed. There is a different way of allowing for the use of terrorism under certain circumstances within a nonconsequentialist approach to the ethics of violence. It can be argued that, as far as justice and rights are concerned, terrorism is never justified. Furthermore, considerations of justice and rights carry much greater weight than considerations of good and bad consequences, and therefore normally override the latter in cases of conflict. However, in exceptional circumstances considerations concerning consequences – the price of *not* resorting to terrorism – may be so extremely weighty as to override those of justice and rights.

Michael Walzer offers an argument along these lines in his discussion of terror bombing of German cities in World War II (Walzer 2000, chapter 16). On the face of it, the argument is meant to apply only to war and to justify only state terrorism; however, as critics have argued, if sound, it should be applicable to insurgent terrorism too. Walzer introduces the argument in the context of presenting and elaborating his account of *jus in bello* and against the background of his analysis of "the problem of dirty hands"; he understands the former predicament as a special, and extreme, case of the latter.

We sometimes face a situation where different moral requirements pull us in opposite directions, and we can act as required by one only at the price of going against the other. This is sometimes not very difficult to resolve, as one moral requirement can have more weight than the other, whether in general or at least in the particular case. When we decide accordingly, we are not left with a sense of great unease or even guilt. But sometimes the conflict is deep and vexing: it presents us with a moral dilemma, defined by Walzer as "a situation where [one] must choose between two courses of action both of which it would be wrong for [one] to undertake" (Walzer 1972, p. 160). We face such a dilemma whenever we can prevent something extremely bad from happening only by breaking a stringent moral rule. People in all walks of life may have to deal with such a predicament, but those in politics are particularly likely to have to do so. As thinkers such as Niccolò Machiavelli, Max Weber, and Jean-Paul Sartre have pointed out, one cannot govern "innocently" – at least not successfully and for long. Walzer concurs, and adds that we would not want to be governed by those whose primary concern was to keep their hands "clean" by strict adherence to moral rules rather than to safeguard and promote the common good. In politics "sometimes it is right to try to succeed, and then it must also be right to get one's hands dirty. But one's hands get dirty from doing what it is wrong to do. And how can it be wrong to do what is right? Or, how can we get our hands dirty by doing what we ought to do?" (ibid., p. 164). This looks paradoxical, but Walzer embraces the apparent paradox: a political leader facing such a quandary should indeed break the moral rule in order to prevent a development that would be extremely detrimental to the community. His action will be wrong, in that it will be a breach of a stringent moral rule, and it will also be right, in that it will stave off the threat to the community. It will leave him with dirty hands and a sense of guilt, yet he ought to do it; if he does not, he will fail to live up to the duties of his office.

Quandaries of this sort are particularly dramatic in wartime. Such was the predicament Britain seemed to be facing in early 1942. The government feared an impending defeat; it also feared that there was nothing its military could do about it, at least as long as they were fighting "clean" – that is, in accordance with the rules of war. Moreover, Britain's defeat was not going to be yet another defeat of a country by another, entailing such things as loss of some territory, war reparations, political concessions, and the like. Britain was perceived as the only remaining obstacle to the subjugation of most of Europe by the Nazis. Now the rule of the Nazis over most of Europe would have meant, as Churchill put it, "an age of barbaric violence" (quoted in Walzer 2000, p. 245). It would have involved extermination of some peoples and something very much like enslavement of others. In Walzer's words, "Nazism was an ultimate threat to everything decent in our lives, an ideology and a practice of domination so murderous, so degrading even to those who might survive, that the consequences of its final victory were literally beyond calculation, immeasurably awful." It was "evil objectified in the world . . . in a form so potent and apparent that there could never have been anything to do but fight against it" (ibid., p. 253).

Thus Britain was thought to be facing what Walzer (borrowing the term from Churchill) calls "supreme emergency": (a) an imminent threat of (b) something utterly unthinkable from a moral point of view. In such an emergency, and in such an emergency only, we may act in breach of such a basic and weighty moral rule as that of civilian immunity, if that is the only way we can hope to prevent the catastrophe. Accordingly, Churchill's government decided that Britain would no longer fight "clean" and unleashed the Royal Air Force on the civilian population of Germany. The onslaught continued almost to the last days of the war. Most of that killing and destruction cannot be defended by this line of argument, since it soon became obvious that Germany was not going to win the war. But in its first stage, in Walzer's judgment, the terror bombing of Germany was morally justified (albeit a crime too). It was morally justified as the only possible response to the supreme emergency Britain was facing.

What if it is only one country, rather than many, that is facing a threat of enslavement or extermination? Walzer holds that the argument of supreme emergency would still apply. He writes:

Can soldiers and statesmen override the rights of innocent people for the sake of their own political community? I am inclined to answer the question affirmatively, though not without hesitation and worry. [. . .] . . . It is possible to live in a world where individuals are sometimes murdered, but a world where entire peoples are sometimes massacred is literally unbearable. For the survival and freedom of political communities – whose members share a way of life, developed by their ancestors, to be passed on to their children – are the highest values of international society. Nazism challenged these values on a grand scale, but challenges more narrowly conceived, *if they are of the same kind*, have similar moral consequences. (2000, p. 254)

Walzer ends his chapter on supreme emergency by emphasizing that the rules of war in general, and the principle of civilian immunity in particular, may not be breached in the face of defeat *simpliciter*, but only in the face of defeat "likely to bring disaster to a political community" (ibid., p. 268).

Objections to the Supreme Emergency View

Walzer's defense of (state) terrorism as a response to supreme emergency has generated much critical discussion. In this section I review and comment on a string of objections to Walzer's position. This should prepare the ground for sketching an alternative view of the limits of the prohibition of terrorism in the final section of this chapter.

Walzer portrays supreme emergency as paradoxical; Brian Orend seeks to remove the paradox. In such an emergency we have two options, each involving a "serious moral violation," and we must choose one. In Orend's view, this predicament is best described as a "moral blind alley" or "moral tragedy." Whatever we do will be wrong. Therefore we are beyond morality: morality can offer no guidance and no justification. Yet we must choose. Moreover, the options we face in supreme emergencies are matters of life and death; therefore our choice will inevitably be determined by the irresistible pull of survival, and we will be forced to use deadly violence against innocent people as the way to survival. Accordingly, "while wrong, [our] actions may nevertheless be excused on grounds of the most extreme duress" (Orend 2000, p. 133).

Orend deploys an interpersonal analogy. A attacks B in an attempt to murder him, and B seeks to save his life by using C, an innocent bystander, as human shield. Our first response to this would be to say that B acted as "a selfish and despicable coward." Yet, upon reflection, we may come to understand that B made a "desperate choice" in the face of an extremely terrifying threat. Thus our more considered moral judgment of B and B's action may be more discerning and less harsh:

> We might be willing to excuse B's actions, on grounds that the terrible duress and mortal fear operative on him in the situation drove him to make the terrible choice he did. Like any animal filled with mortal terror, he desperately reached out for any means necessary to stave off death. This doesn't make his choice *right* or morally justifiable; it makes it *understandable* and, depending on the exact circumstances, *excusable* from criticism or punishment. It will be excusable if we determine that the pressure . . . was so extreme that B acted more out of animal instinct than out of a morally culpable decision-making capacity. We would say . . . that *he was forced to do something terribly wrong.* (Orend 2005, p. 144)

The same applies to those who act on behalf of a polity that is facing a supreme emergency. In such a plight, Orend writes, "as a matter of fact any country . . . will do whatever it can to prevail. The animal instincts are going to kick in, just as in our inter-personal analogy" (ibid., p. 149). Like Walzer, Orend too has a single historical example, that of terror bombing of German cities by the RAF.

The view of supreme emergency as a moral tragedy that takes us beyond the realm of morality, into a Hobbesian struggle for survival in which we resort to *any* means whatsoever, eliminates all appearance of paradox. "Walzer suggests that, in a supreme emergency, you have a right to do wrong, and/or a duty to violate duty, whereas no such claims are here made, resulting in a more coherent understanding. You don't have the right to do wrong, or a duty to violate duty; if you do wrong, you do wrong, even under the pressure of supreme emergency conditions" (Orend 2005, p. 149).

Some of Walzer's wordings seem deliberately paradoxical, and the sense of paradox is reinforced when he portrays supreme emergency as a case of "dirty hands" conundrum (Walzer 2000, pp. 323–5). But, as I will argue in the next section, supreme emergency can be sufficiently described without any reference to the contentious issue of dirty hands, a right to do wrong, or a duty to violate duty.

The main question, though, is whether Orend's understanding of supreme emergency is superior to that of Walzer. Walzer speaks of a difficult *moral* conflict, in which extremely weighty consequential considerations lead the agent to decide against extremely weighty deontological considerations. The right decision in such a case makes one's action morally *justified*, all things considered. Orend sees the same predicament as a conflict *beyond morality*, in which an irresistible survival instinct prevents the agent from settling the issue by rational moral thinking and makes her decide under duress. Once she does, her action cannot be justified – it is morally wrong – but she can be *excused* for having performed it.

Some situations in war fit this description. A soldier on the battlefield might fall into the grip of the survival instinct to the extent that he can no longer think rationally or act in a significantly voluntary way and, say, kill some civilians in order to save his life. But supreme emergency is not something that faces a single soldier on the battlefield. It is rather a problem facing a nation at war or, more accurately, those who lead the nation and decide on its behalf whether to go to war and how to fight it. Again, we can imagine a case where a nation's leaders find themselves under duress in some Dr Strangelove-type situation. But that sort of thing hardly ever happens. What *is* likely to happen is that the option to resort to intentional large-scale killing of enemy civilians – that is, to a type of state terrorism – gets discussed in high political and military committees, in conditions reasonably conducive to rational thinking, on the assumption that such thinking will be engaged in in appropriate detail and without undue haste, and that the pros and cons of that option will be carefully assessed and weighed against alternatives. Should a political or military leader involved show signs of thinking, feeling, or acting "like [an] animal filled with mortal terror," he or she would be excused from the deliberations rather than be allowed to help determine their outcome. Both Walzer and Orend offer the same historical example of deliberate killing of a large number of enemy civilians justified, or excused, by a supreme emergency: that of the bombing of German cities in World War II. The decision-making process that led to that campaign is well documented, not least in the voluminous writings of the person who bears the greatest part of the overall responsibility for it, Prime Minister Churchill. We know that its participants were not "filled with mortal terror" and did not "act out of animal instinct," but rather exercised their "morally culpable decision-making capacity."

There is one important point of concurrence between Orend and Walzer: both – albeit for different reasons – refuse to condemn morally those who in a supreme emergency resort to large-scale killing of civilians. Other critics of Walzer reach a different conclusion: that civilian immunity must be respected even in such an emergency, and that those who fail to do so are to be morally condemned.

One is C. A. J. Coady, who takes Walzer to task for his bias in favor of the state. Several critics have highlighted a certain degree of this bias in Walzer's ethics of war in both its parts. In Walzer's account of *jus ad bellum*, it comes to the fore in particular in his restrictive view of the legitimacy of military intervention, based on an argument about the "fit" between the state and the political community's traditions and way of life. In his account of *jus in bello*, it is apparent in his restrictive view of the availability of the supreme emergency argument to various agents, which is the question on which Coady focuses. Walzer presents this argument in his *Just and Unjust Wars*, which for the most part deals with war between states; and he discusses it solely in that context, as an option political and military leaders of a state may have to consider. In his discussion of non-state terrorism in that book and in a later essay titled "Terrorism: A Critique of Excuses," supreme emergency is never mentioned. Walzer argues that non-state terrorism can never be justified or excused. If it is engaged in a liberal and democratic state, it is not justified because it is not necessary: there are ample opportunities and venues for voicing and addressing grievances without recourse to violence. If employed in the struggle against a totalitarian state, it is not justified because it is bound to fail; totalitarian states are "immune" to resistance of any kind, including terrorism.[13] And yet the sole historical instance of wholesale deliberate killing of civilians Walzer considers justified as a response to supreme emergency, the bombing of German cities in World War II, is a case of (state) terrorism employed against a totalitarian state. "Why," asks Coady, "should states enjoy the supreme emergency license when other groups do not?" (Coady 2004, p. 784). To reply, as Walzer does, that the "survival and freedom of political communities" are "the highest values of international society" will not do, if this society is understood – as it is in Walzer's account – as comprising established and internationally recognized political communities.

Some insurgent organizations, too, can reasonably claim to be acting on behalf of political communities. In certain extreme circumstances, such an organization might mount a supreme emergency argument in favor of resort to terrorism. Then again, "why not allow that the [supreme emergency] exemption can apply to huge corporations, the existence of which is central to the lives and livelihoods of so many? Or . . . to individuals when they are really against the wall?" (Coady 2004, p. 787). So long as he has produced no cogent argument for restricting the exemption to states, Walzer seems bound in consistency to make it available to non-state agents as well. But, if he did, that would compromise the "rarity value" of the exemption:

> As the name suggests, the supreme emergency story . . . gets its persuasiveness from the idea that its disruptive power to override profound moral prohibitions is available only in the rarest of circumstances. Any broadening of the reach of these circumstances tends to reduce the rarity value of the exemption and hence increase the oddity of the idea that it can be right to do what is morally wrong. [. . .] . . . The more we move in this direction, the more the currency of supreme emergency is devalued. (Ibid.)

Thus we are facing a choice: we can either concede that the supreme emergency exemption applies more generally than Walzer allows – to states, but also to a range of non-state agents – or decide that it applies to no one, and that civilian immunity and the prohibition of terrorism it entails are absolute and allow for no exceptions whatever. Coady opts for the latter choice: "My own conviction is that we surely do better to condemn the resort to terrorism outright with no leeway for exemptions, be they for states, revolutionaries, or religious and ideological zealots of any persuasion" (ibid., p. 789).

Now Coady is clearly right as far as Walzer's bias in favor of the state is concerned. A stateless people and an organization fighting on its behalf should in principle be as entitled as an established and recognized state to consider resorting to deliberate attacks on civilians, when facing a supreme emergency. Corporations and individuals, on the other hand, seem to be in a different position in this respect. It may yet be possible to argue for restricting the exemption to the former and deny it to the latter without inconsistency and while preserving its rarity value.

Stephen Nathanson, too, takes a critical look at Walzer's position and reaches the conclusion that the supreme emergency argument should not be allowed to undermine our absolute commitment to civilian immunity and consequent rejection of all terrorism. Nathanson first takes a close look at the ways in which Walzer describes such emergency. This brings to the fore two different conceptions of supreme emergency: a broad and, to a significant degree, subjective conception and a specific and objective one. When focusing on the Nazi threat, Walzer uses a broad brush and lays on highly emotional colors: Nazism presented a threat to civilized values, to civilization itself, to "everything decent in our lives," and this threat properly evokes responses such as abhorrence and horror. When looking beyond that particular case, Walzer portrays supreme emergency as "a threat of enslavement or extermination directed at a single nation."

The first, broad and subjective version of supreme emergency is much too flexible and open-ended to provide the kind of ethical guidance we expect of such a criterion. Walzer focuses on World War II and highlights Nazi atrocities while placing the atrocities committed by the Japanese armed forces in that war at a lower point on the atrocity scale, where they fall short of supreme emergency. Yet the latter atrocities, too, were systematic and large-scale, and when portrayed vividly and in detail tend to evoke the same emotional response as those committed by the Nazis. They, too, strike us as incompatible with civilized values and as a threat to "everything decent" in our lives. Vivid and detailed accounts by survivors of the terror bombing of German and Japanese cities in that war will also evoke a response of horror and abhorrence in a decent person. Moreover, "if people are subjected to brutal rule over many years and cannot live normal, secure lives, they are likely to see their own situation as a supreme emergency for them. [. . .] It is not clear that Walzer could show why these people are mistaken since any form of extended oppression is a threat to civilized values" (Nathanson 2006, p. 22).

Should we, then, discard the first, broad and subjective approach to supreme emergency and adopt the second, specific and objective conception, according to which only an imminent threat of extermination or enslavement of a nation amounts to such an emergency? Nathanson finds this version of the supreme emergency criterion clear enough but faults it for two reasons. First, it does not support Walzer's account of the British predicament at the early stage of war, since Britain was not facing such a threat. Second, it is likely to be rejected as too demanding by people facing the threat of lesser, but still huge disasters. Generally, Nathanson submits, people are likely to perceive any urgent, threatening situation as a supreme emergency:

> Consider the American reaction to the September 11 attacks. Though serious and frightening, these come nowhere near satisfying Walzer's criterion, and yet many people would find the expression "supreme emergency" quite apt to describe the post-September 11 situation. They feel that their way of life is threatened, that their civilization is threatened, that any means of combating future acts of terrorism are justified. Likewise, supporters of Bin Laden and the September 11 attackers probably see both the United States and Western culture generally as "an ultimate threat to everything decent" in *their* lives. (Nathanson 2006, pp. 23–4)

The supreme emergency criterion, then, does not provide clear and reliable ethical guidance. Those who adopt it are stepping on a very slippery slope, and are liable to end up violating civilian immunity in many cases in which Walzer himself would not condone doing so. Therefore we should rather endorse this immunity and the consequent rejection of terrorism as an absolute rule of morality.

Now the first, broad understanding of supreme emergency is indeed unacceptably subjective. If it were all we had to go by, such emergency would be in the eye of the beholder. On the other hand, Nathanson's objections to the narrow conception are not very damaging. That conception may not apply to the historical illustration of supreme emergency offered by Walzer, the terror bombing of German cities in World War II, but then so much the worse for that particular illustration. (I will discuss the morality of that bombing campaign in some detail in chapter 8.) People facing a major crisis that falls short of extermination or enslavement are indeed liable to feel, and claim, that theirs is a supreme emergency too. But any moral rule can be misunderstood, misinterpreted, and misapplied. I will come back later to the slippery slope argument Nathanson grounds on his second point.

I am thus in agreement with some of Coady's and Nathanson's objections to Walzer's supreme emergency view but cannot endorse others, and I want to resist their conclusion that civilian immunity must be upheld as an absolute moral rule and that, therefore, terrorism cannot be morally justified in any actual or hypothetical circumstances. I will now present a position that is structurally similar to Walzer's view but is not exposed to the objections of bias in favor of the state, loss of the rarity value of the exemption, its vagueness, and the slippery slope. I propose to term this position the moral disaster view.

Terrorism and Moral Disaster

Let me retrace some of my steps. Just what kind of choice is at issue?

Put in the most general terms, it is a choice between two *prima facie* moral requirements, both applying to the circumstances in which we find ourselves, but pulling us in opposite directions. We cannot act in accordance with one without at the same time going against the other and thereby, in that respect, doing something wrong. Yet that is exactly what we must do; there is no third option. This is a case of moral conflict. Walzer, however, calls this a moral dilemma; but his definition of "moral dilemma," quoted earlier, although perhaps in line with everyday usage, is much too wide for philosophical discussion. Not every moral conflict is a moral dilemma; the latter term is better reserved for a certain type of such conflict. In any case of moral conflict, whatever we do, we do something that is in a certain respect wrong. But in some such cases the two courses of action are not equally wrong: one is more so than the other, whether in general or only in that particular case. Accordingly, there is a solution to the conflict: we ought to choose the other course of action. When we do that, we do what, all things considered, we ought to do. But this does not wipe out the *prima facie* wrongness of our action as a violation of the moral requirement that has been overridden; that accounts for the conceptual room and the moral call for awareness of the moral price paid and regret that it had to be paid. This is moral conflict *simpliciter* (see Ross 2002, chapter II).

Sometimes, however, the conflicting moral requirements are equally weighty, the two possible courses of action equally wrong. There is no solution to the conflict, nothing that, in the end, we ought to choose. This is a moral dilemma, as the term is usually used in philosophy (see Sinnott-Armstrong 1988, chapter 1). In this sense, cases that Walzer presents and discusses as instances of dirty hands, including that of supreme emergency, are not moral dilemmas but, rather, instances of moral conflict *simpliciter*.

Moreover, it is not clear just what is gained by portraying a case of supreme emergency as one of dirty hands. Walzer's discussion of the dirty hands problem, seminal though it is, fails to tell us what is *distinctive* of the problem: what distinguishes it from any case of very serious moral conflict – that is, moral conflict in which the conflicting moral requirements are very weighty indeed. None of the possibilities suggested by Walzer's discussion – conflict between public and private morality, or between role morality and universal moral requirements, or between deontological and consequential considerations – seems to capture that. Some progress has been made in an essay by Stephen de Wijze, who argues that cases of dirty hands are those of very serious moral conflict in which our choice is forced by the circumstances created by an immoral person or persons, so that we end up collaborating with them, furthering their evil project (de Wijze 2007). In this sense, however, a supreme emergency is *not* an instance of dirty hands.

What is it, then? Rather than wade any further into ethical theory and try for a general account of supreme emergency, I will stay within the bounds of the ethics of war and focus on the immunity of civilians or common citizens. Just what would it take for us to be justified in overriding this immunity and engaging in terrorism?

A careful reading of Walzer's book and his more recent essay "Emergency Ethics" shows that, although he promises a "touchstone against which arguments about extremity might be judged" (Walzer 2000, p. 253), what he offers under the heading of supreme emergency is actually a range of answers to this question:

- a crisis in which morality itself seems to be at stake. How, asks Walzer, "can we, with our principles and prohibitions, stand by and watch the destruction of the moral world in which those principles and prohibitions have their hold?" In such a crisis, "our deepest values are radically at risk," and the threat we are facing "devalues morality itself and leaves us free to do whatever is militarily necessary to avoid [it]" (Walzer 2004a, pp. 37, 40).
- the threat that was facing Great Britain and much of Europe in the early stages of World War II: that of entering an age of barbaric violence, in which entire peoples are exterminated or enslaved.
- the threat of extermination or enslavement facing a single nation.
- a threat to "the survival and freedom of a political community."

We should put both the first and the last understanding of supreme emergency to one side. I find the idea of a threat to "morality itself" unintelligible, because I cannot envisage human existence, however damaged and constrained, bereft of all morality. An essential part of being human is being capable of, and given to, moral deliberation and action. Human beings demonstrate this even in the most trying circumstances; there is, for example, ample evidence that, even in Nazi and Soviet camps, both inmates and guards engaged in moral thinking and acted accordingly.

The notion of a threat to "survival and freedom" of a political community, on the other hand, is unhelpful, because ambiguous. In one sense, it is a threat of extermination or enslavement of its people. This takes us back to the third understanding of supreme emergency to be found in Walzer. In another sense, it is a threat to political independence of a state. This kind of threat, however, can hardly have the moral weight required by Walzer's supreme emergency argument. A state may or may not have moral legitimacy. If it does not, its demise may well be morally preferable to its continued existence. But, even if it does, its loss of political independence, however deplorable, surely does not amount to the loss of "everything decent in our lives," something that must be staved off by means of wholesale killing and maiming of civilians.

We are left, then, with extermination or enslavement of entire peoples. If such a threat facing a single people is enough to put onslaught on enemy civilians on the agenda, the same threat facing a number of peoples will provide an even more compelling reason to do so. However, the expression "extermination or enslavement" needs to be unpacked, for the two differ in important respects. First, it is clear what "extermination" of a people amounts to, whereas "enslavement" can refer to different things: the status of slaves in the ancient world, or the fate the Nazis had in store for the "racially inferior" peoples of Eastern Europe, or a less extreme type of totalitarian oppression (as in the Cold War phrase "the enslaved nations of Eastern Europe"). Any such fate, appalling as it is, would still be seen as preferable to extermination. Second, extermination, once perpetrated, cannot be reversed, while those enslaved (in any sense of the word) can always hope to be set free. Enslavement of a people, then, is not quite in the same class of moral enormity as extermination; nor does it have the finality that defines the latter.

I believe that extermination of a people amounts to a moral disaster, and that its imminent threat may put deliberate killing of civilians or common citizens (on a *much* smaller scale) on the agenda. But, if so, why not the same threat facing a smaller group? Why not extend the same moral exemption to a single individual who is about to be murdered and could save his life by using an innocent bystander as a human shield? Part of the answer is: both individual and mass murder are *murder*, but the difference in scale between the two surely has considerable moral significance. Part of the answer is the moral import of continued existence of a large and comprehensive community such as a people – that is, the community that provides the framework and resources for human life in all its aspects, and relates the life of the individual to a collective past remembered and a collective future hoped for. Walzer puts this point well. He cites Burke's famous portrayal of the political community as a partnership between the living, the dead, and those yet to be born, and goes on to say:

> This commitment to continuity across generations is a very powerful feature of human life, and it is embodied in the community. When our community is threatened, not just in its present territorial extension or governmental structure or prestige or honor, but in what we might think of as its *ongoingness*, then we face a loss that is greater than any we can imagine, except for the destruction of humanity itself. We face moral as well as physical extinction, the end of a way of life as well as of a set of particular lives, the disappearance of people like us. And it is then that we may be driven to break through the moral limits that people like us normally attend to and respect. (Walzer 2004a, p. 43)

However, a people can be threatened in its "ongoingness" in a way that falls short of extermination but may be no less effective: by being ethnically cleansed from its land. Strangely enough, Walzer does not advert to this. A people needs a homeland in which it can evolve and maintain its way of life, its traditions and cultural and political institutions. Uprooting a people from its land puts an end to its "ongoingness" almost as effectively as does its extermination. Indeed, the two are closely related: more often than not, those seeking to annex another people's land, but not its inhabitants, carry out massacres with a view of terrorizing those who survive into fleeing. But, while ethnic cleansing is by definition carried out by means of violence, this violence need not reach wholesale extermination of a people. Therefore ethnic cleansing cannot be subsumed under extermination, but constitutes a moral disaster in its own right.

The moral disaster position, then, is structurally similar to that of supreme emergency. Both uphold civilian immunity as an extremely weighty moral rule that expresses the demands of justice, as it applies in wartime, and determines the rights of civilians. Both also concede that this immunity may be overridden *in extremis* – that is, when extremely weighty consequential considerations enjoin that, and, of course, on a *much* smaller scale. But the idea of moral disaster differs from that of supreme emergency in its contents and scope. While supreme emergency ranges from "threats to morality itself" to threats to the political independence of a state, moral disaster includes only the extermination and ethnic cleansing of an entire people from its land.

The moral disaster view refers to peoples rather than to states or political communities; therefore it cannot be charged with pro-state bias. Nor is it exposed to the charge of being vague and overly inclusive; for its crucial terms are, I believe, sufficiently clear. While "genocide" is a legal term whose definition is a matter of some disagreement, "extermination" is an ordinary language word, but nonetheless quite unequivocal. So is the phrase "extermination of a people." "Ethnic cleansing" is by now a legal term. It is also used in ordinary discourse, much too often in loose and sometimes outright irresponsible ways. But that is not to say that it cannot be properly defined. I find the following definition, offered by Bosnian legal scholar Dražen Petrović, quite helpful: "Ethnic cleansing is a well-defined policy of a particular group of persons to systematically eliminate another group from a given territory on the basis of religious, ethnic or national origin. Such a policy involves violence and is very often connected with military operations" (Petrović 1994, p. 351).

By restricting the notion of moral disaster to extermination or ethnic cleansing of entire peoples – two wrongs that, in view of their enormity *and* finality, constitute a category apart – the present view goes a long way in preserving the rarity value of the exemption it proffers.

It might be objected that this position is indeed tighter than Walzer's but is still dangerously vague. The source of its vagueness is largely the word "entire": does it mean, literally, every single member of the threatened people, or does it allow for something short of that, and, in that case, where is the line to be drawn? Moreover, a degree of vagueness lurks in the term "people": just what is a people, and which large human groups qualify?

The first thing to say in response is that the phrase "extermination or ethnic cleansing of an entire people" should indeed not be taken to mean the killing or expulsion of every individual belonging to that people. One can put an end to the collective existence of a people, its "ongoingness" as that particular people – the "ongoingness" of its way of life, its traditions and cultural and political institutions – without killing or expelling every single member of the people. Killing or expelling a large enough number of its members will normally be enough to achieve this result even if some are left alive or even allowed to stay in their land. Just how large must this number be? And just which large human groups qualify as peoples? Here I believe a general point made by Aristotle and echoed by many others since bears repeating: "Our discussion will be adequate if it has as much clearness as the subject-matter admits of, for precision is not to be sought for alike in all discussions, any more than in all the products of the crafts. [. . .] . . . It is the mark of an educated man to look for precision in each class of things just so far as the nature of the subject admits" (Aristotle 1963, pp. 2–3). Now ethics does not always admit of drawing hard and fast lines. My position will not be readily applicable in each and every instance; there will be borderline cases. But that is only to be expected, given the nature of the subject.

Furthermore, when facing such cases, we are not left without a clue. The course of action we are considering is one of the worst atrocities human beings can perpetrate: deliberate killing and maiming of innocent civilians or common citizens. Therefore our approach must be one of restraint. In view of the enormity of what we are considering doing, we may decide to do it only if our predicament is clearly that of moral disaster rather than a borderline case of such disaster. When in doubt, we must desist.

The rarity value of the moral disaster view is further ensured by attending to an issue that Walzer deals with only very briefly and that has been completely neglected by his critics. The *meaning* of "supreme emergency" is defined by the nature of the danger and its imminence. But for such an emergency to amount to a *justification* of deliberate large-scale attacks on civilians or common citizens, a third condition must be met: such attacks must be the way, and the only way, of staving off the danger. Just how certain must we be of that? One might argue that, when *in extremis*, we cannot apply stringent epistemic standards in deciding how to cope – indeed, if we cannot really know what will work, we must take our chances with what might. This is Walzer's view. In such a predicament, he argues, there can be no certainty. Nor is it a matter of calculating probabilities, for there is no method of quantifying them. What we can, and must, do is study the situation closely, take the best available advice, and then "wager" the "determinate crime" of large-scale killing and maiming of civilians against the "immeasurable evil" that is otherwise in store for us. "There is no option; the risk otherwise is too great" (Walzer 2000, p. 260).

I do not accept this position. It highlights the enormity of the threat, while failing to give due weight to the enormity of the means proposed for fending off the threat – the enormity of deliberately killing and maiming innocent people. When that is taken into account, the conclusion should rather be that, even *in extremis*, if deliberate onslaught on innocent people is to be justified, the reasons for believing that it will work, and that nothing else will, must be very strong indeed. If we lack such reasons, we must desist. Even in a most desperate plight, we should not "wager" with the lives of people who are enemy civilians, but *innocent* civilians nonetheless.

In a recent reassessment of civilian immunity in just war theory, Frederik Kaufman writes: "Just shy of absolutism, the supreme emergency is a threshold view; it requires that we refrain from intentionally killing innocent people until the costs of doing so become too high plausibly to do anything else" (Kaufman 2007, p. 105). I have sought to show that, as a characterization of the supreme emergency view, this is only half correct. That view is, indeed, a threshold view; but because the threshold it sets is neither clear enough nor high enough, it is not *just* shy, but rather *well* shy of absolutism. The moral disaster view *is* just shy of absolutism: it maintains that deliberate killing and maiming of civilians in war, or of common citizens in conflict that falls short of war, is *almost* absolutely wrong.

Is the moral disaster view vulnerable to the slippery slope objection? If we allow *any* departure from civilian immunity, do we not make a dent in the prohibition which is likely to become ever wider? Once the rule is no longer absolute, even if some departures from it are justified, there are likely to be others which are not. The exemption will lend itself to misapplications – both those made in good faith, as a result of mistaken beliefs, and those not so made.

I do not believe this type of argument can be assessed in the abstract. Its force varies with the circumstances in which it is deployed. In general, it seems to me that, other things being equal, slippery slope arguments become less convincing as the cost of abiding by the rule at issue becomes higher. Thus in some cases a slippery slope argument may carry great weight, while in others its force may be doubtful. In truly extreme cases, such an argument may no longer seem to the point.

Think of a people facing an imminent threat of extermination or of being ethnically cleansed from its land, and unable to defend itself against an overwhelmingly stronger enemy while fighting in accordance with the rules of *jus in bello*. Suppose we said to its political and military leaders: "Granted, what you are facing is an imminent threat of a true moral disaster. Granted, the only way of preventing the disaster is by breaching the rule of civilian immunity and attacking enemy civilians. But you must not do that. For, if you do, that will make a dent in the rule, and that, in turn, will make possible, and indeed likely, other, unjustified breaches." Would that be a good moral reason for them to acquiesce in their fate?

Stephen Nathanson considers this a powerful, yet ultimately unsuccessful criticism of the view of civilian immunity as an absolute moral rule. He holds that the problem cannot be settled at the level of particular cases. My description of the case is one-sided; a fair description would also include the predicament of the potential victims of terrorism. Such an expanded description might well leave us undecided. For at this level there is simply one plight, that of a people facing an imminent threat of extermination or ethnic cleansing, contrasted with another plight, that of innocent civilians or common citizens to be killed or maimed; one right, that of self-defense of a people against a particularly vicious type of aggression, pitted against another right, that of innocent civilians or common citizens not to be deliberately killed or maimed. But there is no proof that one plight takes precedence over the other, that one right overrides the other. My argument presupposes, rather than proves, that the plight of the former has greater moral weight than the plight of the latter, that the former right overrides the latter. If the problem is to be solved, we need to move to another level, that of moral rules (Nathanson 2010, pp. 208–11).

However, my argument is not meant as a *proof* that the immunity of civilians or common citizens is not absolute. It is rather meant to refute the slippery slope argument for absolutism: to suggest that, when an entire people is facing an imminent threat of extermination or all-out ethnic cleansing, concerns about the hazards of making a dent in the moral rule at issue which may well make for unjustified departures from it further down the line will probably not seem to the point. It is also meant to challenge the absolutist conception of civilian immunity by shifting the burden of argument onto defenders of this conception. If they claim that the rule must be upheld even in those circumstances, what is the argument for this claim?

Nathanson seeks to ground absolute immunity of civilians or common citizens and absolute prohibition of terrorism it entails in a rule-consequentialist ethical theory – a version of consequentialism that holds that an act is morally right or wrong by virtue of conforming to, or violating, the relevant moral rule, and that moral rules are selected and justified by reference to the rationally expected good consequences of their adoption (2010, pp. 191–208). His first step is to argue that the moral rule relating to the treatment of civilians in war that a rule-consequentialist would adopt would prohibit targeting civilians. This rule would be preferred for two reasons: adopting it would reduce the killing and destruction in war more than adopting any alternative rule or no rule at all, and it would not stand in the way of effective fighting because it is by killing soldiers, rather than civilians, that one weakens and ultimately destroys the enemy's fighting capacity. The second step is to show that this rule should be adopted as absolute, allowing for no exceptions whatsoever. Nathanson seeks to show that by considering the consequences of construing the rule as enjoining civilian immunity in most cases, but also allowing for exceptions in supreme emergencies. The consequences would be worse than the consequences of adopting civilian immunity as absolute, for three reasons. The idea of supreme emergency is vague. The criteria for issuing supreme emergency exemptions are liable to be applied in arbitrary and subjective ways. Finally, there is the slippery slope argument: "permitting [departures from the rule of civilian immunity] even under the direst circumstances will lower the bar for justifying such acts . . . broadcast the message that such behavior may sometimes be justified and . . . thus lend its weight to increasing the use of such methods" (ibid., p. 207).

Unlike Nathanson, I do not consider rule-consequentialism the best ethical theory. As I explained in the final section of chapter 4, I do not see it as a significant improvement upon act-consequentialism. But assuming rule-consequentialism for the sake of argument, I too think that, when brought to bear on the question of treatment of civilians or common citizens in armed conflict, it would enjoin their immunity. However, I am not convinced by Nathanson's arguments that this immunity would have to be absolute. The idea of supreme emergency, as presented and deployed by Walzer, is indeed unacceptably vague; earlier in this chapter, I concurred with Nathanson's critique of Walzer on this point. That is precisely why I propose an alternative, structurally similar yet much more stringent position – that of moral disaster. The notion of moral disaster – including, as it does, only extermination or ethnic cleansing of an entire people – is not similarly vague. A further safeguard against its inappropriate deployment is the provision that in borderline or otherwise unclear cases one must desist from attacking civilians. Moreover, Nathanson's point about the dangers of misapplication is not specific to the issue of civilian immunity, but rather a worry concerning moral rules generally. Any moral prescription or proscription may be misapplied because of human ignorance, sloppy thinking, or bias in favor of one's own interests and those of people one cares about. But that is not reason enough to construe it as an absolute moral demand, to be complied with come what may. Finally, as I said earlier, I do not believe that the hazard of stepping on a slippery slope should prevent a people facing extermination or ethnic cleansing from resorting to terrorism, if that is the only effective means of staving off the disaster.[14]

The immunity of innocent civilians or common citizens against being deliberately killed or maimed in a violent conflict and the prohibition of terrorism this entails are not absolute after all. But they *are* almost absolute: they may be overridden only in the face of a true moral disaster.

7

Is Terrorism Morally Distinctive?

Some Answers to the Question

Whatever else it does, the experience of a terrorist act or campaign, and even a report on it, leaves the vast majority of people with a sense of moral atrocity. Moreover, many feel that terrorism is not only morally atrocious, but atrocious in a distinctive way – in a way different from other moral atrocities such as mass murder, ethnic cleansing, or torture. This is not to say that they feel that terrorism is more morally abhorrent than these other atrocities, but rather that it is abhorrent in its own way. Yet it is not easy to articulate this feeling and provide a clear and convincing account of the distinctive moral wrongness of terrorism. There is a string of such accounts in the literature but, although each may be saying something interesting about *some* terrorism, none seems to have captured the distinctive moral atrociousness of *all* terrorism, terrorism as such.

Thus, Samuel Scheffler argues that what is morally distinctive about terrorism is its use of violence and fear with the aim of destabilizing or degrading an existing social order. This aim is achieved by violence against the innocent and the fear it induces in society at large. In a standard case, an act of terrorism kills and maims some innocent people, strikes fear or anxiety in the hearts of many more, and ultimately affects all by helping erode the quality or stability of the entire social order. The fear generated by terrorist attacks disrupts social life and undermines political and social institutions in many ways: by derailing the political process, eroding confidence in the government, bringing about repressive legislation, harming the economy, etc. Over time, the corrosive power of fear tends to affect the willingness of common citizens to engage in some everyday activities, whether by making them suspicious of other participants or fearful of being in places where they might be targeted by terrorists. The minimum features of a standard case of terrorism, then, are: "1) the use of violence against civilians or non-combatants, 2) the intention that this use of violence should create fear in others, including other civilians or non-combatants, and 3) the further intention that this fear should destabilize or degrade an existing social order, or at any rate that it should raise the specter of such destabilization or degradation. The destabilization or degradation of the social order may itself have many different aims" (Scheffler 2006, p. 6). These three features, taken together, make terrorism morally distinctive.

Scheffler goes on to distinguish terrorism and terror. The latter is the same mechanism of violence and intimidation that is characteristic of terrorism, when employed with a view to stabilizing or preserving, rather than undermining, the existing social order. Both terrorism and terror can be used by insurgents and state agencies alike.

This account of the use of violence against the innocent in order to induce fear in society at large and thereby disrupt social life and destabilize the entire social order is an accurate depiction of much terrorism – in particular the kind of terrorism driven by radical ideologies. However, it is not true of all that we would want to recognize, and condemn, as a clear-cut case of terrorism. In his analysis of terrorism-induced fear, Scheffler draws on Thomas Hobbes's famous portrayal of the state of nature and the crucial role of all-pervasive fear that makes that state so horrible. Accordingly, he concentrates on the kind of fear that spreads throughout society and affects all and sundry. But there are also cases of attacks on innocent civilians or common citizens where intimidation is focused on a relatively small group of decision-makers, such as a government. In such cases, the terrorists hijack a plane, or take over a building, turn those who happen to be there into hostages, and announce their conditions for freeing them. In some cases these conditions are quite restricted. During the 1972 Munich Olympic Games, members of Black September, a Palestinian terrorist organization, infiltrated the Olympic village and took eleven Israeli athletes and coaches hostage. Their demands included the release of 234 Palestinian and other prisoners from jails in Israel and of two convicted German terrorists from a jail in Germany. In other cases, the objective may be far-reaching, yet nevertheless quite specific too. In their attack on a school in Beslan, in southern Russia, on September 1, 2004, Islamic militants took hostage some 1,100 civilians, mostly children. The conditions for freeing the captives were an end to the occupation of Chechnya, recognition of its independence, and the release of some thirty detainees. As far as one can tell, in neither case did the terrorists aim at anything so grand as destabilizing or degrading an entire social order (in the Munich Olympics case, it is not clear which social order would have been the target). On Scheffler's account, unless a *further intention* on the part of the perpetrators to induce fear in society at large and help undermine its social order can be shown, neither of these cases qualifies as a standard case of terrorism (2006, p. 10). Yet attacks of this sort are much too common – indeed, much too typical – to be relegated to the "sub-standard."

Another problem with Scheffler's account is that the distinction between terrorism as revolutionary and terror as conservative seems morally arbitrary. The distinction is formal. Conceptually, it is clear enough. It may be important for social science research, which explores the psychological, social, and political mechanisms at work in the use of this kind of violence and responses to it. But what *moral* difference does it make whether an act or campaign of violence against the innocent, aiming at inducing fear, ultimately seeks to help destabilize or degrade, *or* to stabilize or preserve, an existing social order? Surely what matters from a moral point of view are the moral credentials of the existing order. If the existing social order is morally valuable or at least acceptable, that will tell against any terrorist (and, indeed, any violent) attempt to subvert it. If it is unjust or oppressive, its demise will be morally desirable. In the latter case, we may still oppose the use of terrorism in an attempt to overthrow it, but then we will be motivated by our objection to what terrorism is *independently* of its revolutionary or conservative orientation. The fact that, in that case, terrorism would help subvert the existing order will be a point *in its favor*, morally speaking (although one that is not enough to justify its use), rather than the *locus* of its distinctive moral wrongness. The same applies to terror (in Scheffler's special sense). Now if Scheffler's distinction between terrorism and terror does not articulate a morally significant difference, then the revolutionary teleology of terrorism – the *further intention* of the terrorist that the fear caused by her violent action should help destabilize or degrade an existing social order – cannot help explain its distinctive moral wrongness.

Michael Walzer discusses terrorism in terms of just war theory. Terrorism is random killing of innocent people in order to produce fear which will serve some political purpose; thus it inevitably offends against civilian immunity. Now this immunity protects not only individual civilians but also civilians as a class. An individual civilian is protected because, unlike a soldier, she has done nothing to waive or forfeit her right to life and bodily security. The class of civilians is protected because, unlike the class of soldiers, it is not a collective trained, equipped, organized, disciplined, and engaged in fighting. Moreover, whatever happens to the two armed forces and whichever wins the war, the class of civilians on both sides – both peoples – must be present, and must be somehow accommodated, at its end; this, Walzer writes, is "the deepest meaning of noncombatant immunity" (Walzer 2006, p. 4). Accordingly,

> terrorists attack both these immunities. They devalue not only the individuals they kill but also the group to which the individuals belong. They signal a political intention to destroy or remove or radically subordinate these people individually and this "people" collectively. Hence, while all terrorists are murderers, all murderers are not terrorists. Most murderers intend to kill specific people; terrorists kill at random within a specific group of people. The message they deliver is directed at the group: *We don't want you here.* We will not accept you or make our peace with you as fellow-citizens or partners in any political project. You are not candidates for equality or even co-existence. (Ibid., p. 5)

This message is most obvious in terrorism driven by nationalism or religion. State terrorism, too, can be motivated by nationalism or religion. But it can also be addressed to the entire population of the state. In that case, the message is one not of extermination or removal, but of radical subordination – that is, tyranny.

Walzer's portrayal of the distinctive wrongness of terrorism is vulnerable to the same objection I made to Scheffler's account: while it depicts some cases of terrorism, it cannot be applied to others no less typical. The most radical type of state terrorism, that characteristic of totalitarian states, does convey a message of radical subordination. But a state can also resort to terrorism while at war; in chapter 8 I will review and discuss one such case, the terror bombing of German cities in World War II. That bombing certainly conveyed a message of utter contempt for life, limb, and property of German civilians and for Germany's history and culture. None of that was considered indispensable, if its destruction was thought to be useful to the Allies' war effort. But there was no message (and no intention) of destruction of the entire German people, of its total removal from Germany, or even of subjecting it to tyranny. Walzer adverts to this problem in his remarks on the dropping of nuclear bombs on Japanese cities: "there can't be any doubt that the destruction of Hiroshima and Nagasaki implied, at the moment the bombs were dropped, a radical devaluation of Japanese lives and a generalized threat to the Japanese people" (2006, p. 5). This is true, but – as in the German case – it falls short of "a political intention to destroy or remove or radically subordinate" an entire people.

Similarly, insurgent terrorism may serve such an extreme design on another people. But, then again, it may not; it may rather seek to achieve much more limited objectives. The two cases of terrorism of the latter type I cited when discussing Scheffler's position – the Munich Olympics and the Beslan school – are to the point here too. Walzer deals with this problem by granting that "sometimes, perhaps, terrorists do have limited purposes – though it might be better to say that sometimes political militants with limited purposes are called terrorists but don't quite fit the definition," so that "'terrorism' may not be the right word" for what they do (2006, pp. 5–6). This seems just as arbitrary and implausible as Scheffler's relegation of cases that do not conform to his understanding of terrorism to the limbo of the "sub-standard."

A number of authors find the distinctive wrongness of terrorism in what they see as its radical rejection of all rules pertaining to violence and war, or even all rules and values of politics and morality. The former view is advanced by Michael Baur. He points out that terrorist violence is random or indiscriminate in three important ways: in its choice of targets, in its choice of time and place, and with regard to the identity terrorists assume when at work. This, Baur argues, "implies that the terrorist in principle does not recognize any rules of armed conflict" – that is, any rules "that effectively remain 'above the conflict,' and that can govern the terms of an eventual transition by the parties from a state of conflict to a state of peace" (Baur 2005, pp. 16–17). Therefore terrorism makes impossible a transition to "a genuine state of peace based on mutual agreement or recognition." To be sure, if the conflict with terrorists has reached a stalemate, it may be possible to secure the suspension of open hostilities; but that is fully consistent with persistence of a state of war (ibid., p. 19). Baur's conclusion is that "the terrorist *qua* terrorist is implicitly committed to the principle of uncontained and perpetual war – that is, to the kind of war that can never end through mutual recognition or a negotiated truce, but only through the ongoing suppression or complete obliteration of the adversary. And this, in a word, is what is distinctively wrong with terrorism" (ibid., p. 18). This is true even if the declared aims of a terrorist organization fall well short of open-ended suppression or utter obliteration of the enemy: "even if a particular group claims to have only limited objectives, its terroristic *modus operandi* shows that it really cannot be trusted to recognize any limits if there is actual (or future) disagreement or conflict" (ibid., p. 19).

This argument is flawed. Someone's rejection of *a* rule – even the most important rule – regulating a type of activity does not necessarily indicate rejection of *all* rules pertaining to that activity. A terrorist group will be flouting the rule of immunity of innocent civilians or common citizens against deadly violence; that, after all, is what makes it a terrorist group. But, for whatever reason, perhaps only out of self-interest, it may still choose to comply with other rules aimed at restraining violent conflict, such as, for example, that of safe passage for negotiators and mediators. Moreover, Baur's conclusion flies in the face of history. In the 1950s and 1960s many movements for national liberation from colonial rule resorted to terrorism, but nevertheless managed to negotiate and reach a permanent settlement of their conflict with the colonial power. Former terrorists becoming nationally and internationally recognized political leaders is a well-known result of the decolonization process.

Some authors portray terrorists as rejecting all national and international laws or all norms and values of politics and morality – indeed, as rejecting civilization itself. Accordingly, terrorists are deemed to be no longer protected by law, or even to be no longer civilized human beings and holders of moral rights like the rest of us. This view of terrorism is widespread and comes in several versions.

Burton Leiser likens terrorists to latter-day pirates: not merely enemies of a specific policy or law, or a certain government, or a certain state and its laws and institutions, but *hostes humani generis*, enemies of humanity. This makes it possible to say of terrorists some of the things that used to be said of pirates. Since they act "as if they were a law unto themselves" and commit "hostilities upon the subjects and property of any or all nations, without any regard to right or duty," it is right and proper that they should be considered "enemies to mankind with whom no faith or oath ought to be kept" – in effect, "brutes and beasts of prey" (Leiser 1979, pp. 388–93).

One problem with Leiser's argument is that it is focused too narrowly. It relates only to insurgent terrorism; state terrorism may, but need not be, in breach of the laws of the state engaging in it. The most radical type of state terrorism, that characteristic of totalitarian states, is normally provided for and regulated by state law. With regard to non-state terrorism, although much of it, especially in the last few decades, is an international and even global phenomenon, not all terrorist organizations engage in violence across national boundaries. Moreover, Leiser's conclusion seems too radical. It cannot be true that the nature of terrorists' actions, the atrociousness of their crimes, can be adopted in such a direct and sweeping way as the standard of our dealing with them. They may have forfeited many, perhaps most, legal and moral rights, but surely not *all* such rights. If nothing else, when apprehended, surely they have a right to a fair trial. How else can we establish that they are indeed guilty of the terrorist acts or campaigns ascribed to them?

In a similar vein, D. J. C. Carmichael considers the terrorist as a savage living in our midst, but not in our, or indeed any, civilization. To live in the civilized world means to live in *a* civilization, *a* community. An individual may have weighty objections to particular standards accepted in his community and may attempt in various ways to change them. But he has to recognize all along that the community has the final say in the matter. This prior authority of the community to determine its standards is part of what makes it a civilization. A terrorist, unlike a common criminal, not only violates these standards but also claims a *right* to do so. He thereby rejects the community's authority to determine its own standards – that is, the community's claim to count as a civilization. By the same token, he excludes himself from membership in it. Since the terrorist takes this attitude to every existing community, he places himself beyond the bounds of all possible civilizations and in a belligerent state of nature in relation to them. In Carmichael's words, "each person becomes a moral being only within the civilized standards of his political community; beyond the community, there are only beasts and gods. Civilized men recognize this. By contrast, in rejecting the authority and standards of the community, the terrorist plays at being a god and renders himself, thereby, a beast" (Carmichael 1982, p. 25).

One flaw in this argument is that it is not at all clear that terrorists who mount a radical challenge to their own community's standards thereby implicitly adopt the same attitude to every other community. Carmichael does not deny that some terrorist organizations expressly acknowledge the authority of some community other than the one whose standards they contest. But he argues that this is incoherent: by applying the distinction between legitimate and illegitimate communities, the terrorist arrogates the role of a judge of these matters, and is therefore no longer in a position to acknowledge any community as "a prior moral authority" (Carmichael 1982, p. 17). Yet if the individual cannot engage in independent moral thinking and apply the distinction between morally legitimate and morally illegitimate communities as best she can, who else can do that? Carmichael's insistence that a community is by definition a *prior* moral authority in effect does away with this distinction. Furthermore, his contrast between terrorists and common criminals applies with equal force to insurgents, and even to conscientious objectors: these, too, not only offend against their community's standards but also claim a moral right to do so. Therefore this claim of right cannot be the *locus* of the distinctive evil of terrorism; if the terrorist is a savage, so are the insurgent and the conscientious objector.

Some authors portray terrorists as essentially amoral. Thus Paul Wilkinson writes that terrorists reject not only all laws and moral rules pertaining to war but all moral bounds as well. He speaks of their "nihilistic rejection of all ethical and legal constraints" and of their making "war on all ethics and legality." To be sure, some terrorists claim to act in accordance with a morality of their own. But that does not count, since this "revolutionary morality" is "informed by a confusing and often self-contradictory collection of self-justificatory beliefs, myths and propaganda" (Wilkinson 1986, pp. 55, 66–7, 100).

It is true that many terrorists seem to be oblivious to the moral import of their actions. Some terrorists and fellow travelers even flaunt their amoralism, as did the nineteenth-century anarchist writer Laurent Tailhade when he said: "What do the victims matter if the gesture is beautiful!" (quoted in Laqueur 1987, p. 117). But such attitudes are by no means universal. Terrorism of the radical left, at least, can claim a rich apologetic tradition. This tradition has been evolving for a century and a half, from the writings of Mikhail Bakunin and Sergey Nechaev – in particular the latter's "Catechism of the Revolutionist" (Nechaev 1978) – to some of the works of Leon Trotsky, Herbert Marcuse, and, most recently, Kai Nielsen. In the present context, Trotsky's views are of particular interest, not least because he was not only a philosopher of terrorism but also its practitioner. I discussed them in chapter 4 and will not repeat any of that discussion here. I hope to have shown that Trotsky's views and arguments cannot be described as "informed by a confusing and often self-contradictory collection of self-justificatory beliefs, myths and propaganda" or characterized as amoralism. Trotsky addresses real moral issues, and does so in the usual moral terms of right and wrong, just and unjust, good and bad; he bases his arguments on what he holds to be the basic principle of morality; he makes a serious attempt at answering objections. The judgments he passes exhibit the formal traits widely considered definitive of moral judgment: they are action-guiding, universalizable, and of overriding importance to those who make them. What Trotsky rejects is not all morality, morality as such, but only the conventional morality of his society, which he considers to be but an ideological reflection of the *status quo*. In the same breath, he proclaims "the interests of the Revolution" to be the supreme *moral* law. Trotsky's views may not amount to a convincing moral position; many find them deeply flawed, indeed repugnant, and so do I. But they do amount to *a* moral position. To think otherwise is to confuse one's own moral outlook with the moral point of view as such.

Killing the Innocent with and without Intent

None of the answers to the question of distinctive wrongness of terrorism discussed in the preceding section seems satisfactory. Each singles out some trait that terrorism may have, or some consequence that it may bring about, or may be intended to bring about. Thus each may be true of some terrorism, but none seems to apply to all terrorism, terrorism as such.

If so, perhaps the final moral evaluation of terrorism should rather be based on what terrorism – all terrorism – is. According to the definition I offer in chapter 1 and work with throughout this book, all terrorism is deliberate violence against the innocent. This is the worst thing about it, morally speaking. In this sense one can agree with Stephen Nathanson that, with regard to terrorism, the deliberate killing and maiming of innocent people is "the heart of the matter," morally speaking (Nathanson 2010, pp. 33–4). However, there is still the possibility that the feature of terrorism that is the worst thing about it, morally speaking, is not morally *distinctive* of it. For it may not be significantly different, morally speaking, from a type of violence against innocent people we would not call terrorism, because the innocent are not killed or maimed with intent but only with foresight, as a side effect of otherwise legitimate acts of violence or war.

Is there, then, a significant moral difference between killing innocent civilian or common citizen A with intent and killing innocent civilian or common citizen B without intent, but as a foreseen side effect of an otherwise permissible act? Many, perhaps most, people tend to say that there is such a difference: that killing A is worse, morally speaking, than killing B. But this initial response proves difficult to justify. As I pointed out when touching on this question in chapter 4, B is just as dead as A. If we want to deal with the morality of killing human beings in terms of a right to life that all human beings have to start with, then B's right to life has been violated just as A's has. It is sometimes said that a moral evaluation of an act of killing a human being must take into account the attitude to human life, or to the right to life all humans have, that comes to the fore in the act. A person who kills another without intent, as a foreseen side effect of an otherwise morally permissible act, does so with regret and would prefer to carry out the act without bringing about this side effect, if that were possible. But there is no reason why a person who kills another intentionally, as a means of achieving a morally legitimate objective, should not do so with regret as well, and should not prefer to achieve that objective by other means, if that were possible. In both cases, the killing is the direct outcome of a free and considered choice made by the killer. Neither the regret nor the preference for achieving the end in a different way is reason enough not to kill. In both cases, the life of the person killed is treated as dispensable: an acceptable price for achieving one's end, rather than something valuable enough to constrain the pursuit of that end. Looking at the matter from the point of view of the victim and supposing one were bound to be killed, but could choose between being killed with intent and being killed without intent, but as a side effect of the killer's pursuit of his end, would there be any reason for preferring the latter fate to the former?

Thomas A. Cavanaugh has argued that the claim of moral asymmetry between intention and foresight should be tied to Kant's principle of humanity as end in itself, which prohibits treating others as mere means: "the intended/foreseen distinction does not account for its own ethical relevance, but relies on the end-not-means principle to do so" (Cavanaugh 1999, p. 185). The direct victim of terrorism is reduced to mere means to the terrorist's pursuit of his end, whereas the person killed as a side effect of an otherwise legitimate act of war is not used as a means to anything. That, Cavanaugh says, is what makes the former case of killing morally worse than the latter. Yet it is not clear why it is morally worse to kill an innocent person as mere means to one's end than to kill an innocent person as an unintended but foreseen side effect of the pursuit of one's end. Again, the person concerned is dead in both cases, and her right to life has been violated in both cases. Again, in both cases the killing is the direct result of the killer's free and considered choice. In both cases, this result may be regretted, and the killer may prefer to achieve his end without killing, but neither the regret nor the preference prevents him from killing. The life of the person killed proves equally dispensable in both cases. Again, from the point of view of the victim, there seems no reason for preferring being killed without intent but with foresight, as a side effect of the killer's pursuit of his end, to being killed with intent, as mere means to the killer's end.

Cavanaugh's proposal is vulnerable to another objection. At a minimum, Kant's prohibition of treating another as mere means requires that the other should be able to "share in the end" of our action – that is, to consent to it (Kant 2005, pp. 107–8). But if the possibility of the other person's consenting to our action affecting her is the touchstone of not treating her as mere means, that does not help establish and clarify but, rather, tends to blur the moral difference between reducing the other to mere means and harming the other as a side effect of our action. The other cannot "share in the end" of our action that reduces her to mere means – that is, consent to our action. But can the other "share in the end" of our action that inflicts major harm on her without intent but with foresight, as a side effect – that is, consent to our action? Cavanaugh illustrates his argument with a typology of bombing, in which the central distinction is that between terror bombing and tactical bombing – that is, bombing that focuses on military targets. Normally, an innocent civilian to be killed by terror bombing cannot "share in the end" of the bomber's action – that is, consent to it. But is an innocent civilian to be killed as a foreseen side effect of tactical bombing normally in a better position to "share in the end" of the bomber's action – that is, to consent to it?

It seems, then, that we do not have a good explanation why killing innocent civilian or common citizen A with intent would be significantly worse, morally speaking, than killing innocent civilian or common citizen B without intent but with foresight, as a side effect of our action. If so, the deliberate killing of innocent people is not, after all, what makes terrorism distinctively morally wrong.

The Distinctive Moral Wrongness of Terrorism

Do we have to conclude that terrorism is not distinctively morally wrong? It seems we do, if we assume (as almost all the authors discussed do) that its moral distinctiveness must lie in a single trait or consequence of terrorism. But we need not assume that; its moral distinctiveness may rather lie in a conjunction of several traits.

The deliberate use of violence against innocent people is the worst thing about terrorism, morally speaking. It is not what is morally distinctive about it, because there seems to be no significant moral difference between such violence and violence against innocent people inflicted without intent but with foresight, as a side effect. But the deliberate use of violence against the innocent is only the most morally salient thing about terrorism; there is more to terrorism, morally speaking. The terrorist does not inflict violence on innocent people for its own sake, but as a means to something else: to intimidating some other people and coercing them into doing something they otherwise would not do. Now both intimidation and coercion are morally wrong. Neither is morally wrong always, whatever the circumstances; sometimes we have good moral reasons to resort to one or the other, or even both. But both are wrong *prima facie* – that is, as long as there is no moral consideration in favor of resort to them weighty enough to override their initial, intrinsic wrongness. Normally, we are not required to justify influencing someone's beliefs and attitudes by reasoned argument, but any resort to intimidation is exposed to a demand for justification. Normally, we are not required to justify getting someone to do something by persuasion or provision of incentives, but any resort to coercion is exposed to a demand for justification. Intimidation and coercion, too, are part of the answer to the question of what makes terrorism wrong.

Thus terrorism is, after all, morally distinctive. What is distinctive about it, morally speaking, is that it is deliberate violence against innocent people – innocent civilians, in the context of war, or common citizens, in a conflict that falls short of war – perpetrated for the sake of intimidation and coercion. No other type of action, however similar to terrorism in some respect, exhibits this particular combination of wrongs. Innocent people are victimized in incidental killing in armed conflict and in violent crimes in peacetime; but, unlike terrorism, neither of these is perpetrated with a view to intimidation and coercion of further, indirect victims. By *compounding* violence against the innocent by deliberate intimidation and coercion, terrorism differs from both and constitutes a distinctive moral wrong.

8

Case Study:
Terror Bombing of German Cities

The Bombing Campaign

In the preceding chapters, I discussed the fundamental philosophical questions posed by terrorism: how "terrorism" should be defined, whether it can ever be morally justified, and whether it is morally distinctive. If I mentioned any particular act or campaign of terrorism, I did so briefly, by way of illustrating a point, rather than in any detail and for the sake of its intrinsic interest. Accordingly, my entire discussion so far has proceeded at a fairly general level. This chapter and the next should complement that. I will discuss in some detail two cases of sustained use of terrorism on a large scale and for a long time: the terror bombing of German cities by the Allies in World War II and the use of terrorism in the Israeli–Palestinian conflict. Each case is of considerable interest in its own right; moreover, they provide good opportunities for seeing at work the ethical approaches, positions, and arguments introduced and discussed in the previous chapters.

In this chapter, then, I look into the main ways in which the bombing of German cities in World War II has been, or might be, morally defended. For the sake of brevity, I will focus on the Royal Air Force bombing campaign. The terror bombing of German cities was designed by the British political and military leadership; it was started, and for the most part implemented, by the RAF. The United States Army Air Force focused initially on military targets and joined the RAF in deliberate attacks on German civilians only at a later stage. My discussion applies to the part of the USAAF in the terror bombing as well. Moreover, some of the things I say about the bombing of Germany apply, *mutatis mutandis*, to the USAAF terror bombing, conventional and nuclear, of Japan's cities.

The Allied bombing campaign against German cities was not the first case of the use of air force in indiscriminate attacks on civilians. Germany, France, and Britain occasionally engaged in such bombing in World War I. In the aftermath of that war, European colonial powers repeatedly resorted to terror bombing to pacify the natives. Compared to what was to come in World War II, these cases of "terror from the sky" were rather limited; in none of them did the score of civilians killed reach a five-digit number. But they were enough to suggest the enormous destructive possibilities of the new weapon and the temptations it would pose to political and military leaders in future wars.

In the period between the two world wars, attempts were made to ensure that the provisions concerning civilian immunity already contained in the international laws of war should also be applied to air power. Although the 1907 Hague Convention prohibited "any attack on undefended towns, villages, residential places or buildings by any means whatsoever" (Article 25), the word "undefended" was open to different interpretations, and that threatened to undermine the intent of the provision. A committee of jurists from Britain, France, Italy, the United States, and Japan – the major military powers at the time – convened in The Hague in 1922–3 and issued a draft of "Rules of Aerial Warfare" which went some way in remedying that flaw. The draft prohibited "aerial bombardment for the purpose of terrorising the civilian population, of destroying or damaging private property not of a military character, or of injuring non-combatants" and "the bombardment of cities, towns, villages, dwellings or buildings not in the immediate neighbourhood of the operation of land forces." It determined that "aerial bombardment is legitimate only when directed at a military objective," defined as "an object of which the destruction or injury would constitute a distinct military advantage." The draft also addressed the problem of harming civilians incidentally. It prohibited bombing "in cases where [legitimate military] objectives are so situated that they cannot be bombarded without the indiscriminate bombardment of the civilian population." On the other hand, it permitted the bombing of cities, towns, and villages in the immediate vicinity of the operations of land forces when "the military concentration is sufficiently important to justify [it]" (Articles 22 and 24) (quoted in Grayling 2006, pp. 143–4). Another important attempt to set limits to air warfare was made at the Disarmament Conference in Geneva in 1932. The conference reaffirmed the position that bombing civilians was prohibited by the laws of war. It discussed ways of constraining air warfare in general, and even considered prohibiting the production and use of long-range bomber aircraft.

For various reasons, the Geneva conference never reached an agreed outcome. The Hague rules were never ratified by the states represented on the drafting committee and therefore were not legally binding on any World War II belligerent. Nevertheless, they had considerable moral significance and thus, indirectly, certain legal relevance too. As Stephen A. Garrett points out, they were part and parcel of what Michael Walzer calls "the war convention": the body of ethical and religious arguments and principles, traditions and customs, legal regulations, professional codes, and conventions that inform our judgment of actions and policies of warriors and political leaders of states at war (Garrett 1993, p. 28; Walzer 2000, p. 44). Accordingly, both on the eve of World War II and immediately after it had broken out, the British government made known its view that the bombing of civilian population would be illegal, immoral, and barbaric. When, on September 1, 1939, President Roosevelt appealed to European countries to undertake not to bomb civilians in the impending conflict, the governments of Britain, France, and Germany promptly did so. A fortnight later, Neville Chamberlain, British prime minister at the time, announced in the House of Commons: "Whatever be the lengths to which others may go, His Majesty's government will never resort to deliberate attack on women and children and other civilians for purposes of mere terrorism" (quoted in Garrett 1993, p. 29).

In the event, these commitments were not honored. Britain followed a policy of restraint in the first months of the war. But on May 15, 1940, its war cabinet authorized RAF attacks on the cities east of the Rhine. That was the beginning of ever heavier bombing of Germany's cities, reaching ever deeper into its territory. RAF attacks soon reached as far eastwards as Berlin. It was the beginning of a slide that eventually led to "area bombing" – that is, systematic bombing of extensive urban areas and killing large numbers of civilians living there. The slide is succinctly described in Sven Lindqvist's *A History of Bombing*:

> Churchill's decision to begin bombing Germany originally applied only to military targets, which included, however, communication and transportation links; that is, railway stations; that is, targets that often lay in the center of large cities.
>
> On June 20, 1940, the definition of "military targets" was expanded to include industrial targets, which meant that the workers' homes adjacent to those industries also became targets.

On September 6, Hitler responded with the Blitz against English cities that went on for half a year and killed 40,000 British civilians.

On October 16, the British government decided to open what would later, during the war in Vietnam, be called "free fire zones." These were areas where bombing was unrestricted when weather or other conditions made it impossible to find military or industrial targets.

Two weeks later, there was a question as to whether it was worth going to the trouble to find military or industrial targets at all. According to Churchill's statement of October 30, he wanted to maintain the rule that targets should always be military. But at the same time, "the civilian population around the target areas must be made to feel the weight of war." . . . His wording echoed General Sherman's famous promise that he would let the American South feel "the hard hand of war" by burning their cities.

This was precisely the Bomber Command's new assignment: twenty to thirty German cities were to be attacked with incendiary bombs followed by attacks with high-explosive bombs to prevent the Germans from fighting the fire.

"Thus, the fiction that the bombers were attacking 'military objectives' in towns was officially abandoned," says the official British history of the air war. "This was the technique which was to become known as 'area bombing.'" (Lindqvist 2001, sect. 181)

There are two types of area bombing. An entire urban area can be bombed because some specific military or strategic (industry and transportation) target within it is to be destroyed but cannot be pinpointed. It is foreseen that large numbers of civilians living in the area will be killed or injured as a side effect, but their life and limb are considered expendable. Alternatively, an urban area can be bombed with the aim of killing and maiming as many civilians living there as possible, in order to terrorize the civilian population at large and break its morale. A further slide took place in the period between May 1940 and February 1942: a slide from the former to the latter type of area bombing. On February 14, 1942, Bomber Command was issued a directive that determined that the "primary object" of its raids should be German civilians. Its operations "should now be focussed on the morale of the enemy civil population and in particular, of the industrial workers." A list of German cities to be "destroyed" was provided. The next day, this was followed by a minute from the chief of the air staff, Sir Charles Portal, meant to rule out any misunderstanding: "Ref the new bombing directive: I suppose it is clear that the aiming points are to be the built-up areas, *not*, for instance, the dockyards or aircraft factories . . . This must be made quite clear if it is not already understood" (quoted in Webster and Frankland 1961, vol. I, pp. 323–34). A week later, Arthur Harris, a life-long adherent of terror bombing as *the* way of pacifying natives in the colonies and winning wars in our time, took over as the commander-in-chief of Bomber Command.

These two events mark the beginning of terror bombing of German cities as the expressly stated primary task of RAF Bomber Command. The first German city to fall victim to this campaign was Lübeck, a city of no military or strategic importance, famous for its medieval architecture and the manufacture of marzipan. It was chosen because many of its old buildings were made of timber, which meant that the city could be burned down easily and thoroughly. It was raided in the night of March 28–9 by 234 RAF aircraft. Much of the Old Town was destroyed; 320 civilians were killed, 785 were injured, and some 39,000 were made homeless. Next in line was Rostock, bombed for four nights in late April, with similar results; then Essen, Dortmund, Kiel, Stuttgart, Mannheim, and other cities throughout western Germany, many of them raided repeatedly. Since the results were not thought impressive enough, Harris decided to carry out a spectacular bombing raid that would silence all skeptics once and for all. In Operation Millennium, a thousand RAF bombers attacked Cologne, the third largest city in Germany, in the night of May 30–1. Civil defense proved very efficient and only 460 civilians were killed; but some 45,000 were made homeless, and the overall destruction was immense.

At a conference in Casablanca in January 1943, President Roosevelt and Prime Minister Churchill and their chiefs of staff decided on a collaboration of their air forces in the bombing of Germany. A division of labor was worked out whereby the RAF would carry on with terror bombing at night, whereas the USAAF would bomb military and strategic targets by day. By early 1944, however, the USAAF, too, took to terror bombing (see Lackey 2010).

Much of the bombing in 1943 concentrated on the cities of the Rhineland and the Ruhr district, some of which were almost completely devastated. But the high point of the campaign that year was Operation Gomorrah, the stated aim of which was "to destroy Hamburg," Germany's second largest city. It involved a string of night and day raids by the RAF and USAAF from July 24 to August 2. The second major RAF raid, in the night of July 27–8, is known as the Firestorm Raid. By dropping a carefully calculated mix of explosives and incendiary bombs, the planes induced innumerable fires, which then joined together and created a hurricane of fire engulfing much of the city. The heat was so high that metal and glass melted, bricks exploded, and streets were turned into rivers of boiling asphalt. By the morning, some 40,000 civilians were dead. Up to 900,000 residents were made homeless.

The Hamburg firestorm was the first ever to be induced by bombing. But it was not the last; the Allies saw it as a great success and something to strive to repeat throughout the campaign. As Martin Middlebrook writes, "what happened in Hamburg may have been an extreme example of Allied success but the results obtained were the results that were hoped for every time the Allied heavy-bomber forces set out for Germany. . . . What happened at Hamburg was what happened when Bomber Command 'got everything right'" (Middlebrook 2000, pp. 11–12). The RAF and USAAF went on to produce firestorms in fifteen German cities, in some cases killing only a few hundred civilians, in others thousands, and in still others – Brunswick, Darmstadt, Dresden, Kassel, and Pforzheim – tens of thousands.

However, the RAF failed to bring about the one firestorm meant to decide the outcome of the war: to "Hamburgize" Berlin. In a message to Churchill, Harris said: "We can wreck Berlin from end to end . . . It will cost between 400–500 aircraft. It will cost Germany the war" (quoted in Webster and Frankland 1961, vol. II, p. 48). The Battle of Berlin lasted from November 1942 to March 1943, caused extensive destruction, killed 6,166 and seriously injured 18,431 civilians, and made about 1.5 million homeless. But, as Churchill conceded, for various practical reasons, "it fell short of what had been achieved in Hamburg" (Churchill 1948–54, vol. V, p. 460).

The spring and summer of 1944 brought some respite to German civilians, as Bomber Command had to join the other branches of the Allied military in the preparations for the landing in Normandy and in the subsequent offensive on the ground. By the fall of that year, however, it reverted to terror bombing, now joined by the USAAF and enjoying virtual freedom of action in the skies of Europe, as by that time the German air force had been crippled beyond repair. The bombing was now on a much larger scale than ever before, and by the end of 1944 some 80 percent of all German cities of 100,000 or more inhabitants were devastated or seriously damaged.

The campaign continued in 1945, focusing on cities that had not been greatly damaged up to that point, and also engulfing small towns and even villages across Germany. The high point was the destruction of Dresden in the night of February 13–14. The city, called Florence on the Elbe for its beauty and rich cultural heritage, had been spared until then. Its population had almost doubled, as the city was swamped by refugees fleeing the advance of the Soviet army. The bombing induced a firestorm similar to that in Hamburg and caused loss of life and destruction on the same scale. For a number of reasons, the destruction of Dresden attracted much attention internationally. That prompted Churchill to send the following message to Portal:

> It seems to me that the moment has come when the question of bombing of German cities simply for the sake of increasing the terror, though under other pretexts, should be reviewed. Otherwise we shall come into control of an utterly ruined land. We shall not, for instance, be able to get housing materials out of Germany for our own needs . . . The destruction of Dresden remains a serious query against the conduct of Allied bombing. [. . .] . . . I feel the need for more precise concentration upon military objectives, such as oil and communications behind the immediate battle-zone, rather than on mere acts of terror and wanton destruction, however impressive. (Quoted in Webster and Frankland 1961, vol. III, p. 112)

Churchill later revised the message in response to Portal's objections to its much too explicit wording. Terror bombing continued unabated almost to the very end of the war. It devastated yet another string of Germany's historic cities, such as Worms, Mainz, Pforzheim, Würzburg, and Potsdam. It ended with the RAF air staff directive to Bomber Command of April 16, 1945, three weeks before Germany formally capitulated.

The campaign of terror bombing of Germany's civilian population lasted more than three years. The RAF, later joined by the USAAF, killed about 600,000 civilians. Some were killed quickly, by being blown to pieces or crushed by the walls of their homes. Others died slowly, asphyxiated, burned alive, or buried alive under the ruins. Another 800,000 civilians were seriously injured. Some 13 million were made homeless. Many cities and towns across the country were devastated. Untold cultural treasures were destroyed. As the official history of the RAF put it, by early 1945, "the destruction in Germany was . . . on a scale which might have appalled Attila or Genghis Khan" (Richards and Saunders 1954, p. 271).[15]

Dispensing with Civilian Immunity

The bombing of German cities was a deliberate attack on the civilian population with a view to undermining their morale and terrorizing them into pressuring the Nazi government to halt the war and accept unconditional surrender. Civilians are normally considered innocent and therefore morally protected against such an attack. The bombing campaign was a violation of the centerpiece of the *jus in bello* part of just war theory (and any other plausible ethics of war), the rule of civilian immunity. Those who seek to defend the bombing usually accept this rule and try to show that there were good reasons for departing from it in the case at issue, so that the bombing was justified, all things considered. But one might also try to exculpate those who designed and implemented the strategy by rejecting the point of departure of most of the debate – the idea that, in war, civilian life, limb, and property are, at least *prima facie*, off limits.

In chapter 3, I touched upon one instance of this approach to the Allied bombing campaign and, by implication, to targeting civilians in war more generally: Hans Magnus Enzensberger's argument that German civilians were not really innocent but were getting their just deserts for bringing the Nazis to power and supporting their war of aggression. I hope to have shown that his argument will not do. Here I want to look into another example of this approach to the bombing, offered by George Orwell. Like Enzensberger, Orwell knew what he was talking about from personal experience: he had lived through the bombing of London by the German air force. Yet, like Enzensberger, he had no time for the idea of civilian immunity in war.

In his column in *The Tribune* on May 19, 1944, Orwell rejected the objections to the bombing of German cities advanced by Vera Brittain. Brittain's was one of the very few prominent voices raised in Britain at the time against the bombing. She was a pacifist; however, her criticism of the bombing was not couched in pacifist terms but was rather based on the rule of civilian immunity and the view that "it is better to suffer disadvantage in war than to descend to the lower levels of barbarity," such as "the slaughter of civilians by bombing or starvation, and the avoidable destruction of humanity's cultural heritage" (Brittain 1942, p. 89).

Orwell has some understanding for pacifism, but none for the distinction between barbaric and civilized ways of waging war. The idea of constraining warfare by some such rule as civilian immunity, and indeed all talk of limiting or humanizing war, is "sheer humbug." Orwell cannot see why it is worse to kill civilians than to kill soldiers. "Obviously one must not kill children if it is in any way avoidable," he writes, "but it is only in propaganda pamphlets that every bomb drops on a school or an orphanage." While "legitimate" warfare kills "the healthiest and bravest of the young male population," a bomb dropped on a city kills a cross-section of the population. That is a preferable outcome, because

> war is not avoidable at this stage of history, and since it has to happen it does not seem to me a bad thing that others should be killed besides young men. I wrote in 1937: "Sometimes it is a comfort to me to think that the aeroplane is altering the conditions of war. Perhaps when the next war comes we may see that sight unprecedented in all history, a jingo with a bullet hole in him." We haven't seen that yet ... but at any rate the suffering of this war has been shared out more evenly than the last one was. The immunity of civilians, one of the things that have made war possible, has been shattered. Unlike Miss Brittain, I don't regret that. I can't feel that war is "humanised" by being confined to the slaughter of the young and becomes "barbarous" when the old get killed as well. . . . War is of its nature barbarous, it is better to admit that. If we see ourselves as the savages we are, some improvement is possible. (Orwell 1968, pp. 151–2; see also pp. 181–3)

Orwell's argument has two parts: a deontological and a consequentialist one. At this stage of history, at least, war is inevitable, like a natural disaster, rather than a matter of someone's responsibility. It is therefore better, for it is more just, that the suffering it brings should be distributed more evenly, rather than inflicted for the most part on healthy young men in the field. Moreover, as long as we cling to our illusions about "civilized" warfare, we will continue to wage wars. Only if war is allowed to play itself out in all of its destructiveness and barbarity, and if it is clearly perceived and acknowledged as such by all, do we stand a chance of progress toward a world without war.[16]

We can understand, perhaps, how Orwell came to think along these lines against the background of trench warfare in World War I, in which an entire generation of young men had been decimated. The soundness of his argument is another matter. War is not at all, or at least not entirely, something that descends on human beings like an earthquake, completely unrelated to human choice and responsibility. Orwell, too, knew this. If it were, one could not think it a good thing to see "a jingo with a bullet hole in him." What people choose to do and not do does matter. To be sure, if one advisedly helps bring about an unjust war, or supports such a war, one deserves to pay a price for it. But it is not obvious that one deserves to pay the *ultimate* price. And, in any case, not all civilians are jingoes.

Children, in particular, are not, and indeed cannot be, jingoes. Any large civilian population is bound to include a significant proportion of children. If distributive justice requires that the killing and destruction in war be distributed evenly across the entire civilian population, independently of individual choice and action, as Orwell claims, then it is not at all obvious that "one must not kill children." Yet Orwell is unwilling to accept this implication of his argument. Instead, he points out that not every bomb dropped on German cities hit a school or an orphanage. That is true, but not to the point, given Orwell's position. The remark is also disingenuous: the bombing did kill some 100,000 children.

War Is Hell

Orwell defends the bombing by rejecting the rule of civilian immunity, which is the paramount requirement of the *jus in bello* part of the ethics of war. But Orwell's disparagement of all attempts at constraining and civilizing war as "humbug" suggests a more radical defense: one based on a rejection of *jus in bello* as a whole. That is how Air Marshal Sir Robert Saundby, second-in-command to Arthur Harris, defended the destruction of Dresden and, by implication, the entire bombing campaign:

> It is not so much this or the other means of making war that is immoral or inhumane. What is immoral is war itself. Once full-scale war has broken out it can never be humanized or civilized, and if one side attempted to do so it would be most likely to be defeated. So long as we resort to war to settle differences between nations, so long will we have to endure the horrors, barbarities and excesses that war brings with it. That, to me, is the lesson of Dresden. (Saundby 1963, p. 6)

This is an instance of the "war is hell" doctrine, originally propounded by General Sherman as the justification of his rampage through Georgia and the shelling, forced evacuation, and burning of Atlanta in the American Civil War. It takes on board the *jus ad bellum* part of the ethics of war while dropping its other part, *jus in bello*. "War is cruelty, and you cannot refine it," Sherman wrote in a letter to the mayor of Atlanta, who was pleading with him to spare the city. "You might as well appeal against the thunder-storm as against these terrible hardships of war." War is started by human choice; but, once started, it cannot be controlled or restrained until it runs its course. Therefore, the only moral issue raised by a war is who is responsible for starting it. Those responsible for starting a war are responsible for whatever is done in its course by *both* belligerent parties. "Those who brought war into our country deserve all the curses and maledictions a people can pour out. I know I had no hand in making this war " (quoted in Sherman 1990, p. 601). The responsibility for the mayhem and destruction Sherman's actions visited on Southern civilians is to be laid at the door of their own government.

Sherman does not support this extraordinary claim with any argument. As it stands, it is certainly not compelling or even plausible. Just why should we see the breaking out of a war as a matter of human choice and responsibility, and at the same time consider what all those who fight in it do in a completely different light, akin to blows inflicted by a thunderstorm? Just why should we embrace the first part of the ethics of war and at the same time dispense with the second?

Interestingly enough, Sherman was not utterly oblivious to the moral requirements of *jus in bello*. In another letter on the same subject, written two days earlier, he had offered a very different justification for the forced removal of the citizens of Atlanta: "God will judge us in due time, and he will pronounce whether it be more humane to fight with a town full of women and the families of a brave people at our back or to remove them in time to places of safety among their own friends and people" (quoted in Sherman 1990, p. 595). In saying this, Sherman is conceding what his "war is hell" view denies: that what we do in war, too, is a matter of our own choice and responsibility; that *jus in bello*, too, is morally binding; and that every one of those who do the fighting can and will be subject to moral judgment for his own choices and actions on the battlefield.[17] This was true of Sherman and is no less true of Robert Saundby and everyone else who played a part in the bombing of German cities in World War II.

Payback

A very different way of defending the bombing is to portray it as payback for what the German air force had done to British cities. This defense has three versions. It might be argued that the bombing was justified as vengeance, that it was justified as belligerent reprisal, or that it was justified as retaliation demanded by British public opinion and required for maintaining its morale. The common core in these three lines of argument is the notion of payback: the idea of harm or injury inflicted in response to harm or injury undeservedly suffered. They differ with regard to the point of paying back for the wrong suffered: such payback may be considered morally appropriate in itself, because deserved and just, or instrumentally, on account of its good consequences of one kind or another.

All three versions are predicated upon the claim that the German air force was the first deliberately to attack British civilians, and that the RAF took to bombing German cities in response. This was indeed the message British propaganda was sending to the public at home and abroad, including the German civilian population that was being bombed. Yet this is very much a moot point.[18] Since I am discussing an issue in applied moral philosophy rather than in history, I will assume for the sake of argument that the German air force was indeed the first to engage in such attacks. Could what the RAF did to German cities, then, be defended by saying that the Germans were only paid back in their own currency?

Many reject the very idea of vengeance. Some do so for religious reasons, trusting God to see to it that their tormentors, should they remain unrepentant, receive their just deserts. Some accept the view of Socrates that "one ought not to return a wrong or an injury to any person, whatever the provocation is" (Plato 1973, p. 34). Others hold that "to strike back and to strike first are two very different things, morally speaking, irrespective of the results they may produce or be intended to produce" (Armstrong 1961, p. 489). I think the latter view correct and believe that, on certain conditions, vengeance is deserved, just, and therefore morally permissible. For an act of vengeance to be morally permissible, it must satisfy three conditions:

- it must be proportionate in severity to the wrong suffered
- it must be inflicted on the wrongdoer, not on someone else in some way related to the wrongdoer, such as the wrongdoer's family, friends, or compatriots
- it must be exacted in the absence of an impartial authority that could provide redress.

The bombing of German cities has sometimes been portrayed as vengeance richly deserved by the German bombing of British cities. During an air raid on London, Harris remarked: "Well, they are sowing the wind, and they will reap the whirlwind" (quoted in Garrett 1993, p. 192). On July 14, 1941, Churchill announced: "We will mete out to the Germans the measure, and more than the measure, that they have meted out to us" (Churchill 1952, p. 25). Vengeance was a recurring theme in the British press throughout the campaign. Thus John Gordon, editor of the *Sunday Express*, wrote in 1942: "Germany, the originator of war by air terror, is now finding that terror recoiling upon herself with an intensity that even Hitler in his most sadistic dreams never thought possible" (quoted in Brittain 1942, p. 92). These quotations indicate one reason why justification of the bombing as vengeance does not succeed. Justified vengeance cannot amount to a "whirlwind" in response to a wind sown, cannot mete out "more than the measure" of the wrong suffered, cannot realize, let alone go beyond, the "most sadistic dreams." It must be proportionate. In terms of the numbers of civilians killed, the RAF and USAAF went ten times beyond what the German air force *and* the attacks by the V-1 and V-2 missiles had done.

This lack of all proportion would be enough to condemn the bombing of German cities when construed as vengeance. But the bombing also failed to satisfy the second condition of morally permissible vengeance: that of being inflicted on the wrongdoer, rather than on someone innocent of the wrong but related in some way to the wrongdoer. For those killed or maimed were neither the crew of the German aircraft that had bombed Britain nor those higher up in the chain of command and responsibility – their military superiors or political masters. Those killed, maimed, and "dehoused" were common civilians.

In saying this, I am assuming the modern view of moral responsibility as pertaining to individuals and their free and informed choice and action. This view does not rule out all talk of collective responsibility. But the only type of such responsibility the modern view allows for is collective responsibility that is ultimately related to some morally significant act or omission of the individual. To be sure, one can assume a pre-modern notion of collective responsibility independent of individual choice and based on an ascribed, rather than a chosen, identity, such as nationality or race. That, indeed, is how the Nazis looked at these matters in some contexts. So did Churchill and Harris, at least as far as the Germans were concerned. Neither had much use for the distinction between the Nazi leaders and the German military, on the one hand, and German civilians, on the other. As Stephen A. Garrett tells us, neither did the majority of the British press:

> [It] had played an important part in circulating German atrocity stories in the first war and was generally noted for its unabashed jingoism. . . . The majority gave more or less unqualified support to the bombing of Germany. The Sunday Dispatch was typical with its comment that "it is right that the German population should 'smell death at close quarters.' Now they are getting the stench of it." Still another outsized headline screamed "NO PITY! NO MERCY!" . . . Especially virulent in

their support for the area offensive were the Beaverbrook newspapers, for which a typical headline was, "Why all this bosh about being gentle with the Germans after we have beaten them when ALL GERMANS ARE GUILTY!" (Garrett 1993, p. 103)

If we are not ready to revert to this pre-modern notion of collective responsibility, then the justification of the bombing as vengeance must be rejected.

Any attempt at justifying the bombing as belligerent reprisal fails for the same reasons. Belligerent reprisal is an act of war. It is a response to a violation of *jus in bello* perpetrated by the enemy, itself constitutes a violation of *jus in bello*, and is carried out with the aim of forcing the enemy to revert to fighting in accordance with *jus in bello*. A reprisal is often bound up with the hazard of causing the enemy to commit further violations of *jus in bello* in response, rather than to desist from them. Nevertheless, the aim of reprisals is to break off the chain of such violations; they are meant to enforce the laws of war. If a reprisal is to be morally justified, it must stand a decent chance of attaining this aim. It must also satisfy the requirement of proportion. The killing and destruction caused by the bombing of German cities by the Allies was out of all proportion to the killing and destruction caused by the bombing of British cities by the German air force. Furthermore, innocent people – whether civilians or prisoners of war – must not be harmed by way of reprisal, even if that is precisely what the enemy has done. As Walzer explains, "with regard to the most important of the rules of war [such as civilian immunity], the violation of the rules for the sake of law enforcement is ruled out. The doctrine of reprisal . . . refers only to the lesser parts of the war convention, where the rights of the innocent are not at stake" (Walzer 2000, p. 215). Yet, that is exactly what the Allied terror bombing was: a systematic, large-scale violation, over more than three years, of the centerpiece of *jus in bello* – the rule of civilian immunity.

Finally, could the bombing be defended as payback demanded by British public opinion? Even if one believes that the satisfaction of vindictive feelings in a community is, in itself, a good thing, one cannot seriously claim that it is good to such a degree that it justifies the killing and maiming of large numbers of innocent civilians as a means of achieving it. Could the killing of German civilians be defended as a demand of the British public that had to be met in order to maintain *its* morale? Here the moral argument presupposes a positive answer to a factual question: did the morale of British civilian population really need to be sustained in this way? It seems it did not: Gallup opinion surveys made in the course of war never showed more than half of the respondents voicing approval of retaliation by bombing German civilians (Garrett 1993, p. 192). If a vast majority had done so, that might have been an indication (but not a definite proof) of a significant connection between the bombing and British civilian morale. But the fact that not even a simple majority ever did approve of the bombing of civilians does show that their morale was not conditional on the deliberate bombing of German civilian population centers.

Supreme Emergency

Civilian immunity, which was systematically violated by the bombing, is the centerpiece of the *jus in bello* part of just war theory. Yet there is also a way of defending the bombing in terms of this theory. Such a defense is offered in a major statement of the theory, Walzer's book *Just and Unjust Wars* (Walzer 2000, chapter 16). The bombing campaign is portrayed as a response to a "supreme emergency." As I explained in chapter 6, supreme emergency is a predicament in which a political community is facing an imminent threat of a fate that is utterly unacceptable, indeed unthinkable, from the moral point of view. One of the main flaws of Walzer's account of supreme emergency is its vagueness: instead of spelling out a single understanding of the nature of the threat, Walzer actually refers to a range of threats, with a crisis in which morality itself is at stake at one end and a threat to the "survival and freedom" of a single political community at the other. That, however, poses no problem for the present chapter; for the sole historical example of supreme emergency Walzer offers is Britain's plight in the early stages of World War II. The prospect was that of a Nazi victory that would have ushered in "an age of barbaric violence" in Europe, in which some peoples would be exterminated, some others enslaved, and still others impressed into the Nazi-designed and controlled "new order." After the defeat of France, Britain appeared to be the only remaining obstacle to Nazi victory. But it seemed about to be defeated, at least if it continued fighting in accordance with the laws of war. The government took the view that the only promising way of carrying on the fight was to send the RAF to attack major population centers in Germany and break the morale of the German people. That, and that only, was the way to prevent defeat and eventually win the war. This strategy was adopted, and German civilians were deliberately and systematically bombed in their homes, their places of work, and public spaces almost to the last days of the war. Walzer does not propose to justify the entire campaign, for it soon became clear that Germany was not going to win the war. In its first stage, however – that is, until that became clear – the terror bombing of Germany was in his view morally justified as the only feasible response to the emergency Britain was facing.

If such a weighty moral rule as that of civilian immunity in war is to be breached at all, that can only be allowed *in extremis*. Now the threat of Nazi rule in most of Europe was by any standard an extreme threat, morally speaking. It certainly qualified as a supreme emergency. (It also qualified as a threat of moral disaster, in the sense in which I introduced the term in chapter 6.) What is at issue here, then, is whether the empirical part of the supreme emergency defense of the terror bombing campaign is sound. Was the danger imminent? Were there good grounds for believing that the bombing would indeed eliminate it?

Although the slide toward what Churchill described as "an absolutely devastating, exterminating attack by very heavy bombers . . . upon the Nazi homeland" (Churchill 1948–54, vol. II, p. 567) began as early as mid-1940, the time span with which I am concerned can be demarcated quite precisely. It begins on February 14, 1942, when Bomber Command was ordered to concentrate on terror bombing, and ends with the April 16, 1945, RAF air staff directive to stop it. Was the danger of German victory imminent at any point within this period?

Here, it seems to me, one could argue for three different assessments.

- According to the first, Britain was indeed facing the threat of defeat after the rout of its expeditionary force at Dunkirk and the capitulation of France. The German air force was seeking to achieve dominance in the air, a precondition for the invasion of the country by German ground forces. The Battle of Britain, which lasted from July to October 1940, was supposed to secure this dominance, but it was the RAF that prevailed. As a consequence, Hitler had to shelve his invasion plans. On this assessment, the danger of imminent German victory over Britain lasted for several months in mid-1940.
- On another assessment, although Germany had to give up its plans of invading Britain for the time being, it still stood a good chance of winning the war on the continent and subsequently bringing Britain to heel. Hitler decided to deal with the Soviet Union first and settle

accounts with Britain afterwards. He launched the Russian campaign, which was initially highly successful. But by December 1941
the German army was stopped at the gates of Moscow, and the
entire campaign stalled. Another momentous event in the same
month was Pearl Harbor, which brought the United States into the
war. That put paid to any chance of Germany winning the war.[19]
- On yet another assessment, at that time Germany still stood
  some chance of winning. But, after its defeats at El Alamein in
  November 1942 and at Stalingrad in February 1943, it was clear
  that it no longer had any such chance.

Those who adopt the first or the second assessment must conclude
that, at the time British political and military leaders decided that
the RAF was to concentrate on terror bombing, the country was
no longer facing an imminent threat of German victory and that,
accordingly, the bombing campaign was never justified as a response
to a supreme emergency. Those who find the third assessment of
war prospects plausible will say that Britain was, indeed, facing the
danger of defeat and subjugation by Nazi Germany at the time its
leaders decided to launch the campaign of terror bombing and that,
in its first year, the campaign was a response to a supreme emergency, although that was no longer the case in subsequent years. But
they can claim that the campaign was a *morally justified* response to
a supreme emergency only if an additional condition was satisfied:
if those who took the decision had good reasons to believe that the
bombing would achieve its aim of undermining the morale of the
German people and forcing its leadership to halt the war and accept
unconditional surrender. This condition is also the condition on
which the last line of justification to be considered here – the consequentialist one – would depend.

The Balance of Consequences

In just war theory, civilian immunity is a matter of civilians' rights
and justice mandating respect of those rights. Accordingly, civilian
immunity is considered an extremely weighty moral rule; breaching it might be justified, if ever, only in cases where not doing so
would mean failing to prevent some *moral* catastrophe. This rule is
also enjoined by the other major approach to the morality of war –
consequentialism. In consequentialist ethics of war, however, civilian
immunity is understood not as a matter of justice and rights but,

rather, as a rule whose adoption has better consequences overall than the adoption of any alternative rule or of no rule at all. Respecting civilian immunity is the best way of reducing the killing and destruction of war. A rule that is justified because it is useful binds only insofar as it is useful. That means that in consequentialist ethics of war civilian immunity has considerably less weight than it does in just war theory. It is justified because it reduces killing and destruction and accordingly binds only insofar as it does so. In cases where it does not – where it is only by attacking civilians that the best outcome will be achieved – civilian immunity has to give way.[20]

Given that in World War II the best outcome overall was for the Allies to defeat the Axis powers, does that war present us with such a case? Did British political and military leaders have good reasons to believe bombing enemy civilians would undermine their morale and make them force their leaders to call a halt to the war or, alternatively, rise up and replace their leaders with another, peace-minded lot? To understand the assessments British leaders made and the decisions they took, we need to recall a view about air force strategy developed in the 1920s by two air warfare theorists, Basil H. Liddell Hart and Giulio Douhet. Both were concerned that the next major war should avoid trench warfare, which made for a prolonged deadlock rather than quick victory and involved unacceptably high casualties, and both argued that air force offered a promising alternative. There was no need to try to destroy an enemy's armed forces when his will to fight could be broken at its source, in the rear, by concentrated air force attacks on civilian population centers that dislocate normal life and undermine civilian morale. "If we can demoralize one section of the nation," Liddell Hart wrote, "the collapse of its will to resist compels the surrender of the whole" (Liddell Hart 1925, p. 27). This strategy was only seemingly brutal, since "a swift and sudden blow of this nature inflicts a total of injury far less than when spread over a number of years," as it used to be in "the cannon-fodder wars of the past" (ibid., p. 50).[21]

Douhet adopted the same approach:

Take the center of a large city and imagine what would happen among the civilian population during a single attack by a single bombing unit. ... Its impact upon the people would be terrible. ... What could happen to a single city in a single day could also happen to ten, twenty, fifty cities. And, since news travels fast ... what, I ask you, would be the effect upon civilians of other cities, not yet stricken but equally subject to bombing attacks? What civil or military authority could keep order, public services functioning, and production going on under such a threat? . . . A complete breakdown of the social structure cannot but take place in a country subjected to this kind of merciless pounding from the air. The time would soon come when, to put an end to horror and suffering, the people themselves, driven by the instinct of self-preservation, would rise up and demand an end to the war – this before their army and navy had time to mobilize at all! (Douhet 1942, p. 58)

Douhet's answer to those who believe that civilians should not be deliberately attacked in war was the same as Liddell Hart's. "Mercifully, the decision will be quick in this kind of war, since the decisive blows will be directed at civilians, that element . . . least able to sustain them," and so much less blood will be shed overall (ibid., p. 61).

This view of air force strategy gained important followers in Britain between the world wars. It exerted considerable influence on the nature and structure of RAF Bomber Command and the understanding of its role in future wars (see Bond 1991, p. 43). It came into its own in the directive of February 14, 1942, that it should concentrate on bombing Germany's civilian population and breaking its morale. Over more than three years, almost to the last day of the war, the RAF, later joined by the USAAF, did its best to carry out this task. It killed some 600,000 German civilians, seriously injured 800,000 more, made millions homeless, and devastated many German cities. Yet it did not achieve the aim it had set out to achieve: it did not break the morale of the German people and force its leadership to surrender. One of the propaganda slogans that could be read on the ruins of German cities was: "Our walls break, but not our hearts!" Much too often, propaganda slogans are not true. But this one was.

This might be thought puzzling, but it can be explained if we take into account that – contrary to the implicit assumption of the architects of the bombing campaign – morale is not of a piece. Throughout the war years, Germany was covered by a web of informants of the Security Service (*Sicherheitsdienst*), the SS intelligence branch. They were closely following attitudes and concerns of the population, as expressed in people's comments and actions, and sending regular reports to a string of party and government offices.[22] These reports made use of a distinction between two layers of morale: mood (*Stimmung*) and conduct (*Haltung*). The picture that emerges is one of a gap between the two. The former sank; the latter held up.

Obviously, the bombing could not fail to affect the *mood* of the people. One can hardly remain of good cheer when one's spouse and children have been killed, one's home has been destroyed, and one's city is being reduced to rubble. The trust in the *Führer*, other leading figures of the regime, and the Nazi party and the faith in eventual victory were undermined. But, at the same time, the message of dehumanization, unrelenting mass killing and unbridled destruction conveyed by the bombing, as well as the demand for unconditional surrender and various proposals for "punishing" Germany after the war, tended to strengthen, rather than weaken, the will to hold out. Furthermore, as Olaf Groehler writes, the authorities responded to the crisis with "a long-term program of social bribery, population transfers, and demagogic measures meant to preserve stability in the big cities," which had considerable success (Groehler 1990, pp. 295–6). On top of all that, there was the drive to survive which, in the words of Hans Mommsen, "enabled the individual to achieve immense physical feats, and the community to show a never to be repeated solidarity and willingness to help" (Mommsen 2003, p. 115). Thus, as far as the *conduct* of the civilian population was concerned, the overall effect of the terror bombing was the opposite of what it was supposed to be:

> The population affected by the bombing war responded with discipline and determination and acquitted itself with willingness to help and solidarity to a degree that surprised the authorities. "In their outward and inner comportment most people present a sight that until a short time ago one would not have thought possible," reported the public prosecutor in Darmstadt at the beginning of 1944; "the Germans are in the process of becoming a true national community." (Ibid., p. 117)

A telling indication of this development was a fact highlighted by Hans Rumpf. Normally, soldiers on the battlefield are held up as the example of courage, determination, and devotion to duty for civilians to admire and seek to emulate. However, "towards the end of the war it was the other way round: the Wehrmacht orders of the day now held up the civilian population, who still defied the bombing terror, as the shining example for the soldiers" (Rumpf 1963, p. 206).

The other side of the coin was that there was no sensible alternative to continuing to do one's job and at least passively complying with state policies. After all, Nazi Germany was a totalitarian state. The population was closely monitored by a web of government and party officials and informants. Draconian penalties, including death, were meted out for a wide range of offenses against the war effort itself or the morale required for that effort (see Friedrich 2006, pp. 296–300). This is not a matter of hindsight, but rather something the architects of the terror bombing campaign could and should have known. They had no good reason to believe that the bombing would achieve its objective. Indeed, they had no reason at all to believe that. As the campaign unfolded, they had no serious evidence it was succeeding. Indeed, they had no evidence at all. Nor did they try to produce convincing arguments and solid evidence. Much thinking went into dealing with the technical questions: what should be the proportion between explosive and incendiary ordnance, how to produce firestorms in cities, which cities were most likely to be thoroughly burnt down, etc. (see Friedrich 2006, pp. 8–18, 91–101). But apparently no one ever gave any sustained thought to the question of *just how* an assault on the morale of German civilian population would produce policy or regime change in Germany. A minute by Lord Cherwell, Churchill's principal advisor on scientific matters, sent to Churchill on March 30, 1942, provides a telling example:

> In 1938 over 22 million Germans lived in 58 towns of over 100,000 inhabitants, which, with modern equipment, should be easy to find and hit. Our forecast output of heavy bombers . . . between now and the middle of 1943 is about 10,000. If even half the total load of 10,000 bombers were dropped on the built-up areas of these 58 German towns the great majority of their inhabitants (about one-third of the German population) would be turned out of house and home.
>
> Investigation seems to show that having one's house demolished is most damaging to morale. People seem to mind it more than having their friends or even relatives killed. [. . .] There seems little doubt that this would break the spirit of the people. (Quoted in Webster and Frankland 1961, vol. I, pp. 331–2)

Lord Cherwell saw no need to explain just how a people whose spirit had been broken was to proceed to force the hand of the Nazi leaders to halt the war or, alternatively, to overthrow them and put a peace-minded government in their place.

Not only did the British political and military leaders have no reason to believe that the terror bombing campaign would succeed; they had several good reasons to believe that it would not. The lesson to be drawn from the bombing of British cities by the German air force and V-1 and V-2 missiles was that, after an initial shock, bombing does not break, but rather stiffens, the will of the civilian population to hold out. The intelligence concerning the way German civilians were bearing up under the bombs, gathered from a range of sources, was in line with the British experience (see Garrett 1993, pp. 164–9). Finally, sheer common sense could have told them that a population ruled by the Nazis and policed by the Gestapo was not in a position to change government policy or replace the government with one that would surrender.

Thus, the consequentialist justification of the terror bombing fails. By the same token, Walzer's supreme emergency argument also fails, since its second factual premise is false. (The same would be true of any attempt to justify the bombing as a necessary means of averting a moral disaster in the sense I give to this term.)

I have now discussed the main ways in which the terror bombing of Germany's cities in World War II has been or might be morally defended: as a way of ensuring a more equitable distribution of inevitable suffering and loss brought about by war; in terms of the "war is hell" doctrine; as vengeance, reprisal, or retaliation; as a violation of *jus in bello* that was permitted and indeed enjoined by a supreme emergency (or moral disaster); and as a means justified by the aim it was to achieve. I have argued that all these attempts at justification fail. If so, the bombing campaign was an unmitigated atrocity.

Beyond that, it was a campaign of state terrorism – perhaps the longest such campaign in wartime, and the deadliest in terms of the number of victims. In terms of the spirit if not the letter of international law at the time, it was a war crime of immense proportions that deeply compromised the just cause for which the Allies were fighting. Viewed historically, it was a crucial stage in a process of ever more comprehensive and systematic victimization of enemy civilians as a supplement to, or even a substitute for, fighting enemy soldiers. This process had begun in earnest with the British naval blockade of Germany in World War I and was soon to lead to the conventional and then nuclear terror bombing of Japanese cities, and beyond.

9

Case Study: Terrorism in the Israeli–Palestinian Conflict

Palestinian terrorism

The use of terrorism in the conflict between the Zionist movement and the state of Israel, on the one hand, and the Palestinian people, on the other, is a good subject for a case study for several reasons. The conflict is now almost a century old but still shows no signs of abating. It is a complex and extremely violent ethnic, religious, and political conflict; the violence has involved extensive use of both insurgent and state terrorism. The literature on the conflict is immense.[23] Yet there is little in the way of sustained philosophical discussion of the rights and wrongs of terrorism employed in this conflict.

With regard to the use of terrorism, in particular, in much public discourse the conflict is much too often portrayed in a one-sided way. The Palestinians are cast as the villain of the piece: the party that has been using terrorism, unrelentingly and almost throughout the conflict. This is a very inaccurate version of the course of events. The Palestinians have not been the only party employing terrorism; they were not the first to resort to it on a large scale; and their terrorist actions and campaigns do not account for the majority of civilians deliberately killed in the course of this conflict.

What *is* true is that the Palestinians were the first to resort to violence, and to violence against the innocent at that. That happened in the first decade of British rule in Palestine. Palestinian mobs rioted in several towns in 1920–1, and again in 1929; scores of Jewish civilians were killed, many more were wounded, and much civilian property was destroyed. The most atrocious was the massacre of some sixty Jewish residents of Hebron in 1929. Such riots were outbreaks of blind mob rage rather than advised acts of violence aiming at intimidation and coercion. Thus they fall short of terrorism, although this is not to say that they are much less morally repugnant. Similar riots took place as part of the 1936–9 Palestinian revolt against British rule. But that revolt was a much more complex and prolonged affair, involving both economic and political struggle and political violence. The primary targets of the guerrilla bands roaming the countryside were British military and police; but they also attacked Jewish settlements and killed both their armed defenders and civilians. What should count as terrorism were focused attacks on Jewish traffic, farmers in the field, and homes in towns. The same holds of one major urban attack, which David Hirst describes in the following way:

> Once, in Tiberias, the rebels came down to find and kill as many Jews as they could. This was retaliation for bombs – presumed Jewish – which had slaughtered scores of Arabs in various public places. At nine o'clock one October [1937] evening, a large band entered the town; they had earlier cut all its telephone communications with the rest of the country; five minutes later, on a whistled sign from the adjoining hills, the massacre began. As one group attacked British and Arab police barracks, others set fire to the synagogue and houses in the Jewish quarter and killed their inmates. In all, nineteen Jews, including three women and ten children, some of them mere babies, died. [. . .] It was not the largest, but it was certainly the most deliberate massacre since Palestinian violence began. (Hirst 2003, p. 214)

The 1948–9 war included one major case of Palestinian terrorism: the ambush of a convoy taking doctors and nurses to the Hadassah Hospital on Mount Scopus, Jerusalem, in which more than seventy civilians were killed. It was committed in response to the massacre in Deir Yassin (described in the next section).

It is only since the late 1960s that the Palestinians resorted to terrorism in a sustained way and on a large scale. The Palestine Liberation Organization was established in 1964. After its attempts to bring about a popular uprising in the territories Israel occupied in the 1967 war had come to naught, the PLO, later joined by an array of other resistance organizations, took to terrorism. They carried out numerous attacks against civilian targets in Israel and the occupied territories, and against Israeli and Jewish targets abroad. Many still remember some of their particularly spectacular and gory exploits in the 1970s and 1980s, such as the attack at the Munich Olympic Games in 1972, in which eleven Israeli athletes and coaches were killed, or in Ma'alot in 1974, which claimed the lives of twenty high school pupils. They also focused on air traffic. As Benny Morris points out, "the Palestinians, though not its authors, perfected the genre [of airplane hijacking]. [. . .] And they were the first to turn jetliners into targets of light weapons and rocket attacks . . . They were also the first to bomb jetliners out of the skies with time- or altimeter-detonated bombs . . . [. . .] Palestinian terrorists were also the first to massacre passengers at airport check-in counters and in preflight waiting rooms" (Morris 2001, p. 377). Nor were they past attacking targets in Arab countries whose governments had caused their ire.

In the last two decades, Palestinian terrorism has gone through ebb and flow. The mid-1990s and the second Palestinian *intifada* (2000–5) were the heyday of suicide bombers. Some attacked Israeli soldiers and accordingly should be considered guerrilla fighters, although Israelis perceived them, too, as terrorists. Others targeted civilians. Some of these attacks claimed dozens of victims. In recent years, some Palestinian groups operating in the Gaza Strip have carried out numerous home-made missile attacks on civilian population centers in Israel.

Were the Palestinians justified in resorting to terrorism? Are they justified in employing terrorism today? They have had a just cause for armed struggle against Israel: theirs is a struggle for national liberation. But, as I have argued in earlier chapters, although virtually every case of foreign rule, and every case of oppression of one nation by another, is a moral enormity, not every such case is such an enormity that terrorism, too, may be used in order to put an end to it. I reject the consequentialist view that terrorism, like any other course of action, will be justified whenever its rationally expected consequences are good on balance. Terrorism is such a great moral wrong in itself that it is almost absolutely prohibited. In this, as in any other case, this extremely weighty moral prohibition can be overridden only when two conditions are satisfied: when an entire people is facing a true moral disaster, such as extermination or "ethnic cleansing," and when terrorism, and only terrorism, will prevent, put an end to, or reverse, that disaster.

I submit that the first condition is satisfied. The Palestinians have had a just cause for armed resistance from a very early stage of the Zionist settlement. That settlement was taking their land from them and appropriating it for Jewish settlers. This applies both to the lands and homes of individual Palestinians and to the country as a whole. Nonviolent political struggle proved impotent against the combined strength of the Zionist movement and the British, whose mandate was to help set up "a national home for the Jewish people in Palestine."

In the 1948–9 war, the Zionist enterprise achieved a decisive success: the state of Israel was secured, with boundaries way beyond what the United Nations resolution enjoining the division of Palestine had allocated to it, encompassing about 78 percent of the country. No Palestinian state came into being in the remaining parts of Palestine; they were taken over by Jordan (the West Bank) and Egypt (the Gaza Strip). Some 700,000 Palestinians who had lived in what was now Israel were "ethnically cleansed" – scattered all over the region and beyond, about half of them in refugee camps.[24] All were denied the prospect of ever returning to their homes. Their towns and villages were either given over to Jewish settlers or systematically razed to the ground in order to make sure there was nothing for the Palestinian expellees and refugees to return to. Those Palestinians who remained within Israel's borders (about 100,000) became an ethnic minority in their own homeland, second-class citizens in the Jewish state. An entire society, with its history and culture, was uprooted and pulled apart. Surely this qualifies as a true moral disaster. Indeed, that is what the Palestinians call it: *al nakbah* – the Disaster.

Subsequent developments cemented and compounded this disaster. In the 1967 war, Israel conquered the remaining parts of Palestine. Another 200,000 to 300,000 Palestinians fled or were expelled from these territories (Morris 2001, p. 327). Those who remained were subjected to an intrusive and oppressive regime of occupation, dispossession, and economic strangulation, geared to forcing ever more Palestinians to leave. Jews started settling in the conquered territories with a view to eventually annexing all or at least large parts of them to Israel.

Back in the late 1960s, Palestinian resistance, when taking stock of the past and considering its options for the future, might well have felt justified in resorting to terrorism so far as the first of the two conditions – that of a community being hit by a true moral disaster – was concerned. The second part of the justification is another matter. To be sure, both nonviolent politics and guerrilla warfare had proven of no avail. If Israel was to be pushed out of the territories conquered in 1967, if the Palestinians were to attain self-determination, and if at least some of the consequences of the *nakbah* were to be reversed, the only remaining method of struggle seemed to be terrorism. Yet, from the fact that non-terrorist methods have failed, it does not follow that terrorism will succeed. Not every problem has a solution; not every catastrophe can be reversed, or even significantly mitigated.

Palestinian terrorism did bring certain results. It mobilized Arab public opinion behind the Palestinian cause and put their plight on the international agenda. It made the international community understand that the problem was not merely humanitarian – one of more tents and blankets for the expellees and refugees – but rather one of liberation, self-determination, and repatriation of an entire people. Yet internationally Palestinian terrorism also had a very different effect: it greatly undermined the sympathy for the Palestinian cause. It had a similar contradictory effect so far as Israel was concerned. Israelis found it ever more difficult to ignore the political nature of the problem; but, at the same time, every wave of terrorism brought about further hardening of attitudes.

Even the most desperate type of terrorism, the suicide mission, has been of no avail. Palestinian resistance first took to such missions back in the 1970s. David Hirst explains the rationale:

> The efficacy of the "suicide mission" seemed beyond dispute. . . . In cold economic terms, it was very cost-effective. The difference between a conventional high-risk and a *kamikaze* operation was a quantum leap in one's kill rate. Hitherto, that had generally been in the Israelis' favour, but in the two most "successful" of a series of "suicide missions" – Qiryat Shmona and Ma'alot – it was forty-eight dead Israelis against six dead Palestinians. Only with the bombardment of the refugee camps did the Israelis restore the balance in their favour. For the Israelis, the guerrillas believed, such losses were hard to bear, while their own people, who had little to lose but their camps, could absorb death and destruction with . . . fatalistic serenity. The implication of the "suicide mission", they believed, must also be deeply disturbing to the Israelis, who could not but see in it a measure of Palestinian determination never to give up the struggle. (Hirst 2003, p. 460)

This rationale proved flawed. Israel could indeed always send its air force to bomb Palestinian refugee camps and restore the kill rate; that is just what it did. The waves of suicide bombings in the mid-1990s and in the second *intifada* did generate much insecurity and fear, especially in Israel's cities, but only for a while. As to the conclusion Israelis tended to draw from such attacks, both in the 1970s and more recently, it has rather been one of the inhuman, or subhuman, nature of the people who could do such things and a willingness to tolerate, and indeed call for, the most extreme measures against them and against the entire Palestinian people.

Overall, terrorism does not seem to have brought the Palestinians any closer to liberation, self-determination, and repatriation. They might have hoped that it would at the very beginning; but they should have been disabused of any such hope fairly early on. Nor does terrorism seem likely to help achieve these aims in the foreseeable future. Therefore, their resort to terrorism does not satisfy the second requirement of what I hold to be the sole acceptable moral justification of terrorism: the requirement of effectiveness. The Palestinians never had strong reasons to believe that terrorism would prove effective, and therefore their recourse to it was not morally justified in the past. They have no strong reasons to believe that today, and therefore they are not morally justified in employing terrorism today. Their continued killing and maiming of civilians is neither rational nor morally defensible.

Tomis Kapitan finds this judgment premature and argues that the question of effectiveness of Palestinian terrorism is still open. Therefore our conclusion should be conditional rather than categorical: "if Palestinian recourse to terrorism is likely to defeat or even diminish a radical existential threat to their community, then given that the other conditions for justified political violence [laid down by just war theory] are met, some instances of Palestinian terrorism can be justified. Whether this antecedent is fulfilled is a deep and complex matter, for . . . there are powerful considerations on both sides" (Kapitan 2008, p. 180). But I can see no powerful considerations in favor of Palestinian terrorism in Kapitan's tally of its results so far. It is true that "many people throughout the world have become more sympathetic and supportive of the Palestinians," but surely this has happened *in spite*, rather than *because*, of acts and campaigns of Palestinian terrorism. Then again, it may be true that this terrorism "has led *some* Israelis to question policies of the Israeli government . . . and, *in a few instances*, . . . has caused the Israeli government to make *some* concessions to the Palestinians" (ibid., p. 177; emphasis added); but how do these achievements amount to *powerful considerations* in favor of indiscriminately killing and maiming common Israeli citizens? Most importantly, the Palestinians have carried out innumerable acts and many sustained campaigns of terrorism of all kinds on land, at sea, and in the air, in Israel/Palestine and abroad, over four decades. Why is it still too early to draw a line under the results so far and conclude that they do not amount to a compelling case for the effectiveness of Palestinian terrorism? And, if it is, when will the right time come?

Jewish/Israeli terrorism

In much of the public discourse in Israel and in the West, the Palestinians' armed struggle is perceived as bound up with, if not reducing to, terrorism. Yet the other party to the conflict, too, has engaged in terrorism. First the military wing of the Zionist movement and then the state of Israel employed terrorism, in a sustained way and on a large scale, in establishing the Jewish state, expanding its borders, and making the state as ethnically homogeneous as possible. The facts of Jewish/Israeli terrorism tend to be ignored, denied, or recast in a very different light. Accordingly, they are, by and large, much less a matter of common knowledge in the West, and (paradoxically) in Israel too, than the facts of Palestinian terrorism. In this section, I want to review some of them.

When Palestinian resistance took to terrorism in the course of the 1936–9 rebellion against British rule, the Zionists responded in the same currency, and with a vengeance. Benny Morris describes the response:

> The upsurge of Arab terrorism in October 1937 triggered a wave of Irgun bombings against Arab crowds and buses, introducing a new dimension into the conflict. Before, Arabs (and, less frequently, and usually in retaliation, Jews) had sniped at cars and pedestrians and occasionally lobbed a grenade, often killing or injuring a few bystanders or passengers. Now, for the first time, massive bombs were placed in crowded Arab centers, and dozens of people were indiscriminately murdered and maimed – for the first time more or less matching the numbers of Jews murdered in the Arab pogroms and rioting of 1929 and 1936. This "innovation" soon found Arab imitators and became something of a "tradition"; during the coming decades Palestine's (and, later, Israel's) marketplaces, bus stations, movie theaters, and other public buildings became routine targets, lending a particularly brutal flavor to the conflict. The Irgun bombs of 1937–38 sowed terror in the Arab population and substantially increased its casualties. Until 1937 almost all of these had been caused by British security forces (including British-directed Jewish supernumeraries) and were mostly among actual rebels, but from now on, substantial proportion would be caused by Jews and suffered by random victims. (Morris 2001, p. 147)

In the next stage of the conflict, that of the 1948–9 war, Jewish terrorism escalated dramatically. By now all three Zionist armed formations – the mainstream Haganah and the smaller Irgun and Lehi – were engaging in terrorism, systematically and on a large scale.

That was the obvious thing to do, as their aim was to set up and defend a Jewish state that would comprise as much of Palestine as possible and would be as ethnically homogeneous as possible. That meant it would be Arab-free, or at least would be ridden of as many of the Palestinians as possible. Given the demographic situation, that called for what we now call "ethnic cleansing" and what the Zionist movement and later the Israeli establishment euphemistically termed "transfer."[25]

Jewish terrorism had two main forms. The two smaller organizations carried out a campaign of bombing in cities and towns. Both of them also cooperated in military operations with the Haganah, which, after the proclamation of Israel's independence on May 14, 1948, became the regular army of an internationally recognized state. These operations included attacking Palestinian villages and towns and killing civilians. That was sometimes done, in part, in the course of the conquest of a village or town, whether by shooting and shelling from outside positions, or when Jewish forces burst in with all guns blazing in every direction, as they did, for example, in Lydda (Lod). There "two . . . companies, mounted on an armoured car, jeeps, scout cars and half-tracks, drove through [the town] from east to west spraying machine-gun fire at anything that moved" (Morris 2004, p. 426). Sometimes it was done in the aftermath of the conquest, when Palestinian civilians were killed in their homes or rounded up and shot. According to Benny Morris, the Zionist military perpetrated "20-odd cases of massacre" in the course of the war (ibid., p. 592). Some claimed a dozen or so victims, some many more. For instance, "at Saliha it appears that troops blew up a house, possibly the village mosque, killing 60–94 persons who had been crowded into it. In Safsaf, troops shot and then dumped into a well 50–70 villagers and POWs" (ibid., p. 481). In Dawayima, soldiers "killed about 80 to 100 [male] Arabs, women and children. The children they killed by breaking their heads with sticks. [. . .] One soldier boasted that he had raped a woman and then shot her. One woman, with a newborn baby in her arms, was employed to clean the courtyard where the soldiers ate. She worked a day or two. In the end they shot her and her baby." The Jewish soldier who witnessed this adds: "cultured officers . . . had turned into base murderers and this not in the heat of battle . . . but out of a system of expulsion and destruction. The less Arabs remained – the better. This principle is the political motor for the expulsions and the atrocities" (quoted ibid., p. 470).

The best-known massacre was that in Deir Yassin, a village in the vicinity of Jerusalem that had signed a non-belligerency agreement with its Jewish neighbors and repeatedly prevented Palestinian fighters from entering it. On April 9, 1948, a combined force of Irgun and Lehi, with some support from the Haganah, attacked the village. They killed some villagers – men and women, adults and children – in the course of the attack and others in its aftermath, when they were in full control of the village; some by lobbing grenades into their homes, others by shooting, and still others with knives. Some villagers were put on trucks and paraded in the streets of Jerusalem, then taken back and shot. The Jewish fighters also engaged in rape and plunder. British officer Richard Catling, who interrogated numerous survivors, reported that there was "no doubt that many sexual atrocities were committed by the attacking Jews. Many young school girls were raped and later slaughtered. Old women were also molested. [. . .] Many infants were also butchered and killed. [. . .] Women had their bracelets torn from their arms and rings from their fingers, and parts of some of the women's ears were severed in order to remove earrings" (quoted in Hirst 2003, p. 250). The number of civilians killed was assessed at 254 at the time; more recent research puts it at 100 to 120.

The question of the causes of the Palestinian exodus from the parts of Palestine that ended up under Israeli control has always been highly contentious. The official Israeli line has been to put the blame entirely at the door of the Palestinians themselves: they left their towns and villages voluntarily. They had been instructed to do so by their highest political body, the Arab Higher Committee, so as not to be in the way of the armies of the neighboring Arab states entering the country to destroy the newly established Jewish state. The official Palestinian line has been that the *nakbah* was the result of systematic implementation of a Zionist plan for cleansing Palestine of Palestinians. In accordance with this plan, they were expelled by force or made to flee by panic deliberately incited by the Zionist military forces.

The first contention has never been substantiated: no one has ever produced the alleged AHC instructions. On the contrary, search for them has brought to light appeals by Palestinian political leaders to the population not to succumb to panic and to stay put in their homes and on their land (see Childers 1995). That, however, does not entail that the second, opposing explanation is true; it is still the subject of a vigorous debate among historians in Israel and abroad.

In the standard work on the subject, *The Birth of the Palestinian Refugee Problem Revisited*, Benny Morris has argued that there was neither a Zionist grand plan for making Palestine, or as much of it as possible, Arab-free, nor a concrete and explicit decision by Israel's political or military leaders to that effect. It was "war and not design, Jewish or Arab, [that] gave birth to the Palestinian refugee problem" (Morris 2004, p. 588). Morris seeks to show in great detail that the Palestinian exodus had a number of causes: expulsion by Jewish forces, fear of Jewish attack or of being caught up in the fighting, assault on the towns and villages by Jewish forces, atrocities committed on civilians by those forces, psychological warfare waged by Jewish forces aimed at getting the Palestinians to flee, instructions to leave given by local Palestinian leaders, and news of the fall of neighboring Palestinian towns and villages or of a flight from them. The relative importance of these causes for the overall outcome cannot be established with any accuracy. But "the atrocity factor" – actually perpetrated atrocities and the threat of atrocities to come hovering over the country – played an important role in this process. The Deir Yassin massacre, in particular, had an immense impact throughout Palestine. It received much publicity in both Arab and Jewish media. And its message of unprovoked attack, slaughter of civilians, rape, and plunder – which was periodically reinforced by subsequent massacres perpetrated by Jewish forces – could not fail to register dramatically with the target audience. According to Morris, Deir Yassin "had the most lasting effect of any single event of the war in precipitating the Palestinian exodus" (ibid., p. 237).

Another prominent Israeli historian, Ilan Pappe, has reached a different conclusion: "When it created its nation-state, the Zionist movement did not wage a war that 'tragically but inevitably' led to the expulsion of 'parts of' the indigenous population, but the other way round: the main goal was the ethnic cleansing of all of Palestine, which the movement coveted for its new state." Accordingly, Pappe's book *The Ethnic Cleansing of Palestine* seeks "to make the case for the paradigm of ethnic cleansing and use it to replace the paradigm of war as the basis for the scholarly research of, and the public debate about, 1948" (Pappe 2006, p. xvi).

I need not go into this vexing question any further. For on December 11, 1948, the United Nations General Assembly passed Resolution 194, calling on Israel to allow the Palestinian expellees and refugees who wished to do so to return to their homes and properties. Israel rejected it, as well as all subsequent initiatives for repatriation of at least some significant number of Palestinians. In fact, as I mentioned earlier in this chapter, throughout the war and well into its aftermath, Zionist armed forces and the authorities of the new state made sure that Palestinians would *not* return – that there was nothing for them to return to. Therefore, the question of the exact degree of responsibility of the Zionist movement and the state it set up in Palestine for the exodus of native Palestinians is not to the point. Whatever that degree was, when Israel put in place policies, legal provisions, and military practices that prevented, and still prevent to this day, their repatriation, it became fully responsible for their exile.

After the war, most of the native population of what was now Israel (some 700,000 out of 800,000) ended up outside the new state's borders, while their homes and lands remained within those borders. Some found themselves in refugee camps close to the new border, their homes and lands within sight but beyond reach. Moreover, as David Hirst writes,

> such was the caprice of the armistice line that more than a hundred villages were cut off from the land their inhabitants had tilled . . . for generations; there it lay before their very eyes, but strangers were tilling it . . . The plight of these border villagers was particularly distressing because, though cut off from their livelihood, they did not qualify for refugee assistance – a refugee, in the UN definition, being one who has lost both land *and* house. (Hirst 2003, p. 303)

The aftermath of war brought about a new phenomenon, Palestinian infiltrators into Israel. Their motives varied. In his study of Israel's "border wars," Benny Morris estimates that less than 10 percent were bent on guerrilla warfare or terrorism. They did cause numerous Israeli casualties. Others came to retrieve possessions, look for missing relatives, or just get a glimpse of their homes. Still others came to steal. The vast majority went unarmed (see Morris 1993, chapter 2). However, Israelis saw them all as terrorists; in common parlance, the Hebrew word for infiltrator, *mistanen*, came to mean "terrorist." The Israeli army responded by laying mines, shooting to kill on sight, executing captured infiltrators, and carrying out retaliation raids. As Morris points out, all these measures, "to one degree or another, involved state-authorized or, at least, permitted killing of unarmed civilians. Together, they reflected a pervasive attitude among the Israeli public that Arab life was cheap" (ibid., p. 166). Some of these measures also qualify as terrorism.

In this connection, Israeli retaliation raids are of particular interest. At first, they were to be directed against the infiltrators who had inflicted Israeli casualties. When these proved elusive, Israel switched to "indirect deterrence": to sending army units across the border to kill civilians and blow up their homes, and thereby force the authorities of the neighboring Arab states to curb infiltration into Israel. This policy was implemented from 1951 to 1953. The numbers of civilians killed and homes destroyed in such attacks varied. What did not vary was that soldiers were deliberately killing innocent civilians for the sake of intimidation and coercion of others, that the numbers of Palestinians killed were disproportionately high relative to Israeli casualties that had triggered the response, and that the Israeli government denied that its army had anything to do with those raids, which they portrayed as vigilante actions of unidentified frontier settlers.

The best known of these raids was the attack on Qibya on October 14, 1953. In response to the killing in Yehud of a woman and two infants by an infiltrator, Unit 101, a special commando outfit led by Major Ariel Sharon, was sent to the village of Qibya in the West Bank (part of Jordan at the time) with orders "to attack and temporarily to occupy the village [and] carry out destruction and maximum killing, in order to drive out the inhabitants of the village from their homes" (quoted in Morris 1993, p. 245). The soldiers blew up 45 houses and killed 69 or 70 villagers, mostly women and children. Some were shot, others were killed by hand-grenades thrown into their homes, and still others were buried alive in the ruins of their houses. There were no Israeli casualties. Responding to foreign criticism, Prime Minister David Ben-Gurion explained that a thorough investigation had shown that "not a single army unit was absent from its base on the night of the attack on Qibya" and ascribed the raid to inhabitants of frontier settlements, "mostly . . . Jewish refugees from Arab countries or survivors of Nazi concentration camps" (quoted ibid., p. 256).

After Qibya, it was decided that this sort of thing was by now causing too much fallout internationally, and that future strikes should focus on military and police targets in neighboring countries. But Israel took to "indirect deterrence" again, on an even larger scale, in the 1970s, trying to fend off guerrilla and terrorist attacks being launched by Palestinian resistance organizations from Jordan, Syria, and Lebanon. Again, the numbers of civilians killed were disproportionately high compared to casualties sustained by Israel. In the late 1970s and throughout the 1980s and 1990s, the strikes were directed mainly against Lebanon. The proclaimed aim of Israeli artillery and air force attacks on towns and villages was to make south Lebanon "uninhabitable," thereby exerting pressure on the Beirut government to curb Palestinian and Lebanese resistance. Thus, in Operation Accountability (July 1993), 118 civilians were killed and 150,000 to 200,000 were sent fleeing to the north. In Operation Grapes of Wrath

(April 1996), 154 civilians were killed and about 300,000 displaced (B'tselem 2000, chapter 5).

Finally, some of the methods Israel has used to maintain its hold on the territories occupied in 1967 can be considered terrorist. One is "pinpointed liquidations" (*hisulim memukadim*) (also known as "targeted killings"). As Benny Morris writes, members of undercover units, "disguised as Arabs, on foot or in vehicles with territorial plates, operated in small teams, night and day, capturing or, more often, killing riot leaders as well as 'wanted' terrorists. The foreign press charged that some of these units operated like death squads, shooting suspects without warning and usually finishing off those who had already been wounded" (Morris 2001, pp. 591–2; see Middle East Watch 1993).

Another terrorist method of keeping the lid on the Palestinians is blowing up family homes as collective punishment. Terrorist violence, for the most part, consists in killing and maiming the innocent in order to intimidate and coerce others; but destroying their property in order to intimidate and coerce others, especially destroying bare necessities, also qualifies. After implementing house demolition policy for decades, in February 2005 the Israeli army came to the conclusion that the policy did not have the deterrent effect that was supposed to justify it, and decided to discontinue it.

These, then, are the main varieties of Jewish/Israeli terrorism against Palestinians and neighboring Arab countries. Can it be morally justified?

I cannot see how any of it can be defended from a moral point of view. The only plausible justification of terrorism, the argument about the only way of preventing an imminent moral disaster, does not apply at any stage. Would losing the 1948–9 war have amounted to such a disaster for the Jewish population of Palestine and what remained of European Jewry? It depends on just what war aim would not have been achieved. If the aim was to establish "a national home for the Jewish people *in Palestine*," then some might want to argue that, in view of the fate of European Jewry in World War II, failure to achieve this aim should count as a moral disaster. But the question whether it should is not to the point; for attaining *this* aim did not require the use of terrorism. If, on the other hand, the aim of the war was to take over *most of Palestine* and *"ethnically cleanse"* it of most of its native population – that is, what the Zionist movement actually achieved – then terrorism was indeed necessary. But there was no moral justification for doing *that*. Indeed, the success of that enterprise was itself a moral disaster: the *nakbah*.

If the argument of preventing an imminent moral disaster does not apply to the 1948–9 war, it has no purchase whatever on the later stages of the conflict. Since its establishment, the state of Israel has faced a series of challenges. Coping with some of them required a resort to violence. But none can seriously be portrayed as a threat of an imminent moral disaster such that fending it off could justify a policy of deliberate killing and maiming of large numbers of innocent civilians. All the campaigns of state terrorism Israel has carried out throughout its conflict with the Palestinians – from the early 1950s to the present – have been morally indefensible.

This conclusion is likely to be disputed. According to a view widespread in Israel and among Israel's supporters abroad, the Jewish state was facing a threat to its very existence at its birth, and has faced the same threat ever since – a threat posed by the Palestinians and the Arab world at large. This was not merely a threat of dismantling the political institutions making up the state, but rather one of extermination or expulsion of its Jewish population. And although today most Arab states no longer seek to wipe Israel off the map, the Palestinians still do; that is why their terrorist organizations are still prosecuting their violent campaign against Israel. Therefore, it might be argued, if the threat of a moral disaster can justify recourse to terrorism, then the campaigns of Israeli state terrorism in the 1948–9 war and since have been morally justified.

This justification raises two questions. The first is about the substance of the threat: have Israel's enemies really sought to exterminate or expel its Jewish citizens, and do they seek to do that today? The second is about the prospect of success and imminence of the threat: assuming that has been their aim, have they ever come close to achieving it? Now whatever the answer to the first question may be, the answer to the second is: no, they have not. Many in Israel and among its supporters abroad like to present the entire Israeli–Arab conflict as one of "the few against the many." Yet even in the 1948–9 war the asymmetry of power was the other way round, and Israel's enemies never came close to defeating it. As Morris explains, "the battle seemed, at least on paper, extremely unequal. The Palestinian Arabs enjoyed a roughly 2-to-1 population advantage – 1.2 or 1.3 million to 650,000 Jews. Moreover, they benefited from a vast hinterland of sympathetic Arab states . . . The Jewish 'hinterland' – the Diaspora – lay many hundreds of miles away." However,

the [Jewish community] enjoyed basic advantages over the Palestinian Arabs in all other indices of strength – "national" organization for war, trained manpower, weaponry, weapons production, morale and motivation, and, above all, command and control. Moreover, [it] enjoyed a demographic advantage in army-age males, resulting in part from the deliberate policy during the previous years of bringing in as many young male immigrants as possible. The disparities between the military strengths of the two sides were rooted in the nature of the two societies as well as in historical circumstances. Facing off in 1947–48 were a highly motivated, literate, organized, semi-industrial society and a backward, largely illiterate, disorganized, agricultural one. (Morris 2001, p. 192; see also pp. 191–6)

The entry into Palestine of armed forces from the neighboring Arab states did not change this imbalance. Israel's armed forces were superior in numbers, in weapons, and in virtually every other important respect to those armies put together (see ibid., pp. 215–18).

Throughout the conflict, Israel has retained its superiority. It has stood its ground against Palestinian terrorism and guerrilla warfare. It initiated four out of the six major wars it has fought and won all six. Since the late 1960s, it has been *the* regional military power, and a nuclear one at that. "The few against the many" is a highly effective propaganda slogan, not a description of what happened (see Morris 2001, pp. 311, 685–90). Therefore, even if many in Israel and abroad may have feared that the Jewish state was threatened with a moral disaster, such a threat has never been real and imminent, and Israeli political and military leaders have never had good reasons to believe that it was.

In my view, then, both Jewish/Israeli and Palestinian terrorism throughout the conflict have been morally unjustified, albeit for different reasons. Others have decided this issue differently. In the next section I will consider the views of a philosopher who has recently discussed the rights and wrongs of terrorism in the Israeli–Palestinian conflict in some detail and has judged much of it to have been morally justified.

Terrorism in the Israeli–Palestinian Conflict and the Principle of Humanity

In a number of writings, Ted Honderich has offered an account of the morality of terrorism and has applied this account to several recent armed conflicts, including that between Israel and the Palestinians. Honderich works with a wide definition of "terrorism" that covers both violence against civilians or common citizens and that against members of the military, security services, and political leadership. But this poses no problems, since his justification of the practice is expressly applied to both. Honderich's justification of terrorism is consequentialist: like everything else, terrorism is morally justified when it serves "the principle of humanity" – that is, when it can be rationally expected to help getting and keeping people out of bad lives. Human lives are bad when they are bereft of, or insufficiently endowed with, the "great human goods": quality and reasonable length of life, freedom and power, relationships with other humans, belonging to human groups, respect and self-respect, and the goods of culture. Now terrorism inevitably makes for some bad lives; but sometimes it is the only method that can be rationally expected to help a larger number of people out of such lives. In such cases, it is morally justified. I discussed Honderich's consequentialist account of terrorism in chapter 4. In this chapter, I assume that account for the sake of argument and look into the way Honderich applies it to the Israeli–Palestinian conflict.

This conflict has involved much violence, including terrorist violence, on the part of both sides. Honderich offers an evaluation of both sides' recourse to terrorism over the entire history of the conflict.

In ancient times, Palestine, or at least much of it, was inhabited by the Jewish people. For some of that time, the Jews had their own state there. But ancient history does not count for much when contrasted with bad lives of large numbers of human beings at present and cannot ground any valid moral claim today. Modern history, on the other hand, tells in favor of the Palestinians, who had inhabited Palestine for many centuries and constituted the vast majority of the population at the time the Zionist settlement began.

But if Zionism could not justify its claim to the country by citing the history of ancient Palestine, it could do so by pointing at the medieval and modern history of antisemitism and its culmination in genocide. This was a compelling argument for enabling the Jewish people to live in its own homeland, like so many other peoples. The founding of "a Jewish homeland of some or other extent in Palestine" was the defining goal of Zionism (Honderich 2006, p. 97). The pursuit of this goal was allowed, and indeed required, by the principle of humanity. Another part of the case for Zionism was the judgment that was reasonable to make at the time the Zionist settlement in Palestine began, and into the late 1940s, that the Palestinians "were not fully a people" (ibid., p. 100). They had not separated themselves from other Arabs, lacked the self-consciousness of a people in its own right, had not formed their own state, and did not have their own borders.

It followed . . . that the Palestinians could not suffer an overwhelming kind of catastrophe. They could not have the pain and suffering of being deprived of a certain kind of the great goods of freedom and power, relationship, respect and self-respect, and culture – that kind that depends exactly on a realized fact of relationship, being fully a people in their own land. There was a way in which they did not have great goods taken from them. (Ibid., pp. 100–1)

To be sure, this judgment later turned out to have been mistaken. The Palestinians were and had been fully a people: their subsequent struggle for self-determination proved as much. But the mistake had been made in good faith and therefore does not undermine the moral justification of Zionism and the founding of Israel.

Now "the State of Israel was brought into being . . . partly by means of Jewish terrorism" (Honderich 2006, p. 99). Honderich finds that this terrorism was morally justified by the same arguments that justify the founding of the state: by the moral requirement that the Jewish people be given a homeland, and by the judgment, reasonably made at the time, that the Palestinians were not fully a people, and that therefore turning most of those who lived in what became Israel into expellees or refugees was not a morally prohibitive price to pay for founding the state.

After the 1948–9 war, Zionism took on the form of support and defense of Israel "within its original borders" or "more or less" within those borders (Honderich 2006, pp. 97, 102). That, too, was a morally justified stand, in part for the same reason that justified the founding of the state, but also because "time since 1948 has changed things." Israel is now the homeland of Jews living there, and their identity is bound up with it. "Their great goods as a people are there. They have escaped discrimination there. Their self-respect, their relationships and their culture are bound up in or with the place" (ibid., pp. 104–5). To dismantle the state of Israel would involve producing many bad lives yet again – a morally absurd proposition.

This moral justification of Zionism and of terrorism involved in the pursuit of its aims stands in sharp contrast with Honderich's moral condemnation of what he calls neo-Zionism and of terrorism employed in the pursuit of *its* aims. Neo-Zionism is the policy, implemented by Israel since its victory in the 1967 war, of seeking "to take possession in perpetuity of more of the remaining 20 per cent of the land of the Palestinians, and control of all of it." This policy cannot be pursued without terrorism. Thus "neo-Zionism has been and is terrorism by a national state. Its attacks, killings, maimings, destructions and depredations of every kind could be nothing else" (Honderich 2006, p. 102). By adopting neo-Zionism as its national project and resorting to terrorism in its attempt to realize it, Israel "has become vicious . . . a violator of another people" (ibid., p. 104). Israel's state terrorism used in implementing the neo-Zionist enterprise is utterly indefensible from the moral point of view.

The other party to this conflict, the Palestinians, has also resorted to terrorism from an early stage of the conflict and to this day. Honderich argues that this, too, has been morally justified. The justification is grounded in the principle of humanity. The result of the 1948–9 war was that the state of Israel was set up on the ruins of Palestinian society. The Palestinians were largely driven out of their homeland and turned into expellees and refugees scattered throughout the Middle East and beyond, many in refugee camps to this day, living bad lives and denied any hope that this might ever change. In 1967, Israel conquered the remaining part of Palestine and subjected the Palestinians living there to a brutalizing occupation, thus making them, too, live bad lives. Moreover, the judgment that by the 1940s they were still not fully a people was in fact mistaken. Therefore, over and above what the Palestinians suffered in terms of great human goods as individuals, families, and local communities, "they could and did suffer an overwhelming kind of catastrophe owed to deep relationships, a deprivation of a singular kind of great goods" bound up with being fully a people and being denied self-determination and uprooted from its own land (Honderich 2006, pp. 109–10).

All the attempts of the Palestinians to prevent, stop, or reverse at least some of these developments and to attain freedom and self-determination in the small part of Palestine beyond Israel's 1949–67 borders by nonviolent means have come to naught. Therefore they have been justified in resorting to terrorism, their "only means to a viable state" (Honderich 2006, p. 117) and what that will bring into their lives as a people and as individuals.

Honderich finds this a terrible, but inescapable conclusion. It is not an extraordinary one, though: "there is a clear history of such assertions by us all." For instance, "ordinary morality" has sanctioned such things as terror bombing of German and Japanese cities in World War II (Honderich 2006, pp. 113–14).

It is interesting to note that Honderich's position on the morality of terrorism in the Israeli–Palestinian conflict tends to be misunderstood or misrepresented. More often than not it is perceived, and criticized, as one of extreme partiality to the Palestinians. To be sure, some of Honderich's wordings, such as that "terrorism has been a moral right of the Palestinians" or that "the suicide bombers have been morally permitted if not obliged to do what they have done" (2006, pp. 118, 111), have often been found provocative, and the provocation may well have contributed to the misperception. But one can see Honderich's position in this light only if one completely disregards his defense of Zionism and the terrorism employed by the Zionist military formations. That this is indeed disregarded so often tells us something about the state of public debate about this conflict. Yet what Honderich has tried for is a balanced evaluation of terrorism in this conflict: one that impartially proffers moral justification both for Ma'alot or the Munich Olympic Games *and* for Deir Yassin or Qibya.

However, an evaluation may be balanced and still wrong, and in my judgment Honderich's evaluation of terrorism in the Israeli–Palestinian conflict is a case in point. I take exception to his assessment of both Jewish/Israeli and Palestinian terrorism and to the historical account he offers as the background.

The distinction between Zionism and neo-Zionism makes it possible for Honderich to justify the terrorism employed by the Zionist movement and the state of Israel up to the 1967 war, while condemning the terrorism Israel has employed since. This is in line with a moral and political stance many people adopt: Zionism was morally justified and politically sound as long as it sought to set up and then support a Jewish state in some four-fifths of Palestine. However, expanding beyond that means denying the Palestinians any prospect of self-determination and a viable state, and is therefore morally wrong and politically unacceptable. But I find the distinction between Zionism and neo-Zionism unwarranted and the clean bill of health issued to Zionism too quick. To address the latter issue first, there was a good case *in the abstract* for setting up "a Jewish national home" after World War II. But that is not the same as a good case for doing so *in Palestine*, if that country was not, as the Zionists were claiming, "a land without a people awaiting a people without a land" to come and settle it. As soon as we turn from the former to the latter aim, we need to consider the immense price the Palestinians were made to pay in the process.

Honderich argues that, back in the 1920s, 1930s, and 1940s, the Zionist movement was right to decide that this price was not too high, because it was reasonable to believe that the Palestinians were not "fully a people"; but he does nothing to support this claim with facts about Palestinian society, culture, and politics in those decades. He points out that the Palestinians had no state and no borders "of their own." Yet they did have their own borders: the fairly well-established historical borders of their country, Palestine. If statehood were a necessary condition of peoplehood, quite a few peoples would have to be demoted; but of course it is not. The Basques or the Kurds are each fully a people, although neither have ever had their own state. In fact, the Palestinians not only were fully a people in the 1920s, 1930s, and 1940s, they could and should have been recognized as such by the Zionist movement and everybody else. That did not need to be established retrospectively, in the light of their armed resistance to the Zionist and neo-Zionist attempt to put an end to their collective existence *as* a people, as Honderich submits. Thus the price for realizing the aim of Zionism – for setting up the state of Israel in almost four-fifths of Palestine and "cleansing" it of most of its native Palestinian inhabitants – *was* prohibitive, morally speaking, and could and should have been recognized as such at the time. Zionism, too, is deeply morally compromised.

Honderich's acceptance of Zionism and rejection of neo-Zionism is predicated on seeing the former as aiming at a limited goal that can be made compatible with Palestinian self-determination and statehood, and the latter as pursuing an extreme agenda utterly irreconcilable with legitimate Palestinian aspirations. But this contrast has no basis in history. From its inception, the Zionist movement sought to take over Palestine in its entirety, or at least as much of it as it could conquer and keep. Its acceptance of the idea of partition at some stages of the conflict was never in good faith. As Benny Morris writes,

> the original goal of Zionism was the establishment of a Jewish state in the whole of Palestine. The acceptance of partition, in the mid-1930s as in 1947, was tactical, not a change in the Zionist dream. "I don't regard a state in a part of Palestine as the final aim of Zionism, but as a means toward that aim," Ben-Gurion wrote in 1938. A few months earlier, Ben-Gurion told the Jewish Agency Executive that he supported partition "on the basis of the assumption that after we constitute a large force following the establishment of the state – we will cancel the partition of the country and we will expand throughout the Land of Israel." To his wife, Paula, Ben-Gurion wrote: "Establish a Jewish state at once, even if it is not in the whole land. The rest will come in the course of time. It must come." (Morris 2003, p. 9)

And, of course, both Zionism and neo-Zionism have engaged in ethnic cleansing as the inescapable way of ridding the expanding Jewish state of the native Palestinian population. In this regard, so far the achievements of Zionism have greatly overshadowed those of neo-Zionism.

Thus I cannot accept Honderich's justification of Zionist terror-ism. What of his assessment of Palestinian terrorism as morally justi-fied? Since I am assuming, for the sake of argument, Honderich's consequentialist approach to the issue, the decisive question is: Does Palestinian terrorism satisfy the condition of effectiveness? Is it the way, and the only way, to their attaining their morally legitimate aims of self-determination and a viable state? Honderich thinks so: "Their struggle proved itself to have been necessary to their having a chance of justice. That it has produced so very little has surely established that anything less would have produced nothing. Their struggle in its resolution, surely, has also established . . . that they will succeed in the end. The Palestinians will not give up and they will achieve what they otherwise would not achieve, their country" (Honderich 2006, p. 110).

Yet what is clear is only that Palestinian terrorism over four decades has produced very little indeed. It has helped rally Arab public opinion to the cause and has put the issue on the international agenda. At the same time, it has also lost the Palestinians much sym-pathy internationally and hardened the attitudes of Israelis. Even the most desperate type of terrorism, that of suicide attacks, has proved counterproductive. Terrorism has not brought the Palestinians closer to reversing the consequences of the *nakbah*. That other methods have failed is no good reason to believe that terrorism must succeed. That every problem has a solution, every drama a good ending, is an article of faith that has no place in consequentialism – an approach to ethics that prides itself on its hard-nosed reliance on empirical facts. Honderich does not base his moral justification of Palestinian terrorism in the wide sense – their attacks on Israeli military, politi-cal assassinations, *and* wholesale killing and maiming of common citizens, including children, in Israel and elsewhere – on careful empirical investigation of the consequences it has achieved so far and can reasonably be expected to achieve in the future but, rather, on a leap of faith. This is odd, and casts doubts on his consequentialist commitments.

At one point, Honderich appears to be hedging his bets: "In World War 2, Jews in the Warsaw ghetto fought to the end. They fought hopelessly, it is still said. They could not hope to live. They bring to mind that there can be a realism in what is hopeless. You can fight, rightly, not for yourself or your time, but for those who come after you. The Jews did so. The Palestinians can do so" (2006, p. 110). This analogy is signally inapposite. Unlike Palestinian terrorists, the Jews who rose up in the Warsaw ghetto did not attack innocent civilians, but took on German soldiers. What they did was not terrorism (in my preferred, narrow sense of the term) but, rather, guerrilla warfare. As a witness at the Eichmann trial put it, the idea driving the uprising was: "if you could not save your life it might still be worth your while to save your honor" (quoted in Arendt 1963, p. 108). One does not save one's honor and send an edifying message to future generations by killing and maiming innocent civilians.

As for the support Honderich's justification of Palestinian terrorism is said to receive from the fact that "ordinary morality" considers the bombing of Hamburg and Dresden, Hiroshima and Nagasaki, to have been morally justified, I hope to have shown in the preceding chapter that the bombing was *not* morally justified. If "ordinary morality" indeed issues those bombing campaigns with a clean bill of health, that only goes to show yet again that we should not look to it for moral guidance: not in everyday moral discourse, and certainly not in moral philosophy.

Therefore I do not accept Honderich's "terrible conclusion," insofar as it means that, since the Palestinians have a just cause for armed struggle, they also have a moral right to resort to terrorism. Or, more accurately, I do not accept this conclusion if "terrorism" is used in my preferred sense of violence against the innocent. To be sure, Honderich's understanding of "terrorism" is wider, and also includes what I would rather call political assassination or guerrilla warfare – that is, violence against those who are not innocent (in the relevant sense). Insofar as Honderich's argument refers only to the latter type of violence, I and many others may well grant the conclusion. But *that* conclusion is not terrible; or, at any rate, it is not terrible in the sense and to the degree in which the previous one is.[26]

Summing Up

This book is a philosophical investigation of terrorism. Therefore I have not sought to describe and explain the main stages of the historical development of terrorism or to display its political, economic, cultural, and psychological causes and consequences. Such topics are the province of historical and social science research. Philosophy may draw on results of such research, but its focus is on conceptual and moral questions of the sort not explored – or, at any rate, not explored systematically and in depth – in history or the social sciences. With regard to terrorism, philosophy asks how it is to be defined and what is its moral standing.

In discussing the first, conceptual question, I have had to advert to the confusions, double standards, and relativism that plague so much public discourse about terrorism. I have argued that these obstacles to rational discussion and judicious evaluation of terrorism can be overcome if we avoid definitions that focus on the identity of those who resort to violence, as well as definitions that highlight the ultimate aims of resorting to it. We should rather understand terrorism in terms of just what is done and what the proximate aim of doing it is. Moreover, we should not try for a definition that would be best in any context, for any type of discourse, but should rather seek one that is going to be particularly helpful in discussing the moral questions posed by terrorism. The definition need not be purely descriptive and need not cover the entire range of ordinary use of the term; it may legitimately be prescriptive too – although, of course, not to such a degree that the connection with actual use is seriously undermined. This approach leads to defining terrorism as the deliberate use of violence, or threat of its use, against innocent people, in order to intimidate some other people and coerce them into doing what they otherwise would not do. In this connection, I do not use the word "innocent" in the everyday, morally highly demanding sense of not being implicated in any wrongdoing whatsoever, but rather in the special sense of not having done anything that makes one deserve or become liable to be targeted with deadly violence. In wartime, this is true of innocent civilians; in a violent conflict falling short of war, it is true of ordinary citizens.

This definition is largely in line with ordinary use, both historically and at present, since such use assumes that terrorism is a type of violence and that it aims at striking terror (great fear) in the hearts of people not directly attacked. But the definition also departs from ordinary use in restricting this violence to attacks on innocent people. Thus defined, the term no longer applies to a number of nineteenth-century anarchist or nationalist organizations widely perceived as terrorist, because they engaged in what I prefer to call political assassination. There is a world of difference, morally speaking, between killing highly placed officials of what one considers an unjust, oppressive government and indiscriminately killing ordinary citizens. This difference, I have argued, is best acknowledged by departing from ordinary use and applying the term "terrorism" in the latter but not in the former case.

Since my definition of terrorism is agent-neutral, it allows for the type of terrorism that many definitions used by state agencies and the media, and taken for granted in much everyday political and moral debate, make logically impossible: state terrorism. I have reviewed the main types of state involvement in, or with, terrorism, and have sought to show that, morally speaking, state terrorism is, by and large, worse than insurgent terrorism.

In line with my definition of terrorism, the focus of my discussion of its morality is narrower than that of a number of other philosophical discussions of the subject and much of everyday political and moral discourse: it is a discussion of violence against the innocent perpetrated with a view to intimidation and coercion of some other people. The innocence of the direct victims of terrorism is a major obstacle to any attempt at its moral justification. Thus one way of seeking to justify it is to argue that civilians or common citizens are not really innocent of the wrongs terrorists fight against. Such arguments rely on some notion of collective responsibility. I have discussed a number of attempts along these lines and argued that they either deploy some crude and therefore untenable conception of collective responsibility or operate with a plausible understanding of collective responsibility which, as a matter of fact, does not apply to the vast majority of direct victims of terrorism. The overwhelming majority of direct victims of terrorism *are* innocent in the relevant sense of the word.

If terrorism is to be morally justified, then the innocence of its direct victims will have to be conceded. One will then have to show that there are moral considerations in favor of resorting to terrorism, and that they are weighty enough to override the moral protection against violence grounded in the innocence of direct victims. One way of doing so is to argue that, in certain circumstances, resort to terrorism has better (or less bad) consequences on balance than any other available course of action. I have argued that consequentialist justifications of terrorism fail. Some fail because of the ideological character of the aim that is supposed to justify the use of terrorism as a means. But all fail because they fail to attend to the grave intrinsic wrongness of terrorism and judge it exclusively in terms of its consequences. In doing so, they offend against some of the fundamental moral convictions many, perhaps most of us, share: the separateness of persons, respect for persons, the paramount significance of the distinction between guilt and innocence, the need for moral dialog, and the basic moral equality of human beings.

Another type of moral justification of terrorism is in terms of rights and justice. To be sure, terrorism violates some of the most important rights of its direct victims and therefore constitutes a grave injustice. But it has been argued that it is nevertheless permissible and indeed called for, morally speaking, when it is an indispensable means to achieving a society where such rights will be more widely respected, *and* its use makes for more justice in the distribution of violations of basic human rights during the transition stage. I have argued that this justification of terrorism, too, fails. Instead of according proper weight to the basic human rights of the individual victimized by terrorism, it submerges her in the group of rights holders. Accordingly, it is at odds with some of the same basic moral beliefs consequentialism offends against: the separateness of persons, respect for persons, and the distinction between the innocent and the guilty.

Finally, it is sometimes argued that, because of what it is, terrorism is extremely morally wrong most of the time – but not when a political community, or a people, finds itself *in extremis*. According to the most influential version of this position, resort to terrorism may be permissible when a political community is facing a "supreme emergency." A closer look at this position has revealed that, instead of providing a moral touchstone for recourse to killing and maiming innocent people, it provides a range of interpretations of supreme emergency, from a crisis where morality itself is at stake to a threat to the survival and freedom of a single political community. Another problem with this position is that it proposes an unacceptably low epistemic standard: it authorizes the leaders of a political community facing a supreme emergency to "wager" on terrorism as a way of overcoming the crisis.

Accordingly, I have rejected the supreme emergency view as unacceptably permissive and offered my own as an alternative. My view is structurally similar to the supreme emergency position but much more restrictive, both with regard to the kind of crisis that has to be faced and the epistemic standards that have to be met. A people may properly consider resorting to terrorism only in the face of a "moral disaster" – that is, if it is about to be exterminated or ethnically cleansed from its land, *and* if there are very strong reasons to believe that terrorism will prevent, stop, or reverse that, and that nothing else will.

Many feel not only that terrorism is extremely morally wrong, but also that it is wrong in its own distinctive way: not necessarily more or less wrong than other moral atrocities such as mass murder or torture, but different from them in some significant way. I have reviewed a range of attempts to spell out this distinctive moral wrongness of terrorism. These attempts tend to focus on some trait or some consequence characteristic of the most extreme instances of terrorism, such as the aim of destabilizing or degrading an existing social order, or conveying the intention of destroying or removing or radically subordinating an entire people, and to project it on all terrorism, terrorism as such. None of these attempts withstands critical scrutiny. Terrorism – all terrorism, terrorism as such – is bad enough as it is; there is no need to make out that it is inherently as bad as its most extreme instances. It is indeed morally distinctive; but its moral distinctiveness is closer to home. The definition of terrorism I propose in chapter 1 and use throughout the book is meant to be particularly helpful in discussing its moral standing; accordingly, it highlights those features that cause most of us to view it with great moral repugnance. These are deliberate violence against the innocent, intimidation, and coercion. Thus the definition of terrorism already tells us what is morally distinctive about it. Terrorism is morally distinctive in that it is violence deliberately inflicted on innocent people *compounded* by the proximate aims of intimidating and coercing some other people.

The discussion of terrorism in general, which makes up the bulk of the book, is complemented with two case studies of systematic,

large-scale use of terrorism: the terror bombing of German cities by
the Allies in World War II and the use of terrorism in the Israeli–
Palestinian conflict. The lesson to be drawn from both is just how
extremely difficult it is to provide a convincing moral justification
of an actual act or campaign of terrorism. In terms of the account
of the morality of terrorism presented in this book, the "terror from
the sky" the Allies unleashed on the civilian population of Germany
cannot be morally justified. Even if we grant that, for a time, Great
Britain was indeed facing a true moral disaster, there were never
good reasons for believing that terrorism, and only terrorism, would
prevent it. Neither Palestinian terrorism nor terrorism employed by
the Zionist movement and the state of Israel can be morally justified,
albeit for different reasons. The Palestinians did indeed undergo a
true moral disaster – which they call *al nakbah*, the Disaster – in the
1948–9 war, and have lived with the consequences of that disaster
to this day. But those who took up arms on their behalf have never
had good reasons to believe that that disaster would be stopped, or
that its consequences would be reversed, by means of terrorism, and
by those means only. The Jews living in Palestine before the 1948–9
war, and the state of Israel throughout its history, have never faced
an imminent threat of a moral disaster. These cases show that the
standard for moral justification of terrorism proposed by my account
is very demanding indeed.

Is it too demanding? In both case studies, I reach the conclusion that none of the terrorism discussed was morally justified. In
the earlier chapters, I mention a number of acts and campaigns of
terrorism, but never as instances of morally justified resort to terrorism. Does this mean that I have not given, and indeed cannot give,
a single historical example of terrorism that was morally justified
by the standard I have proposed – that of being the means, and the
only means, of coping with a moral disaster? And, if so, does that tell
against my account of the morality of terrorism? Does it show that the
account has no purchase on reality?

It is true that I have not given, and cannot give, an example of
morally justified terrorism taken from history, whether ancient or
modern. But I do not see this as an embarrassment for my view on
terrorism. On the contrary, I believe this is as it should be. If we consider what terrorism is – the deliberate use of often deadly violence
against innocent people, for the sake of intimidating and coercing
some other people – or if we peruse a detailed report of a particular
act or campaign of terrorism, we may well feel that such an extreme
type of violence ought to be extremely difficult to justify. We may not

find it surprising that all the accounts of terrorism discussed in this book, except, perhaps, the moral disaster view, seem much too weak to justify it. If so, we may not find it odd that no case of terrorism so far has been morally justified, or that any recourse to it in the future is extremely unlikely to be. For terrorism is, after all, almost absolutely wrong.

Notes

1 For a wide range of views on the concept and moral justification of violence, see Bufacchi, ed., 2009.
2 For a sample of social science research illustrating a different approach, see Stohl and Lopez, eds, 1984.
3 To be sure, the drastic asymmetry of resources and the consequent asymmetry of destructiveness between state and non-state terrorism could change should an insurgent organization that engages in terrorism get hold of weapons of mass destruction.
4 The willingness to inflict very high "collateral damage" on enemy civilians in order to minimize casualties sustained by one's own military is not a radical innovation introduced by the "war on terrorism." As Martin Shaw has cogently argued, since the Vietnam War, a "new Western way of war" has evolved, characterized by the deliberate and sustained attempt to shift the risk to life and limb from Western soldiers to enemy civilians. This has come to the fore in the two Gulf Wars, in the intervention in Kosovo and the bombing of targets in Serbia, and in Afghanistan (see Shaw 2005). Some commentators have remarked, only half in jest, that the principle of civilian (noncombatant) immunity is being replaced by a principle of Western soldier (combatant) immunity.
5 For discussion of a range of issues posed by the "war on terrorism," see e.g. Shanahan, ed., 2005.
6 For a spectrum of views on collective responsibility, see May and Hoffman, eds, 1991.
7 Bin Laden was not always consistent on this matter. In a letter "To the Americans," dated October 6, 2002, he offered the same justification for the killing of common citizens in the September 11 attacks (Bin Laden 2005, pp. 164–5). But in what appears to be his earliest pronouncement on the subject, an interview given on October 20, 2001, he sought to justify that by pointing out that the Americans and their allies were killing civilians in the Muslim world. When the reporter interviewing

him pressed the point by asking, "So you say this is an eye for an eye? They kill our innocents, so we kill theirs?" Bin Laden replied: "Yes, so we kill their innocents – this is valid both religiously and logically" (ibid., p. 118).

8 To say that they need not try to prevent or stop the war is not to say they need do nothing at all about it. There may well be a good case for protesting against it, although such protest will not change the course of events (see Hill 1979).

9 For a different version of the responsible bystander argument that presupposes the doctrine of double effect and seeks to show that under certain circumstances large numbers of common citizens of a democratic polity may be legitimately attacked, see Dobos 2007.

10 For a comprehensive selection of views and arguments concerning the doctrine of double effect, see Woodward, ed., 2001. For a recent attempt at its defense, see Cavanaugh 2006.

11 For an early statement of rule-consequentialism, see Mabbott 1953.

12 For a forceful statement of this criticism, presented from an act-consequentialist point of view, see Smart 1956, pp. 346–8.

   Brad Hooker has recently revived this discussion. He argues that the objection that, under pressure of atypical circumstances, rule-consequentialism collapses into act-consequentialism assumes that the theory has "an overarching commitment to maximize the good." However, properly understood, rule-consequentialism does not involve such a commitment. It consists of two tenets: moral rules are to be selected solely because their adoption can rationally be expected to maximize the good, and acts are to be judged as right or wrong solely by reference to those rules. "This is all there is to the theory – in particular, there is not some third component consisting in or entailing an overarching commitment to maximize the expected good." Accordingly, "there is nothing incoherent in rule-consequentialism's forbidding some kinds of act, even when they maximize the expected good. Likewise, there is nothing incoherent about rule-consequentialism's requiring other kinds of act, even when they conflict with maximizing the expected good. The best known objection to rule-consequentialism dies once we realize that neither the rule-consequentialist agent nor the theory itself contains an overarching commitment to maximize the good" (Hooker 2008, section 8). However, I do not see how the objection is refuted. *Why* should we assess moral rules solely in terms of their rationally expected consequences and choose those whose adoption will maximize the good, if maximizing the good is not the point of morality? And *why* should we adhere to such a rule even in cases where the reason for its selection, the ground of its justification, does not hold?

13 When the essay was reprinted in a later book, Walzer inserted a bracketed remark on this. His amended view is that non-state terrorism might be justified in a supreme emergency, but only in the face of threat of

genocide. As a matter of fact, though, "this kind of a threat has not been present in any of the recent cases of terrorist activity. Terrorism has not been a means of avoiding disaster but of reaching for political success" (Walzer 2004b, p. 54).

14 It is interesting to note that one can adopt rule-consequentialism as one's ethical theory and yet view the immunity of civilians or common citizens and the attendant prohibition of terrorism as very stringent, but not absolute moral rules. When presenting rule-consequentialism as the theoretical foundation of his argument for this immunity as absolute, Nathanson refers to the work of Richard B. Brandt and Brad Hooker. Yet these philosophers do not view this immunity as absolute. They argue that a set of moral rules selected because of the good consequences of their adoption should include a rule that allows and indeed requires one to prevent disaster even if that means breaking some other moral rule. Even such a stringent moral rule as the prohibition of deliberate use of violence against innocent people may be overridden if the disaster that cannot be prevented in any other way is grave enough. See Brandt 1992, pp. 87–8, 150–1, 156–7, 338 n. 3; and Hooker 2000, pp. 98–9, 127–36. There is thus some convergence between their understanding of the immunity of civilians or common citizens and my own "moral disaster" position at the level of practical conclusions, in spite of the different views of the grounds of this immunity.

15 For a study of all the main aspects of the bombing, see Friedrich 2006. For a detailed, year by year account of how it was to be on the receiving end, see Beck 1986. For a multidisciplinary collection of essays on various issues raised by the bombing, see Primoratz, ed., 2010.

16 Orwell's argument against civilian immunity is structurally similar to Virginia Held's argument in defense of terrorism which I discussed in chapter 5. Both have a deontological and a consequentialist component. Both propose to justify the killing and maiming of civilians or common citizens by appeal to distributive justice as it applies to a period of transition to a morally much more satisfactory world.

17 For an analysis of several versions of the "war is hell" view, see Dombrowski 1983.

18 See e.g. Boog 2005; Rumpf 1963, chapter 2. Rumpf quotes several British authors – both defenders of the bombing, such as J. M. Spaight (*Bombing Vindicated*, 1944), and its critics, such as F. J. P. Veale (*Advance to Barbarism*, 1948), B. H. Liddell Hart (*The Revolution in Warfare*, 1946), and J. F. C. Fuller (*The Second World War 1939–1945*, 1948) – in support of his conclusion that, "in addition to the burden she justly carries, Germany does not carry the further heavy burden of responsibility for the unleashing of total, unrestricted air warfare" (Rumpf 1963, p. 27).

19 Churchill, for one, thought so at the time: "Now at this very moment I knew the United States was in the war . . . So we had won after all! [. . .]

Once again in our long Island history we should emerge . . . safe and victorious. [. . .] Hitler's fate was sealed. Mussolini's fate was sealed. As for the Japanese, they would be ground to powder. [. . .] . . . There was no more doubt about the end" (Churchill 1948–54, vol. III, pp. 539–40).

20 As I hope to have shown in chapters 4 and 6, attempts of some advocates of rule-consequentialism to endow moral rules in general, or civilian immunity in particular, with much greater or even absolute stringency do not succeed.

21 Later, however, Liddell Hart became opposed to this method of warfare. In June 1942, after the raids on Cologne, he wrote: "It will be ironical if the defenders of civilisation depend for victory upon the most barbaric, and unskilled, way of winning a war that the modern world has seen" (quoted in Bond 1991, p. 145).

22 For a selection of these reports, see Boberach, ed., 1968.

23 For a comprehensive history of the conflict from the proto-Zionist immigration into Palestine in the last decades of the nineteenth century to the beginning of the twenty-first, see Morris 2001. For discussion of a number of philosophical issues posed by the conflict, see Kapitan, ed., 1997.

24 The total number of expellees and refugees at the end of the 1948–9 war is a matter of some dispute; see Morris 2004, pp. 602–4.

25 On the idea of "transfer" in the Zionist movement up to the 1948–9 war, see Morris 2004, chapter 2.

26 For more on Honderich's defense of Palestinian terrorism, see Law, ed., 2008. Many of the contributions included in this collection engage critically with Honderich's position.

References and Bibliography

Alexandra, Andrew, 2006. Review of *Terrorism: The Philosophical Issues*, ed. Igor Primoratz. *Iyyun: The Jerusalem Philosophical Quarterly* 55, pp. 111–16.

Anscombe, G. E. M., 1981a. "War and Murder," in Anscombe, *Ethics, Religion and Politics*. Oxford: Blackwell, pp. 51–61.

Anscombe, G. E. M., 1981b. "Mr Truman's Degree," in Anscombe, *Ethics, Religion and Politics*. Oxford: Blackwell, pp. 62–71.

Arafat, Yasir, 1995. "Address to the UN General Assembly (November 13, 1974)," in Walter Laqueur and Barry Rubin, eds, *The Israel–Arab Reader: A Documentary History of the Middle East Conflict*. 5th edn, Harmondsworth: Penguin, pp. 329–40.

Arendt, Hannah, 1958. *The Origins of Totalitarianism*. 2nd edn, Cleveland: World.

Arendt, Hannah, 1963. *Eichmann in Jerusalem: A Report on the Banality of Evil*. London: Faber & Faber.

Aristotle, 1963. *The Nicomachean Ethics*, trans. David Ross. Oxford: Oxford University Press.

Armstrong, K. G., 1961. "The Retributivist Hits Back," *Mind* 70, pp. 471–90.

Ashmore, Robert B., 1997. "State Terrorism and its Sponsors," in Tomis Kapitan, ed., *Philosophical Perspectives on the Israeli–Palestinian Conflict*. Armonk, NY: M. E. Sharpe, pp. 105–32.

Atwell, John E., 1982. "Kant's Notion of Respect for Persons," *Tulane Studies in Philosophy* 31, pp. 17–30.

Bauhn, Per, 1989. *Ethical Aspects of Political Terrorism: The Sacrificing of the Innocent*. Lund: Lund University Press.

Baur, Michael, 2005. "What Is Distinctive about Terrorism, and What Are the Philosophical Implications?" in Timothy Shanahan, ed., *Philosophy 9/11: Thinking about the War on Terrorism*. Chicago: Open Court, pp. 3–21.

Beck, Earl R., 1986. *Under the Bombs: The German Home Front, 1942–45*. Lexington: University Press of Kentucky.

Bin Laden, Osama, 2005. *Messages to the World: The Statements of Osama Bin Laden*, ed. Bruce Lawrence, trans. James Howarth. London: Verso.

Bittner, Rüdiger, 2005. "Morals in Terrorist Times," in Georg Meggle, ed., *Ethics of Terrorism and Counter-Terrorism*. Frankfurt: Ontos, pp. 207–13.

Boberach, Heinz, ed., 1968. *Meldungen aus dem Reich: Auswahl aus den geheimen Lageberichten des Sicherheitsdienstes der SS 1939–1944*. Munich: Deutscher Taschenbuch.

Bond, Brian, 1991. *Liddell Hart: A Study of his Military Thought*. London: Gregg Revivals and King's College London.

Boog, Horst, 2005. "Der strategische Bombenkrieg der Alliierten gegen Deutschland 1939–1945: Ein Überblick," in Lothar Fritze and Thomas Widera, eds, *Alliierter Bombenkrieg: Das Beispiel Dresden*. Göttingen: V&R Unipress, pp. 11–31.

Brandt, Richard B., 1992. *Morality, Utilitarianism, and Rights*. Cambridge: Cambridge University Press.

Brittain, Vera, 1942. *Humiliation with Honour*. London: Andrew Dakers.

B'tselem, 2000. *Israeli Violations of Human Rights of Lebanese Civilians*. Jerusalem: B'tselem.

Bufacchi, Vittorio, ed., 2009. *Violence: A Philosophical Anthology*. Basingstoke: Palgrave Macmillan.

Buzan, Barry, 2002. "Who May We Bomb?" in Ken Booth and Tim Dunne, eds, *Worlds in Collision: Terror and the Future of Global Order*. Basingstoke: Palgrave Macmillan, pp. 85–94.

Carmichael, D. J. C., 1982. "Of Beasts, Gods, and Civilized Men: The Justification of Terrorism and of Counterterrorist Measures," *Terrorism: An International Journal* 6, pp. 1–26.

Carter, Michael Phillip, 1989. "The French Revolution: 'Jacobin Terror,'" in David C. Rapoport and Yonah Alexander, eds, *The Morality of Terrorism: Religious and Secular Justifications*. 2nd edn, New York: Columbia University Press, pp. 133–51.

Cavanaugh, Thomas A., 1999. "Double Effect and the End-Not-Means Principle: A Response to Bennett," *Journal of Applied Philosophy* 16, pp. 181–5.

Cavanaugh, T. A., 2006. *Double-Effect Reasoning: Doing Good and Avoiding Evil*. Oxford: Oxford University Press.

Childers, Erskine, 1995. "The Other Exodus," in Walter Laqueur and Barry Rubin, eds, *The Israeli–Arab Reader: A Documentary History of the Middle East Conflict*. 5th edn, Harmondsworth: Penguin, pp. 122–8.

Churchill, Winston S., 1948–54. *The Second World War*, 6 vols. London: Cassell.

Churchill, Winston S., 1952. *The War Speeches*, comp. Charles Eade, Vol. 2. London: Cassell.

Coady, C. A. J., 2004. "Terrorism, Morality, and Supreme Emergency," *Ethics* 114, pp. 772–89.

Coady, C. A. J., 2006. "How New Is the 'New Terror'?" *Iyyun: The Jerusalem Philosophical Quarterly* 55, pp. 49–65.

Coady, C. A. J., 2008. *Morality and Political Violence*. Cambridge: Cambridge University Press.

Corlett, J. Angelo, 2003. *Terrorism: A Philosophical Analysis*. Dordrecht: Kluwer Academic.

Danner, Mark, 2009. "The Cleansing: A Televised Genocide," *Stripping Bare the Body: Politics, Violence, War*. New York: Nation Books, pp. 145–71.

Dardis, Tony, 1992. "Primoratz on Terrorism," *Journal of Applied Philosophy* 9, pp. 93–7.

de Wijze, Stephen, 2007. "Dirty Hands: Doing Wrong to do Right," in Igor Primoratz, ed., *Politics and Morality*. Basingstoke and New York: Palgrave Macmillan, pp. 3–19.

Dobos, Ned, 2007. "Democratic Authorization and Civilian Immunity," *Philosophical Forum* 38, pp. 81–8.

Dombrowski, Daniel A., 1983. "What Does 'War Is Hell' Mean?" *International Journal of Applied Philosophy* 1, pp. 19–23.

Douhet, Giulio, 1942. *The Command of the Air*, trans. Dino Ferrari. New York: Coward-McCann.

Draper, Kai, 1998. "Self-Defense, Collective Obligation, and Noncombatant Liability," *Social Theory and Practice* 24, pp. 57–81.

Dworkin, Ronald, 2006. *Is Democracy Possible Here? Principles for a New Political Debate*. Princeton, NJ: Princeton University Press.

Enzensberger, Hans Magnus, 1994. *Civil War*, trans. Piers Spence and Martin Chalmers. London: Granta Books.

Feinberg, Joel, 1980. "The Nature and Value of Rights," *Rights, Justice, and the Bounds of Liberty: Essays in Social Philosophy*. Princeton, NJ: Princeton University Press, pp. 143–58.

Frey, R. G., and Morris, Christopher W., eds, 1991. *Violence, Terrorism, and Justice*. Cambridge: Cambridge University Press.

Friedrich, Carl J., and Brzezinski, Zbigniew K., 1965. *Totalitarian Dictatorship and Democracy*. 2nd edn, Cambridge, MA: Harvard University Press.

Friedrich, Jörg. 2006. *The Fire: The Bombing of Germany, 1940–1945*, trans. Allison Brown. New York: Columbia University Press.

Fritze, Lothar, 2007. *Die Moral des Bombenterrors: Alliierte Flächenbombardements im zweiten Weltkrieg*. Munich: Olzog.

Gallie, W. B., 1956. "Essentially Contested Concepts," *Proceedings of the Aristotelian Academy* 56, pp. 157–91.

Garrett, Stephen A., 1993. *Ethics and Airpower in World War II: The British Bombing of German Cities*. New York: St Martin's Press.

Gilbert, Paul, 1994. *Terrorism, Security and Nationality*. London: Routledge.

Gilbert, Paul, 2003. *New Terror, New Wars*. Edinburgh: Edinburgh University Press.

Glover, Jonathan, 1991. "State Terrorism," in R. G. Frey and Christopher

W. Morris, eds, *Violence, Terrorism, and Justice*. Cambridge: Cambridge University Press, pp. 256–75.

Goodin, Robert E., 2006. *What's Wrong with Terrorism?* Cambridge: Polity.

Govier, Trudy, 2002. *A Delicate Balance: What Philosophy Can Tell Us about Terrorism*. Boulder, CO: Westview Press.

Grayling, A. C., 2006. *Among the Dead Cities: Was the Allied Bombing of Civilians in WWII a Necessity or a Crime?* London: Bloomsbury.

Groehler, Olaf, 1990. *Bombenkrieg gegen Deutschland*. Berlin: Akademie.

Harris, John, 1980. *Violence and Responsibility*. London: Routledge & Kegan Paul.

Hart, H. L. A., 1979. "Between Utility and Rights," in Alan Ryan, ed., *The Idea of Freedom: Essays in Honour of Isaiah Berlin*. Oxford: Oxford University Press, pp. 77–98.

Heinzen, Karl, 1978. "Murder," in Walter Laqueur, ed., *The Terrorism Reader*. New York: New American Library, pp. 53–64.

Held, Virginia, 2008. *How Terrorism Is Wrong: Morality and Political Violence*. Oxford: Oxford University Press.

Henry, Emile, 1977. "A Terrorist's Defence," in George Woodcock, ed., *The Anarchist Reader*. Hassocks: Harvester Press, pp. 189–96.

Hill, Thomas E., 1979. "Symbolic Protest and Calculated Silence," *Philosophy and Public Affairs* 9, pp. 83–102.

Hirst, David, 2003. *The Gun and the Olive Branch: The Roots of Violence in the Middle East*. 3rd edn, London: Faber & Faber.

Honderich, Ted, 2002. *After the Terror*. Edinburgh: Edinburgh University Press.

Honderich, Ted, 2006. *Humanity, Terrorism, Terrorist War*. London: Continuum.

Hooker, Brad, 2000. *Ideal Code, Real World: A Rule-Consequentialist Theory of Morality*. Oxford: Oxford University Press.

Hooker, Brad, 2008. "Rule-Consequentialism," in Edward N. Zalta, ed., *Stanford Encyclopedia of Philosophy*, http://plato.stanford.edu/entries/consequentialism-rule/.

Hume, David, 1963. "Of the Original Contract," *Essays Moral, Political and Literary*. Oxford: Oxford University Press, pp. 452–73.

Hyams, Edward, 1974. *Terrorists and Terrorism*. New York: St Martin's Press.

Ivianski, Zeev, 1989. "The Moral Issue: Some Aspects of Individual Terror," in David C. Rapoport and Yonah Alexander, eds, *The Morality of Terrorism: Religious and Secular Justifications*. 2nd edn, New York: Columbia University Press, pp. 229–66.

Jollimore, Troy, 2007. "Terrorism, War, and the Killing of the Innocent," *Ethical Theory and Moral Practice* 10, pp. 353–72.

Kant, Immanuel, 2005. *The Moral Law: Groundwork of the Metaphysics of Morals*, trans. H. J. Paton. London: Routledge.

Kapitan, Tomis, ed., 1997. *Philosophical Perspectives on the Israeli–Palestinian Conflict*, Armonk, NY: M. E. Sharpe.

Kapitan, Tomis, 2008. "Terrorism," in Raja Halwani and Tomis Kapitan, *The Israeli–Palestinian Conflict: Philosophical Essays on Self-Determination, Terrorism and the One-State Solution*. Basingstoke: Palgrave Macmillan, pp. 132–97.

Kaufman, Frederik, 2007. "Just War Theory and Killing the Innocent," in Michael W. Brough, John W. Lango, and Harry van der Linden, eds, *Rethinking the Just War Tradition*. New York: State University of New York Press, pp. 99–114.

Kautsky, Karl, 1973. *Terrorism and Communism: A Contribution to the Natural History of Revolution*, trans. W. H. Kerridge. Westport, CT: Hyperion Press.

Kavka, Gregory S., 1978. "Some Paradoxes of Deterrence," *Journal of Philosophy* 75, pp. 285–302.

Khatchadourian, Haig, 1998. *The Morality of Terrorism*. New York: Peter Lang.

Koestler, Arthur, 1968. *Darkness at Noon*, trans. Daphne Hardy. London: Longmans.

Kolnai, Aurel, 1977. "Erroneous Conscience," in Kolnai, *Ethics, Value and Reality: Selected Papers*. London: Athlone Press, pp. 1–22.

Lackey, Douglas, 2004. "The Evolution of the Modern Terrorist State: Area Bombing and Nuclear Deterrence," in Igor Primoratz, ed., *Terrorism: The Philosophical Issues*. Basingstoke: Palgrave Macmillan, pp. 128–38.

Lackey, Douglas, 2006. "The Good Soldier versus the Good Cop: Counterterrorism as Police Work," *Iyyun: The Jerusalem Philosophical Quarterly* 55, pp. 66–82.

Lackey, Douglas, 2010. "The Bombing Campaign: the USAAF," in Igor Primoratz, ed., *Terror from the Sky: The Bombing of German Cities in World War II*. New York: Berghahn Books, pp. 39–59.

Laqueur, Walter, 1987. *The Age of Terrorism*. Boston: Little, Brown.

Law, Stephen, ed., 2008. *Israel, Palestine and Terror*. London: Continuum.

Leiser, Burton, 1979. *Liberty, Justice, and Morals: Contemporary Value Conflicts*. 2nd edn, New York: Macmillan.

Lewis, H. D., 1948. "Collective Responsibility," *Philosophy* 24, pp. 3–18.

Liddell Hart, B. H., 1925. *Paris or the Future of War*. London: Kegan Paul, Trench, Trubner.

Lindqvist, Sven, 2001. *A History of Bombing*, trans. Linda Haverty Rugg. London: Granta Books.

Luban, David, 2003. "The War on Terrorism and the End of Human Rights," in Verna V. Gehring, ed., *War after September 11*. Lanham, MD: Rowman & Littlefield, pp. 51–62.

Mabbott, J. D., 1953. "Moral Rules," *Proceedings of the British Academy* 39, pp. 97–117.

Marcuse, Herbert, 1968. "Ethics and Revolution," in Richard T. De

George, ed., *Ethics and Society: Original Essays on Contemporary Moral Problems*. London: Macmillan, pp. 133–47.

May, Larry, and Hoffman, Stacey, eds, 1991. *Collective Responsibility: Five Decades of Debate in Theoretical and Applied Ethics*. Savage, MD: Rowman & Littlefield.

McKeogh, Colm, 2002. *Innocent Civilians: The Morality of Killing in War*. Basingstoke: Palgrave.

Meggle, Georg, 2002. "Terror und Gegen-Terror. Erste ethische Reflexionen," *Deutsche Zeitschrift für Philosophie* 50, pp. 149–62.

Meggle, Georg, 2011. "Was ist Terrorismus?" *Philosophische Interventionen*. Paderborn: Mentis, pp. 121–43.

Middle East Watch, 1993. *A License to Kill: Israeli Undercover Operations against "Wanted" and Masked Palestinians*. New York: Human Rights Watch.

Middlebrook, Martin, 2000. *The Battle of Hamburg: Allied Bomber Forces against a German City in 1943*. London: Cassell.

Miller, David, 1984. "The Use and Abuse of Political Violence," *Political Studies* 32, pp. 401–19.

Miller, Seumas, 2009. *Terrorism and Counter-Terrorism: Ethics and Liberal Democracy*. Oxford: Blackwell.

Mommsen, Hans, 2003. "Wie die Bomber Hitler halfen," in Stephan Burgdorf and Christian Habbe, eds, *Als Feuer vom Himmel Fiel: Der Bombenkrieg in Deutschland*. Munich: Deutsche Verlags-Anstalt, pp. 115–21.

Morris, Benny, 1993. *Israel's Border Wars, 1949–1956: Arab Infiltration, Israeli Retaliation, and the Countdown to the Suez War*. Oxford: Oxford University Press.

Morris, Benny, 2001. *Righteous Victims: A History of the Zionist–Arab Conflict, 1881–2001*. New York: Vintage Books.

Morris, Benny, 2003. "The New Historiography: Israel and its Past," in Morris, *1948 and After: Israel and the Palestinians*. Oxford: Oxford University Press, pp. 1–48.

Morris, Benny, 2004. *The Birth of the Palestinian Refugee Problem Revisited*. Cambridge: Cambridge University Press.

Murphy, Jeffrie G., 1973. "The Killing of the Innocent," *The Monist* 57, pp. 527–50.

Nagel, Thomas, 1979. "War and Massacre," in Nagel, *Mortal Questions*. Cambridge: Cambridge University Press, pp. 53–74.

Nath, Rekha, 2011. "Two Wrongs Don't Make a Right: A Critique of Virginia Held's Deontological Justification of Terrorism," *Social Theory and Practice* 37, pp. 679–96.

Nathanson, Stephen, 2006. "Terrorism, Supreme Emergency, and Noncombatant Immunity: A Critique of Michael Walzer's Ethics of War," *Iyyun: The Jerusalem Philosophical Quarterly* 55, pp. 3–25.

Nathanson, Stephen, 2010. *Terrorism and the Ethics of War*. Cambridge: Cambridge University Press.

Nechaev, Sergey, 1978. "Catechism of the Revolutionist," in Walter Laqueur, ed., *The Terrorism Reader*. New York: New American Library, pp. 68–72.

Nielsen, Kai, 1981. "Violence and Terrorism: Its Uses and Abuses," in Burton M. Leiser, ed., *Values in Conflict: Life, Liberty and the Rule of Law*. New York: Macmillan, pp. 435–49.

Nozick, Robert, 1974. *Anarchy, State, and Utopia*. Oxford: Blackwell.

Orend, Brian, 2000. *Michael Walzer on War and Justice*. Cardiff: University of Wales Press.

Orend, Brian, 2005. "Is There a Supreme Emergency Exemption?" in Mark Evans, ed., *Just War Theory: A Reappraisal*. Edinburgh: Edinburgh University Press, pp. 134–53.

Orwell, George, 1968. *Collected Essays, Journalism and Letters*, ed. Sonia Orwell and Ian Angus, Vol. 3. London: Secker & Warburg.

Pappe, Ilan, 2006. *The Ethnic Cleansing of Palestine*. Oxford: Oneworld.

Petrović, Dražen, 1994. "Ethnic Cleansing – An Attempt at Methodology," *European Journal of International Law* 5, pp. 342–59.

Plato, 1973. "Crito," trans. Hugh Treddenick, in Edith Hamilton and Huntington Cairns, eds, *Collected Dialogues*. Princeton, NJ: Princeton University Press, pp. 27–39.

Primoratz, Igor, ed., 2004. *Terrorism: The Philosophical Issues*. Basingstoke: Palgrave Macmillan.

Primoratz, Igor, ed., 2007. *Civilian Immunity in War*. Oxford: Oxford University Press.

Primoratz, Igor, ed., 2010. *Terror from the Sky: The Bombing of German Cities in World War II*. New York: Berghahn Books.

Rawls, John, 1971. *A Theory of Justice*. Cambridge, MA: Harvard University Press.

Richards, Denis, and St George Saunders, Hilary, 1954. *Royal Air Force, 1939–1945*, Vol. III. London: HMSO.

Ross, W. D., 2002. *The Right and the Good*, ed. Philip Stratton-Lake. Oxford: Oxford University Press.

Rumpf, Hans, 1963. *The Bombing of Germany*, trans. Edward Fitzgerald. London: Frederick Muller.

Ryan, Alan, 1991. "State and Private; Red and White," in R. G. Frey and Christopher W. Morris, eds, *Violence, Terrorism, and Justice*. Cambridge: Cambridge University Press, pp. 230–55.

Saundby, Sir Robert, 1963. "Foreword," in David Irving, *The Destruction of Dresden*. New York: Holt, Rinehart & Winston, pp. 5–6.

Scheffler, Samuel, 2006. "Is Terrorism Morally Distinctive?" *Journal of Political Philosophy* 14, pp. 1–17.

Shanahan, Timothy, ed., 2005. *Philosophy 9/11: Thinking about the War on Terrorism*. Chicago: Open Court.

Shaw, Martin, 2005. *The New Western Way of War: Risk-Transfer War and its Crisis in Iraq*. Cambridge: Polity.

Sherman, William Tecumseh, 1990. *Memoirs*. New York: Library of America.

Sinnott-Armstrong, Walter, 1988. *Moral Dilemmas*. Oxford: Blackwell.

Sinnott-Armstrong, Walter, 1991. "On Primoratz's Definition of Terrorism," *Journal of Applied Philosophy* 8, pp. 115–20.

Smart, J. J. C., 1956. "Extreme and Restricted Utilitarianism," *Philosophical Quarterly* 6, pp. 344–54.

Somerville, John, 1981. "Patriotism and War," *Ethics* 91, pp. 568–78.

Sparrow, Robert, 2005. "'Hands up Who Wants to Die?' Primoratz on Responsibility and Civilian Immunity in Wartime," *Ethical Theory and Moral Practice* 8, pp. 299–319.

Steinhoff, Uwe, 2007. *On the Ethics of War and Terrorism*. Oxford: Oxford University Press.

Stohl, Michael, and Lopez, George A., eds, 1984. *The State as Terrorist: The Dynamics of Governmental Violence and Repression*. Westport, CT: Greenwood Press.

Strawson, Peter, 1982. "Freedom and Resentment," in Gary Watson, ed., *Free Will*. Oxford: Oxford University Press, pp. 59–80.

Teichman, Jenny, 1986. *Pacifism and the Just War*. Oxford: Blackwell.

Trotsky, Leon 1961. *Terrorism and Communism*. Ann Arbor: University of Michigan Press.

Trotsky, Leon, Dewey, John, and Novack, George, 1973. *Their Morals and Ours: Marxist vs. Liberal Views on Morality*. 5th edn, New York: Pathfinder Press.

Walter, E. V., 1967. "Policies of Violence: From Montesquieu to the Terrorists," in Kurt H. Wolff and Barrington Moore, Jr., eds, *The Critical Spirit: Essays in Honor of Herbert Marcuse*. Boston: Beacon Press, pp. 121–49.

Walzer, Michael, 1972. "Political Action: The Problem of Dirty Hands," *Philosophy and Public Affairs* 2, pp. 160–80.

Walzer, Michael, 2000. *Just and Unjust Wars: A Moral Argument with Historical Illustrations*. 3rd edn, New York: Basic Books.

Walzer, Michael, 2004a. "Emergency Ethics," *Arguing about War*. New Haven, CT, and London: Yale University Press, pp. 33–50.

Walzer, Michael, 2004b. "Terrorism: A Critique of Excuses," *Arguing about War*. New Haven, CT, and London: Yale University Press, pp. 51–66.

Walzer, Michael, 2006. "Terrorism and Just War," *Philosophia* 34, pp. 3–12.

Webster, Sir Charles, and Frankland, Noble, 1961. *The Strategic Air Offensive against Germany 1939–1945*, 4 vols. London: HMSO.

Weissberg, Alex, 1952. *Conspiracy of Silence*, trans. Edward Fitzgerald. London: Hamish Hamilton.

Wellman, Carl, 1979. "On Terrorism Itself," *Journal of Value Inquiry* 13, pp. 250–8.

Werth, Nicolas, 1999. "A State against its People: Violence, Repression, and Terror in the Soviet Union," in Stephane Courtois et al., *The Black Book of Communism: Crimes, Terror, Repression*, trans. Jonathan Murphy and Mark Kramer. Cambridge, MA: Harvard University Press, pp. 33–268.

Wilkins, Burleigh Taylor, 1992. *Terrorism and Collective Responsibility*. London: Routledge.

Wilkinson, Paul, 1986. *Terrorism and the Liberal State*. 2nd edn, London: Macmillan.

Williams, Bernard, 1973. "A Critique of Utilitarianism," in J. J. C. Smart and Bernard Williams, *Utilitarianism: For and Against*. Cambridge: Cambridge University Press, pp. 75–150.

Woodward, P. A., ed., 2001. *The Doctrine of Double Effect: Philosophers Debate a Controversial Moral Principle*. Notre Dame, IN: University of Notre Dame Press.

Young, Robert, 2004. "Political Terrorism as a Weapon of the Politically Powerless," in Igor Primoratz, ed., *Terrorism: The Philosophical Issues*. Basingstoke: Palgrave Macmillan, pp. 55–64.

Index